Bultmann

Bultmann

Towards a Critical Theology

Gareth Jones

Polity Press

Copyright © Gareth Jones 1991

First published 1991 by Polity Press
in association with Basil Blackwell

Editorial office:
Polity Press, 65 Bridge Street,
Cambridge CB2 1UR, UK

Marketing and production:
Basil Blackwell Ltd
108 Cowley Road, Oxford OX4 1JF, UK

Basil Blackwell Inc.
3 Cambridge Center
Cambridge, MA 02142, USA

ISBN 0 7456 0697 0

British Library Cataloguing in Publication Data
A CIP catalogue record for this book is available from the British
Library.

Library of Congress Cataloging-in-Publication Data
A CIP catalogue record for this book is available from the Library of
Congress.

Printed in Great Britain by Billing & Sons Ltd, Worcester

Contents

Acknowledgements

Much of the research for my work on Bultmann's theology was undertaken as part of my Ph.D. studies. I would like to take this opportunity, therefore, to thank John O'Neill and John Heywood Thomas, my two examiners, for their thoughtful and considerate criticisms of that thesis.

The chance to develop my ideas into the present form has been greatly supported by the Bampton Fund of Oxford University; I would like to take this opportunity to thank its Electors for their support of my research since 1988.

More directly, Nicholas Lash, for three months, and Rowan Williams, for the best part of three years, supervised my Ph.D. research. Throughout that period, James Bradley also offered much friendly and important advice. I will be thanking all of them for many years to come.

In addition, Robert Morgan and John Ashton in Oxford, John Painter in Melbourne, Christopher Rowland in Cambridge, and Josef Wohlmuth and Gerhard Sauter in Bonn, have all commented on various aspects of Bultmann's theology and this study. At the end of my work on this manuscript, John Thompson of Polity Press weighed in with some very timely criticisms. I am very grateful to him for his efforts, and indeed to everyone at Polity for their care, attention, and friendliness.

Throughout the writing of this book, Peta Dunstan has read and re-read the material given to her with considerable care and incisiveness. Her patience and thoughtfulness have been a great bonus, as many other of her friends will already know. And, last but by no means least, Lisa has helped me with my revisions of this manuscript more than she could ever realise, simply by being herself. To her and to everyone mentioned above I am greatly indebted, though – for better or for worse – I am solely responsible for the end result.

This book is dedicated to my father, who has always supported me in my studies in every way he possibly could: I simply would never have achieved as much as I have without his help. Similarly, I could not have contemplated this work without the love and support throughout my Ph.D. studies and beyond of Jane, Miranda, and Jody. They never showed the slightest interest in Rudolf Bultmann, but the greatest of interest in me, which always seemed the fairest of bargains.

All translations from German are my own unless otherwise stated. The use of feminine rather than masculine pronouns throughout is deliberate, and for the obvious reasons. All remarks or references in square brackets are the author's. Finally, I have kept notes to a minimum, referring readers to the Bibliography for publication details of specific texts.

Introduction

Rudolf Bultmann (1884–1976) is commonly regarded as the greatest New Testament scholar of the twentieth century. This is understandable, given the nature and extent of his publications in this field: *The History of the Synoptic Tradition*, first published in 1921; *The Gospel of John*, of 1941; *The Theology of the New Testament*, first published in 1953. These are simply the major scholarly works of an individual who dominated German New Testament studies from 1921 until his death fifty-five years later.

Bultmann, however, has also come to be regarded as the creator of the so-called 'existentialist' reading of the New Testament and the gospel, in which its religious message is reduced to an understanding of the individual's historical predicament, expressed in broadly anthropological and psychological terminology. So prevalent has this reading become, and so secular a discipline is existentialism perceived to be, that certain commentators have questioned the Christian orthodoxy of Bultmann's methodological position. In this respect, the debate concerning 'demythologising' (*Entmythologisierung*), which followed the publication of his essay 'New Testament and Mythology' (Bultmann, 1948), has dogged the appreciation and understanding of Bultmann's thought throughout the post-war period.

It is undoubtedly true that a not inconsiderable proportion of this controversy was created by Bultmann's own refusal to clarify his position, to elucidate once and for all precisely what he meant by his programme of demythologising. Nevertheless, for the most part, contemporary theology's inability to come to grips with Bultmann's work, to recognise its philosophical deep structure in Heidegger's hermeneutic phenomenology, and to advance meaningfully beyond the high ground that it claimed, are the products of a misguided attempt to regard Bultmann as an existential anthropologist, little more than Martin Heidegger's religious amanuensis.

In a sense, this problem has become yet more acute since Bultmann's death in 1976. Its extent can be gauged if one considers Eberhard Jüngel's *Glauben und Verstehen* (1985), which was intended to be the definitive analysis of Bultmann's theology. Jüngel's study, though in many respects impressive, betrays its origins in the work of one of Karl Barth's most impressive followers, with predictable results: one receives the impression that, for Jüngel, Bultmann the existentialist is tied to an era that ended in the 1960s. Bultmann is in danger of being forgotten, lost in the shadows as people attempt to elaborate upon the monument left behind by his contemporary and critic, Karl Barth. This, however, would be a grave loss for modern theology, for as great a figure as the late Karl Rahner has argued that:

> Orthodox Protestant theology and Catholic theology as well have confronted themselves too readily with the thought that the school of Barth has routed the old liberal school in Protestant theology. Granted that a great deal of Barth and his achievements will remain, the fact is that Bultmann has really won the day over Barth in European Protestant theology as a whole. (Rahner, 1968, p. 16)

Admittedly, Rahner's statement is over twenty years old, and it is by no means certain that he would have expressed himself thus today: even as he spoke, the wheel of history turned, and Bultmann's theology went into decline. Nevertheless, the attempt must be made to think through Rahner's insight, for the sake of a world of theology that has itself all but lost sight of Bultmann's contemporary importance.

This study seeks both to remedy this situation and to give a fully comprehensive analysis and understanding of Bultmann's thought: its expression in what came to be known as kerygmatic theology; its philosophical foundations in hermeneutic phenomenology; and its reception by, and implications for, contemporary thought. For this attempt to succeed, however, many of today's preconceptions concerning Bultmann's work must be challenged and, for the most part, overthrown. The view, therefore, that Bultmann is an existentialist theologian – where 'existentialism' is regarded as a crude form of psychology – will be challenged again and again, indeed rejected, to make way for an appreciation of the phenomenological foundations of Bultmann's understanding of the Christ event, or *Ereignis*. Similarly, the opinion that Bultmann's findings as a New Testament scholar can somehow be 'siphoned off' from his 'misguided' forays into demythologising will be called into question. It will be shown that, above all of his other publications, the commentary upon the Fourth Gospel comprises Bultmann's theological and philosophical manifesto, equal to Barth's *Commentary on Romans* of 1919 (Barth, 1963) as a considered expression of its author's position. Finally, and perhaps most importantly, this study will challenge the reception of Bultmann's work and thought by those who have followed him; will challenge the view that a theology of the Word, and its hermeneutics, can ever be divorced (in whatever sense) from the socio-political context in which speech about God and God's actions takes place.

To a great degree, consequently, the present study will be examining Bultmann's thought in terms of its *pedagogic* success; that is, it will consider theology as education. This approach is clearly justified, given the wider context of German Protestantism in which Bultmann's own theology must be located: that of *Glaubenslehre*, the teaching of faith, which stretches back in the modern period as far as its classic advocate, Friedrich Schleiermacher. In so far as Bultmann's thought intends to bring the individual to the encounter with the risen Lord – that is, to educate the subject on the pathway to God – it has a pedagogic intent. As this study develops, the evaluation of this pedagogic intent will come to be regarded as the thin red line that runs throughout its length.

Its format, therefore, is intentionally straightforward. Chapter 1 sets out the essential structure and motifs of Bultmann's theology, in terms of his treatment of Christology. Chapter 2 then examines the philosophical foundations of this theology in terms of Bultmann's ontological reflection, before Chapter 3 considers Bultmann's debt to Heidegger. Chapter 4 will offer an analysis of the heritage of hermeneutic theology established by Bultmann, and Chapter 5 its more critical reception in the work of T. W. Adorno and Dorothee Sölle, and indeed contemporary thought. This will establish the move towards a genuinely critical theology, as advocated in the Conclusion, the promise of which is arguably one of the most exciting prospects of the 1990s.

Before that story can be unfolded, however, it is necessary to establish the precise position of this present study in the vast secondary literature concerned with Bultmann's thought: where it reinforces work already done; where it questions hitherto accepted interpretations; and where it might indeed break new ground. The remainder of this Introduction, therefore, is devoted to identifying these terms of engagement.

1   The Philosophical Deep Structure

For over thirty years, the English-speaking world has been served by John Macquarrie's two studies of the intellectual relationship between Rudolf Bultmann and Martin Heidegger, *An Existentialist Theology* (1955), and *The Scope of Demythologising* (1960). In this respect, Macquarrie (one of the English translators of Heidegger's *Being and Time*) advanced modern theology's understanding of the philosophical background to Bultmann's thought by his careful and precise comparison of the work of these two thinkers. It has been the very precision of that comparison, however, that has caused most problems for the contemporary appreciation of Bultmann's theology. In simple terms, by concentrating upon Heidegger's *Being and Time*, and by examining the relationship between Bultmann's theology and that one book of Heidegger's, Macquarrie – wittingly or unwittingly – has encouraged the view that Bultmann has merely 'borrowed' a specific terminology, a transcendental analysis or deduction of the individual's historical predicament, which he then 'marries' to his explicitly religious and Christian understanding of the human context *coram deo*. On this interpretation, there is very little to say about the philosophical deep structure of Bultmann's thought: it has no deep structure, being merely the reflection and appropriation of a gifted amateur after his encounter with Heidegger in Marburg in the 1920s. Unfortunately – and Macquarrie alone stands out from this situation – this has been the nature of the British reception of Bultmann's theology.

This view of Bultmann's debt to Heidegger has surprising currency even today, and has characterised the readings of Bultmann offered by a wide variety of secondary commentators. Karl Barth's 'Rudolf Bultmann: An Attempt to Understand Him' (1962a), is a classic and notorious example of even a great theologian's failure to appreciate the subtlety of Heidegger's thought. Barth demonstrates knowledge solely of *Being and Time*, and then precious little understanding. The same story can be told of Robert C. Robert's study, *Rudolf Bultmann's Theology: A Critical Appraisal* (1977), which is certainly highly critical, though superficial. Likewise, Anthony Thiselton's *The Two Horizons* (1980), which, hampered by its attempt to cover too great a landscape in too small a space, fails to consider seriously anything more than Bultmann's interpretation of *Being and Time*.

The single common denominator underwriting the work of all of these commentators, then, is their failure to look beyond the torso of *Being and Time*, despite Heidegger's explicit statement that it in no way constituted a complete elucidation of his philosophical position (cf. Heidegger's remark to Jaspers; see Chapter 3 of this volume). This is precisely the task facing the present study: to take seriously Heidegger's strictures, and to entertain the notion that Bultmann understood far more regarding Heidegger's hermeneutic phenomenology than has been acknowledged hitherto. The key that will unlock the philosophical foundations of Bultmann's Christology, and which will reveal its author to be far more than the religious anthropologist of popular folklore, is an understanding of the event theory that lies at the heart of both Heidegger's and Bultmann's methodology. Quite simply, Heidegger's mature and reflective consideration of the event of the ontological difference is not to be found in *Being and Time*. Consequently, *any* reading of Heidegger that is limited to that text amounts to no reading at all. In effect, that is the situation in which contemporary theology finds itself with respect to Bultmann, and which the present study sets out to rectify.

It would be unfair and erroneous, however, to suggest that there have been no studies of the intellectual relationship between Bultmann and Heidegger that escape this general criticism. Helmut Haug's article 'Offenbarungstheologie und philosophische Daseins-analyse bei Rudolf Bultmann' (1958) is an impressive attempt to go deeper into that relationship. Likewise, the article by Jean Colette, 'Kierkegaard, Bultmann, et Heidegger' (1965), and that by G. W. Ittel, 'Der Einfluss der Philosophie Martin Heideggers auf die Theologie Rudolf Bultmanns' (1965). Heinrich Ott's *Geschichte und Heilsgeschichte in der Theologie Rudolf Bultmanns* (1955), and his sub-sequent book, *Denken und Sein. Der Weg Martin Heideggers und der Weg der Theologie* (1959), are both major works of theological end-eavour in their own right. And yet Ott, despite his succession to Barth's chair in Basel in the early 1960s, is largely ignored by con-temporary thought.

Undoubtedly the most massive study of Bultmann's work from a philosophical perspective is Maurice Boutin's *Relationität als Verste-henprinzip bei Rudolf Bultmann* (1974), though its analytical stance sometimes hinders its appreciation of the breadth of Bultmann's vision. Helmut Franz's 'Das Denken Heideggers und die Theo-logie' (1961) attempts a comprehensive consideration of the poten-tial of Heidegger's philosophy for contemporary theology. It is, however, a comparatively short article for such a major theme. Finally, and characteristically, Eberhard Jüngel's *Glauben und Ver-stehen: Zum Theologiebegriff Rudolf Bultmanns* (1985) represents a most learned, though hardly sympathetic, reading of Bultmann's thought, with clear – though often brief – references to important elements within its philosophical foundations.

Thus, despite the fascinating reminiscences of Marburg during the 1920s that Hans-Georg Gadamer has provided in his *Philoso-phical Hermeneutics* (1976) and *Philosophical Apprenticeships* (1985), recent commentary upon Bultmann's intellectual relationship with Heidegger has singularly failed to do justice to its subject matter. This failure is acute: the intellectual relationship between Heidegger and Bultmann is arguably the most important example since the publication of Schleiermacher's *Speeches on Religion* in 1799, of phil-osophy and theology learning directly from each other. Bultmann and Heidegger did so, moreover, against the background of the destruction of the old European order, and the rise to power of National Socialism. A failure to understand their relationship, therefore, and its significance, is a failure of responsibility towards one's own cultural and socio-political history. And there has been such a failure.

In other philosophical areas, too, scant attention has been paid to Bultmann's antecedents. It is true that Bultmann skilfully defended his position against Karl Jaspers's *Die Frage der Entmythologisierung* (1954), but this was hardly a major debate. Of greater interest, therefore, are a number of articles and monographs which examine other aspects of this philosophical background. Ernst Fuchs considered certain epistemological problems regarding Bultmann's theology in his article 'Bultmann, Barth, und Kant' (1951). W. Kirchhoff's important monograph *Neukantianismus und Existential-analytik in der Theologie Rudolf Bultmanns* (1959) examines a tradition other than the phenomenological in Bultmann's thought, as does Otto Schnübbe in his *Der Existenzbegriff in der Theologie Rudolf Bultmanns; ein Beitrag zur Interpretation der theologischen Systematik Bultmanns* (1959).

Undoubtedly the best-known monograph concerned with Bultmann's 'debt' to neo-Kantianism is Roger Johnson's *The Origins of Demythologising: Philosophy and Historiography in the Theology of Rudolf Bultmann* (1974), although Johnson's thesis suffers because of its over-emphasis on one or two short articles from Bultmann's very early career, prior to the meeting with Heidegger in Marburg in 1923. John O'Neill has written 'Bultmann and Hegel' (1970), and most recently Jeremy A. Barash has included some important material on Bultmann in his examination of Heidegger's philosophy, *Martin Heidegger and the Problem of Historical Meaning* (1988). Finally, and arguably the single most important secondary article on Bultmann's thought available in the English language, Paul Ricoeur's 'Preface to Bultmann', in his *Essays on Biblical Interpretation*, sets standards of insight and interpretation hitherto unequalled, even if ultimately Ricoeur fails to appreciate Bultmann's desire to stop 'demythologising' before the roof caves in upon theology. Despite this, Ricoeur succeeds, where so many have failed, in appreciating the textual dynamics of a *critical* hermeneutics in terms of a phenomenological, that is, ontological, analysis of experiential reality. Such, indeed, might be regarded as a simple and basic step. What is surprising, nevertheless, is the number of secondary commentators who fail to appreciate its significance.

In other words, contrary to popular opinion and belief, the

philosophical foundations of Bultmann's thought remain largely uncharted territory. Rudimentary maps, hesitantly marked with paths, are provided by commentators such as Ricoeur, Macquarrie, Boutin, and Haug. Gadamer gives hearty encouragement before the traveller sets out. Jüngel provides a final word of warning. And yet it remains something of a journey into the unknown.

With respect to the philosophical deep structure of Bultmann's thought, therefore, the task is clear. The sensitive commentator must turn to those of Heidegger's writings that demonstrate his understanding of the event of the ontological difference. This is the key to any appreciation of Bultmann's own understanding of the kerygmatic Christ as the event in which God encounters the individual, and she encounters – in the moment of decision – her possibilities of existence. At the same time, the commentator must not lose sight of those other elements – most notably neo-Kantianism – that contributed to Bultmann's philosophical development. This task will be undertaken in Chapter 3.

Precisely why such an examination of the philosophical deep structure of Bultmann's thought, in terms of its intimacy with Heidegger's *phenomenology*, is required, is clear when one considers a collection like that edited by J. M. Robinson (with J. M. Cobb), entitled *New Frontiers in Theology I: The Later Heidegger and Theology* (1963). In attempting to examine the fate of the 'new' hermeneutics in modern theology, this collection of essays presupposes the 'standard' position with respect to Bultmann and Heidegger; that is, it presupposes that Bultmann has 'done' the 'early' Heidegger of *Being and Time*, leaving the way clear for a consideration of the 'later' Heidegger. Therein, however, lies the problem. For the so-called 'early' and 'later' Heidegger are not to be juxtaposed in such discreet a fashion; such is not the nature of Heidegger's *Kehre*. On the contrary, as is made clear in Heidegger's crucial text *Time and Being* (cf. Chapter 3 of this volume), the rethinking of the earlier transcendental deductions, which took place during and after the Nietzsche lectures and seminars of the 1930s and 1940s, is never merely an overturning of those earlier positions in favour of something like the 'new' hermeneutics. This would be clear to *theologians*, if they were able to understand the struggle towards the event of the ontological difference in Heidegger's early transcendental deductions, and if they were able to recognise this struggle being mirrored in Bultmann's understanding of the event of revelation, Jesus Christ. The 'new' hermeneutics, therefore, must learn from the 'old' phenomenology. For without the phenomenological foundations, the turn towards new frontiers in theology, when those frontiers are located in hermeneutics, will be a turn towards ambiguity and confusion. To a considerable degree, that is the contemporary state of hermeneutic theology (cf. Chapter 4).

2 Kerygmatic Theology

Persuading people to recognise the importance of this philosophical deep structure, however, has entailed a considerable struggle in the arena of Bultmann scholarship. The reason for this is not too difficult to identify. When philosophy in Bultmann is reduced to the level of a gifted amateur's appropriation of a certain anthropological conceptuality, found in one single text of Heidegger's which is otherwise too obscure for prolonged consideration, the problem fades away, rather like the Cheshire Cat. For when taken solely as an *anthropology*, the transcendental deduction of *Being and Time* demonstrates quite marked similarities to the Lutheran tradition, from Luther himself, through Kierkegaard, to twentieth-century figures such as Harnack and Herrmann. Certainly, this is an important element in Heidegger's own intellectual make-up (cf. Chapter 3), but it should not be used to deny the existence of an explicitly *philosophical*, that is, phenomenological, element in Bultmann's thought. Whether consciously or unconsciously, however, this is what has taken place, and Bultmann commentators can be divided into two camps, those who acknowledge Bultmann's affinity with Heidegger, and those who do not.

All of these secondary commentators, though, are certain of one thing, namely, that Bultmann's is a *kerygmatic* theology, indeed, *the* kerygmatic theology. Ulrich Asendorf, in his brilliant study *Gekreuzigt und Auferstanden* (1971), makes this perfectly clear. So too does David Cairns in his *A Gospel Without Myth?* (1960), although Cairns is one of those commentators who does not consider sufficiently the role of philosophy in Bultmann's thought. That charge cannot be laid at the door of Schubert Ogden. He has, over the last twenty-five years, been the most persistent of Bultmann's American critics: his *Christ without Myth* (1962) is an important development of certain key themes in Bultmann's work, characterised by a lucid and intelligent philosophical insight of its own. Such an event in Bultmann studies, however, is all too rare: efforts like those of Malet (1969), Malevez (1954), Marle (1956), Miegge (1960), and Owen (1957), whilst laudable in their exposition of certain traditional concepts in Bultmann's thought, do little or nothing to advance towards a meaningful understanding of his lasting impact upon contemporary theology.

Of the most recent studies of Bultmann's theology, that of W. Stegemann, *Der Denkweg Rudolf Bultmanns* (1978), is characteristically deficient in its appreciation of Bultmann's philosophical background. Stegemann's is, however, an excellent guide to Bultmann's theology, as is the classic text in this respect, Walter Schmithals's *The Theology of Rudolf Bultmann* (1968). Schmithals, of course, was a friend and colleague of Bultmann's, and his work, despite pietistic tendencies, displays an insight all too often lacking elsewhere.

In terms of Bultmann's treatment of the question of Christology, Ernst Käsemann's programmatic essay 'The Problem of the Historical Jesus' (1964), introduced a debate that was further developed by the volume, again edited by James Robinson, entitled *A New Quest of the Historical Jesus* (1983). This debate continues today, with the so-called 'third' quest of the historical Jesus (cf. Chapter 1). As an adjunct to this debate, Johannes Korner's *Eschatologie und Geschichte* (1957) is an important piece, despite its insistence upon treating Bultmann's thought solely in terms of New Testament scholarship. N. J. Young's *History and Existential Theology* (1969), though, considers the subject of *Geschichte* in a more overtly theological manner, despite its lack of authentic philosophical sophistication.

Certain of the accusations that Bultmann has faced over the question of the historical Jesus, he has rebutted in his responses to the essays in *The Theology of Rudolf Bultmann* (1966), edited by Charles W. Kegley. As John Painter points out, Bultmann's comments there have too often been ignored since they were published in 1966. Painter's own book, *Theology as Hermeneutics* (1987), is arg-

uably the best guide to Bultmann's Christology, offering a searching analysis of many of the criticisms that have been regularly – and
thoughtlessly – cast in Bultmann's direction.

Finally, two important books, one old and one new, have
examined the earliest origins of Bultmann's kerygmatic theology.
James D. Smart's *The Divided Mind of Modern Theology* (1967)
considers Bultmann in relation to his *alter ego*, Karl Barth, during
the formative years of their theological careers, most significantly
the early 1920s. Martin Evang's *Rudolf Bultmann in seiner Frühzeit*
(1988) is as comprehensive an examination of Bultmann's earliest
career to 1921 as could possibly be desired. It provides important
information derived from archive work, and offers biographical as
well as interpretative detail regarding those years when Bultmann
was under the indirect sway of Marburg neo-Kantianism, in the
guise of his theological teacher, Wilhelm Herrmann. Here, though
on an incidental note, a recent book in English by Simon Fisher,
Revelatory Positivism? (1988), offers an excellent introduction to the
Marburg (as opposed to Baden) school of neo-Kantianism.

The overall impression that one receives, however, from a
consideration of these secondary texts, is disappointment. There are
some excellent studies, but in general failure is inevitable whenever
a commentator dares to examine Bultmann's thought without an
adequate understanding of its philosophical background. In review,
there can be little excuse for this, save the previously cited and
virtually universal acceptance of the thesis that the Bultmann/
Heidegger question is closed. This is not the case.

3   Hermeneutics and Critical Theology

To a certain degree, therefore, important aspects of Bultmann's
thought have been examined – with varying degrees of success – by
a multitude of secondary commentators. Bultmann's intellectual
relationship with Heidegger, if only in terms of the latter's *Being and
Time*, has been extensively considered, as has Bultmann's understanding of demythologising. Again, Bultmann's entire approach to
the question of the historical Jesus has attracted great crowds of

scholars and critics, with a very wide variety of responses. The same could be said of a number of other important areas of Bultmann's theological endeavour.

In terms of more overtly critical studies of Bultmann's thought, however – those that could fairly be expected to consider such items as ethics, the socio-political context in which Bultmann worked, his lasting contribution, or otherwise, to hermeneutics – one quickly identifies a dearth of genuine insight. A volume such as Robert P. Ericksen's *Theologians under Hitler* (1985), for example, mentions Bultmann once, despite his standing as the doyen of New Testament scholars in the 1930s and 1940s. Admittedly, Ericksen's is a study concerned with National Socialist sympathisers – individuals like Hirsch, Althaus, and Kittel – whereas it is universally acknowledged that Bultmann was an opponent of National Socialism, and guardian of his Jewish students. Nevertheless, its lack of a comprehensive perspective upon the years 1933–45 is disappointing.

Similarly, the two collections published to coincide with the Bultmann centenary, *Rudolf Bultmanns Werk und Wirkung* (1984), edited by B. Jaspert, and *Bultmann Retrospect and Prospect* (1985), edited by E. C. Hobbs, are missing a truly critical reading of Bultmann's role in German academic and intellectual life in terms of society and politics. Norman Perrin's *The Promise of Bultmann* (1979) is entirely a-politicial, representative of an attitude towards Bultmann's work that dominates modern theology. Indeed, the two major attempts to examine Bultmann's 'ethics', Thomas C. Oden's *Radical Obedience* (1965) and H. E. Todt's *Rudolf Bultmanns Ethik der Existenztheologie* (1978), can almost be characterised as a-political studies of Bultmann's thought. Two pieces by Hans Jonas, 'A Retrospective View' (1977) and 'Is Faith Still Possible?' (1982), indicate in broad outlines the work that remains to be done in this area. The only explicit studies of politics in Bultmann's work are A. Schwan's impressive *Geschichtstheologische Konstitution und Destruktion der Politik* (1976), all the more telling for linking Bultmann to his National Socialist colleague Gogarten, and Dorothee Sölle's brilliant *Political Theology* (1974), which has received too little attention (but cf. Chapter 5).

In the area of hermeneutics, R. W. Funk's *Language, Hermeneutic, and the Word of God* (1966) is provocative and clearly well informed, yet it pales by comparison with David Tracy's magisterial study, *The Analogical Imagination* (1981), which almost single-handedly has advanced the cause of hermeneutics in theology. Chapter 5 will include an engagement with Tracy, undoubtedly one of the best means by which to consider the hermeneutic heritage, post-Bultmann. Tracy's insights throw into sharp relief the work of 'the little schoolmasters', Fuchs and Ebeling, in *Studies of the Historical Jesus* (1964) and *Word and Faith* (1963) respectively (see Chapter 4), although this should not be regarded as a blanket condemnation of the Tübingen theology of the 1950s and 1960s, nor of much of Ebeling's own creative work in theology.

Despite its brilliance, however, Tracy's book is not a genuinely *critical* theology; that is, it is not a confrontation with the destruction of the Western philosophical tradition, as chronicled, perhaps undertaken, in the work of such figures as Lukacs, Adorno, Marcuse, Bloch, and Benjamin. Nor is it critical in a different sense; that is, in terms of an evaluation of the success of Bultmann's pedagogic intent. Yet it is precisely the work of such individuals as Adorno and Sölle that throws down the gauntlet before Bultmann's attempt to identify the sole *authentic* avenue for speech from and towards God and the divine (not to mention what such thinkers as Benjamin and Lukacs would do to the reception of the work and reputation of Karl Barth). In this respect, T. W. Adorno's *Jargon of Authenticity* (1973), despite its explicit condemnation of Bultmann's theology and its identification and demolition of the ideology of Heideggerian hermeneutics, is virtually unread and unheard of by Bultmann's secondary commentators.

Pieces examining the literary and cultural context from which Bultmann's thought emerged are extremely scarce. The only piece to consider the literary context in which Bultmann's thought developed is the present author's essay, 'The Play of a Delicate Shadow: Bultmann and Hesse in the Magic Theatre' (1988). Bultmann is not mentioned in any of the background studies to the literature of the period 1915–45.

In other words, certain robust and none too discreet conclusions can be readily drawn from this examination of the secondary reception of Bultmann's thought. At an early stage, contemporary theology became convinced that it 'understood' Bultmann and Heidegger, taken as an item; on the strength of one general reading of *Being and Time*, this particular problem was regarded as solved. In a similar fashion, Bultmann's efforts regarding the question of the historical Jesus and the entire nature of demythologising, and the interpretation of the New Testament, became the recipients of standardised treatment. Gradually, and inexorably, Bultmann the incisive thinker has been replaced by Bultmann the existentialist, tied with iron stays to the era of the 1950s and 1960s. There he can be understood or, rather, defused. His challenge to modern theology, the *possibilities* of hermeneutic and critical theology, have been met by returning to the safe haven of epistemology, and forsaking phenomenology and the quest for a fundamental ontology. Today, only Habermas responds to that particular challenge.

Clearly, with a thinker of the stature of Rudolf Bultmann there exists the scope for a new, comprehensive and critical reading of his work and significance for contemporary theology. Indeed, there is more. For as one of his earliest and ablest interpreters, Bultmann is in a position to teach us much concerning the 'hidden king' of twentieth-century philosophy: Martin Heidegger (the appellation is Hannah Arendt's). The stakes, therefore, are high: one possibility of the future of modern theology, a genuinely critical theology, as the reward for renewed interest in the thought of Rudolf Bultmann.

1

Christology: The Question of the Historical Jesus

With a theologian such as Rudolf Bultmann, there are any number of different places where one might begin a consideration of his theology. Many start, for example, with his programme of demythologising. Others concern themselves with the role of specific concepts in his thought. Here, attempts to interpret Bultmann's use of the term *Verstehen* are common, as are examinations of the role of hermeneutics in his theology. Still others adopt a more overtly historical perspective, attempting to regard Bultmann in his own peculiar context, in which he spanned a number of very distinct eras of theological endeavour. All of these different approaches are to be found among those secondary texts considered in the Introduction.

For better or for worse, however, such approaches present a rather static image of Bultmann's theology. They do not attempt, in other words, to consider how his work developed in response to particular issues or questions. Against this trend, the present chapter will concentrate upon precisely one such question, that of the historical Jesus, and examine Bultmann's treatment of it. In so doing, the basic structure of his theology will become apparent.

I should add here that by 'the question of the historical Jesus', I always mean theological reflection upon the role of that individual in human speech about the relationship between God, humanity, and the world. I do not, therefore, mean 'historical-critical research into the facts of Jesus' life' when I discuss the question of the historical Jesus. To understand the expression in this latter sense would be to make precisely that mistake which so many have made before, to the detriment of our understanding of Bultmann's thought.

In contemporary theology, however, one sometimes hears expressed the opinion that 'Bultmann's Christology is a comparatively unarticulated matter, and his grasp of philosophy that of the gifted amateur', the statement delivered in a tone that suggests a certain sympathy with, if not pity for, the New Testament exegete who attempted to wed existentialism to religious experience of the crucified One, only to fail. In many respects, such an opinion is typical of the British reception of Bultmann's thought. It is erroneous, of course, in both of its propositions. The purpose of the present study is to demonstrate precisely how it is erroneous: first, by revealing the clarity and sophistication of Bultmann's understanding of the Christ event; and second, by considering Bultmann the philosopher not as an existentialist, but as a phenomenologist. Only then will it be possible to turn to the reception and development of Bultmann's legacy, in terms of hermeneutic theology and critical theology, in Chapters 4 and 5.

The validity of these twin aims can be readily justified. In his famous paper 'What does it mean to speak about God?' (Bultmann, 1980, pp. 26–37), Bultmann approaches the fundamental question of theological method in characteristically forthright fashion: 'We can only speak of God insofar as we are speaking of his Word spoken to us, of his act done to us' (p. 36). In so far as Jesus Christ is God's Word, so Christology is made central to Bultmann's entire theology, and his stature as the century's greatest Lutheran theologian (by definition, therefore, a theologian of the Word) stands or falls by its articulation. Similarly, Bultmann argues: 'It is clear that if man will speak of God, he must evidently speak of himself' (p. 28). That is, philosophical reflection upon human existence is central to the success of theology. Taken together, these two statements demonstrate Bultmann's conviction that our understanding of Jesus Christ, and our understanding of ourselves, are unified *coram deo*. Only so can speech about God be authentic theology.

For the sake of clarity, these two aspects of Bultmann's theology must be treated separately. Chapters 2 and 3 will consider Bultmann's philosophical reflection upon human existence. The present chapter will examine Bultmann's Christology.

Where, however, does one begin such an examination? Here, at least, the issue seems less controversial. Certainly, Bultmann grew up, theologically, among a number of very divergent influences (see below). And, certainly, after the end of the Second World War he found himself, throughout the 1950s and into the 1960s, the focus of a debate centring upon his essay 'New Testament and Mythology' (Bultmann, 1948). But in terms of the question of the historical Jesus, the period that produced a revolution in European theology was the 1920s, when kerygmatic theology first took hold and began to overturn Liberal Protestantism. The writings of this period prove the best starting-point for the present examination, therefore.

Published in 1925, 'What does it mean to speak about God?' (Bultmann, 1980) might justifiably be described as Bultmann's greatest contribution to the 'new theological movement' named dialectical or *Krisis* theology which, in so far as it made the Word of God the sole medium for speech about God, reiterated the central message of Karl Barth's *Commentary on Romans* (Barth, 1963); the first edition of this was published in 1919, stimulating the rejuvenation of German theology in the 1920s, after the upheaval of the First World War. Bultmann's serious consideration of the question of the historical Jesus began in response to these developments in the 1920s.

As a result primarily of Barth's work, and the influence it immediately enjoyed, the theological heritage of Liberal Protestantism was inevitably compromised. In a lecture of 1957, looking back on that period, Barth wrote:

> For me personally a day in the beginning of August in that year [1914] has impressed itself as the *dies ater*. It is the day on which 93 German intellectuals published a profession of support for the war policy of Kaiser Wilhelm II. Included among the signers I was shocked to have to see the names of pretty much all my teachers – theologians whom I had until then loyally honoured. Having been estranged from their ethos, I observed that I would also no longer be able to follow their ethics and dogmatics, their exegesis and historical interpretation. For me in any case the theology of the nineteenth century had no future any more. (cf. Rupp, 1977, p. 11)

This illustrates one of the accepted axioms concerning the origins of dialectical theology; that is, its radical rejection of Liberal Protestantism, its theology, and its identity of religion with a culture held responsible for the outbreak of the First World War. In this respect – arguably his greatest contribution to twentieth-century theology – Karl Barth was held to have influenced decisively those who followed him.

In so far as Rudolf Bultmann was clearly influenced by Barth's great manifesto, so much so that he became like him (and Gogarten) a leader of the new theological movement, one might have expected Bultmann to share in Barth's judgement of the First World War. This, however, was not the case. In a letter of 1926 to Erich Forster, pastor and professor in Frankfurt, Bultmann wrote:

> Of course, the impact of the war has led many people to revise their concepts of human existence; but I confess that that has not been so in my case. Perhaps I am again going too far towards the other extreme, but I must be frank; the war was not a shattering experience for me. Of course there were a great many individual things, but not the war as such. I am quite clear about this, and I once defended my case in numerous conversations, that war is not so different from peace; a shipwreck, an act of meanness, the sort of thing that happens every day, confronts us with exactly the same questions as the heaping up of events in war. So I do not believe that the war has influenced my theology. (cf. Schmithals, 1968, p. 9)

There is a clear difference of opinion at this point, one that was to contribute to the split between Bultmann and Barth, underway as early as 1922 and readily apparent by 1927. It is a difference, moreover, that has implications not only for the relationship between Bultmann and Barth, but also for their respective relationships with their theological teachers. Barth's statement is unequivocal: he rejects the Liberal Protestantism of his teachers, and its role in his own work; henceforth he would pursue an independent course. Bultmann's comments, by contrast, are almost apologetic in their refusal to acknowledge any significant role to the First World War in the formation of his theology. Indeed, no mention at all is made of the war having modified Bultmann's reception of Liberal Protestantism. The implication is clear: at least as far as a theological understanding of human existence was concerned, Bultmann did not reject the work of his teachers, as did Barth. Whatever the influence of Barth upon Bultmann, and it was considerable, it was not in terms of the former's rejection of Liberal Protestantism.

With Bultmann's theology, therefore, it is not possible to point to the First World War, and to say, as with Barth, that it provides a simple point at which one can see that he rejects the theology associated with it. With Bultmann, the situation is more complex than that. It is not so much a question of rejection, as assimilation, certainly not of the methods of Liberal Protestantism, but perhaps of its ultimate aims. The influence of Barth, in relation to those aims, was to inform that process of assimilation.

This claim appears problematic at first glance. After all, Bultmann published in 1924 an article, 'Liberal Theology and the Latest Theological Movement' (Bultmann, 1964, pp. 1–25), which was highly critical of Liberal Protestantism. Moreover, Bultmann was one of the editors of *Zwischen den Zeiten*, a journal antithetical in stance to *Die Christliche Welt*, the flagship of Liberal Protestantism. Nevertheless, Bultmann did not reject the work of his teachers, as did Barth. On the contrary, throughout his theological career he was at pains to acknowledge his debt to individuals such as Herrmann and Harnack (cf. Harnack, 1957, pp. vii–ix). In this respect, the stays that tie Bultmann to that tradition of *Glaubenslehre* reaching back to Schleiermacher appear as tight as ever.

The riddle is easily solved. Bultmann rejected the form, not the content, of Liberal Protestantism. That is, he affirmed the aims of his teachers, whilst rejecting their methods. This can be seen in his treatment of the 'lives of Jesus' question in liberal theology, where Bultmann acknowledged the need to establish theology and faithful existence in the encounter with Jesus Christ, whilst deploring the images conjured up by specific individuals. In this way, Bultmann was to stand within that tradition of German theology reaching back via Wilhelm Herrmann and Albrecht Ritschl to Friedrich Schleiermacher. Barth, after the publication of the Manifesto of the 93 Intellectuals, stood outside of this tradition. When he reached out to Barth, consequently, and recognised the validity of his emphasis upon the unique significance of God's Word of revelation, Bultmann did so from within the secure confines of liberal theology (cf. Rahner's statement, quoted in my Introduction). In this sense, Bultmann was not a theological innovator, as was Barth. He was, rather, the guardian of that tradition of *Glaubenslehre* going back to the *Speeches on Religion* of 1799. This much will become clear as the present chapter unfolds.

On the question of the historical Jesus, therefore, Bultmann and Barth were to stand in two very different camps. Barth, effectively and momentously, rejected the entire work of his theological teachers. Bultmann, by contrast, sought to correct their mistakes. Ultimately, this disagreement served to distinguish Barth's massive *Church Dogmatics* from the very tradition in which he was trained, whilst, for better or for worse, Bultmann set himself always to be judged by the same criteria as his own teachers.

Who, though, were the theological teachers whose work Bultmann attempted to continue, albeit by means of a radically different theological method? Overwhelmingly, Bultmann was influenced by the theology of Wilhelm Herrmann (1846–1922), himself a disciple of Albrecht Ritschl (1822–89), and the History of Religions (*Religionsgeschichte*) School, comprising primarily Gunkel, Weiss, and Wrede. In their differing ways, both Herrmann and the History of Religions School had a profound and lasting influence upon Bultmann's theological development.

Even a cursory examination of Bultmann's bibliography for the years 1908–23 confirms this interpretation. Bultmann's publications as a New Testament exegete are dominated by *religionsgeschichtliche* concerns, and his overtly theological writings manifest Herrmann's influence. Bultmann's theological youth, in other words (cf. Evang, 1988, especially pp. 63–83), was more or less entirely given over to the development of these twin concerns.

However, these two influences – that is, Herrmann's and that of the History of Religions School – might seem at first sight to be unrelated. One concerns dogmatics and systematic theology, the other biblical criticism and exegesis, and the history of the earliest Christian communities. Such a verdict, though, would forget Bultmann's axiom, that: 'We can only speak of God insofar as we are speaking of his Word spoken to us, of his act done to us' (Bultmann, 1980, p. 36). This concerns the question of Christology. And, in so far as the question of Christology in the debate between Liberal Protestantism and kerygmatic theology centres on the question of the historical Jesus, and how it was to be handled, then both

Herrmann and the History of Religions School and their treatment
of this issue are intimately related at the very heart of Bultmann's
theological method.

In effect, therefore, what we find by 1914 in German theology
is a bottleneck in which the question of the historical Jesus has
become the centre of all attention. Barth, as has been indicated,
simply bypassed it. But Bultmann, reacting to this situation yet
unwilling to reject his own legacy, sought to solve the problem
through his work both as a New Testament exegete and systematic
theologian. In the process, he was confronted not simply by the
work of such figures as Herrmann and Kähler, but also the new
developments underway in the research of, for example, Wrede,
Weiss, and Schweitzer. As a theologian, therefore, Bultmann seeks
to address the issues raised at this juncture by grasping the nettle of
the question of the historical Jesus.

This challenges one of the most cherished of assumptions regarding Bultmann's theology, namely, that he has no interest in the
historical Jesus, the figure of flesh and bones who lived and died
2,000 years ago in Palestine, but rather is concerned solely with
the risen Lord, the Redeemer who is encountered spiritually when
the believer is called to decision in the kerygma and the words of
the minister. Granted that Bultmann's interests lie overwhelmingly with the task of bringing the individual to the encounter with
the risen Lord, however, this task in itself inevitably begs the question: 'What has become of the historical Jesus?' It is at this point
that all of Bultmann's varied occupations – New Testament exegete, historian of the earliest Christian communities, interpreter of
Pauline and Johannine theologies, pastor and preacher – combine.
And it is at this point of contact between every aspect of the theologian's task that the present chapter's analysis of Bultmann's
Christology must commence. In other words, in his attempts to
answer the question of the historical Jesus, Bultmann was obliged
to his various tasks as New Testament exegete, historian of the
early Church, theologian and preacher.

In this respect, Bultmann's theology is rather like an hour-glass.
The neck of the hour-glass is, indubitably, Bultmann's understanding of the Christ event. The first bell of the hour-glass, though,
registers all of Bultmann's concerns with the question of the historical Jesus, the proclaimed, kerygmatic Jesus Christ, and the risen

Lord: from its widest point, his attempts to discern the authentic nature of the Synoptic tradition, and the figure underlying that tradition, to its narrowest, his proclamation of the Word as event, encounter, and decision. Any analysis of Bultmann's theology which would progress beyond the generalisations that have come to dominate its reception in the secondary literature, must follow the course travelled by the grains of his thought. This means nothing more nor less than acknowledging, and beginning with, the role of the question of the historical Jesus in Bultmann's theology. Only then will it be possible to move on to the Christ event proper, and the phenomenology that establishes it.

The decisive advantage of beginning a consideration of Bultmann's theology with his understanding of the question of the historical Jesus, consequently, is that it exposes the basic structures of that entire theology. God's relationship with the individual; faith; encounter; decision; the eschatological nature of authentic human existence: all of these theological motifs are considered, originally, within Bultmann's treatment of this primary question. And, as Käsemann was to acknowledge in his essay, 'The Problem of the Historical Jesus' (Käsemann, 1964), any critique of Bultmann's theology must begin with his treatment of this historical figure, Jesus of Nazareth. In this respect, the question of the historical Jesus becomes the key that unlocks all of the doors into Bultmann's thought.

Pursuing the simile of the hour-glass momentarily, Chapters 4 and 5 will consider its second bell, the areas into which the grains of Bultmann's thought flow. As stated above, these areas are hermeneutic theology and critical theology respectively. But without the analysis of the present chapter, those themes would be without context. For, as will be seen, it is solely the question of the historical Jesus that informs the evaluation of Bultmann's significance for contemporary thought in the fields of hermeneutics and critical theology. With this paradox firmly in mind, it is now necessary to turn to a more detailed consideration of this theme.

The remainder of this chapter will be broken into five sections: the influence of Herrmann; the rediscovery of eschatology; the historical Jesus I: *Historie*; the historical Jesus II: *Geschichte*; and, finally, the risen Lord. The first two sections concern those influences from the two primary wings of Bultmann's teachers,

Herrmann and the History of Religions School, with guided his formative understanding of the question of the historical Jesus. The final three sections explain how Bultmann's Christology works, as the architectonic of his entire theology.

1   The Influence of Herrmann

In an essay entitled 'The Principles of Dogmatics according to Wilhelm Herrmann', Karl Barth quotes Herrmann with respect to what he regards as 'the pinnacle of Herrmann's thought':

> God who brings us in the midst of our dependence on the unlimited to a true life, thereby gives us to understand that he is raising our life from the depths, hidden to us, of the world to which we belong, as a life which is to rule in that world. In the pure offering of trust lies the evidence of the reality of which the living becomes Lord. (Barth, 1962b, p. 247)

Behind this somewhat opaque statement, there lies the basis of an understanding of the religious life of the individual: trust in and dependence upon 'the unlimited', which raises the believer to a new life, in truth and faith. The revelation of this possibility, and the medium of the individual's relationship with God, is Jesus Christ. Certain key theological motifs, therefore – that is, trust, faith, dependence, the essence of the religious life, the personal salvation of the individual – are made dependent upon Herrmann's Christology. God's will is expressed via the divine action in Jesus Christ. Theology, consequently, must concern itself with the interpretation of this Christ event. As will be seen, on this point Bultmann follows Herrmann with great care.

Herrmann's considerable emphasis upon certain personal qualities or characteristics as the basis of the religious life, even though those qualities or characteristics be granted by divine grace, indicates the direction in which his theology will travel, that is, towards the notion of a personal relationship with God, in Christ. Herrmann is doing more than that, however. On the contrary, 'Herrmann is seeking to draw a distinction between on the one hand the material world which is to be interpreted mechanistically, and on the other hand, the personal reality of God and of human experience' (Dyson, 1974, p. 65). This much was revealed in the passage quoted by Karl Barth: our life in the depths of the world to which we belong is to end in faith, as we are raised up in Christ to a new and personal relationship with God. Herrmann the theologian, consequently, makes a clear distinction between the reality of the fallen world to which we belong, and the reality of the resurrection, in which it is possible for us to share, through the grace of God in Christ. The point of Christology is to elaborate the relationship of this distinction, and its soteriological implications for the individual, with the figure of the historical Jesus. Christ, in other words, is the medium by which God and the individual are joined, as the Redeemer in whom the gulf between the divine and the worldly is overcome.

It is important at this juncture to understand that Herrmann is not, in any sense, establishing a metaphysical distinction between two planes of reality. On the contrary, Herrmann is concerned to censure such metaphysical speculation, and deny it a place in genuine theology (cf. Herrmann, 1966, p. 21). Rather, Herrmann wishes to establish an understanding of a 'reality' that is not metaphysically, but experientially or psychologically, distinct. It is something that the individual intuits as her inner life, as that in which religious existence can be raised up by God, in Christ. This is the specific nature of the relationship between religion and reality. Herrmann writes: 'The experience out of which religion may arise...is the realisation on the part of any religious man that he has encountered a spiritual Power in contact with which he has felt utterly humbled, yet at the same time uplifted to a real independent inner life' (Herrmann, 1927, p. 36). It is this humility before a spiritual Power, and its acceptance into the inner life of the individual, that is for Herrmann of the essence of the Christian religion as a *revealed* religion, that is, as the religion of Jesus Christ. In other words, for Herrmann, Jesus Christ is one with the spiritual Power of the resurrection, so much so that the encounter with the risen Christ is one and the same as the encounter with the spiritual Power. 'In Christ', therefore, the individual is raised into relationship with God. This theme, so apparent throughout Bultmann's theology, is perhaps the most obvious point at which he belongs to that tradition stretching back in German thought to Schleiermacher and the origins of romantic idealism.

This approach, it should be noted, does not *require* the divorce of the material world from the plane upon which the relationship between God and the individual takes place. On the contrary, the material world is regarded as the locus in which that relationship, as encounter, takes place. In so far as the categories in which that relationship is described, however, cannot be reduced to the level of the material, there exists the possibility for the neglect of that world. Once again, this is by no means a requirement of the emphasis upon the relationship between God and the individual. But it is a distinct possibility, and a danger against which the theologian must ward. In this sense, it will be recognised as an important element of the critical reception of Bultmann's theology (cf. Chapter 5).

This emphasis upon Christology is maintained when Herrmann writes: 'Christian faith is that renewal of the inner life which men experience in contact with Jesus as he becomes for them the revelation of God which is the foundation of God's rule in their hearts' (Herrmann, 1927, p. 62). This understanding of Jesus Christ's role or purpose is reiterated in all of Herrmann's mature writings on Christology (cf. especially Herrmann, 1966, pp. 149–85; Herrmann, 1967, pp. 282–9). It does, however, beg one question of great importance. That is: 'Who precisely is this Jesus Christ?' It was Herrmann's answer to this question, far more than his emphasis upon faithful dependence as the basis of the religious life of the individual, that influenced Bultmann and was to have a lasting significance for his own Christology. In other words, the basic anthropology that Bultmann and Herrmann seem to share is little more than one element in that broad, Lutheran tradition to which they both belong and aspire. It is at the level of Christology, rather, that is, the manner in which one understands the Christ event, that one begins to perceive the true nature of Herrmann's influence upon Bultmann's theological development. (This is an important point when understanding Bultmann's relationship with Heidegger; cf. Chapter 3.)

Bultmann's debt to Herrmann, therefore, is not to be identified in terms of any specific description of Jesus Christ, but rather in terms of the decision to focus attention upon that figure as the medium by which God and the individual are joined, thereby making the theme of 'encounter' central to Christology. Here, it is possible to witness Bultmann working with the basic themes of his teachers, whilst at the same time correcting their fundamental mistakes from the perspective of his own philosophical reflection. As will be recalled, it was this attitude that characterised Bultmann's response to Liberal Protestantism in the 1920s, under the influence of Karl Barth (see above).

In his Christology, and influenced by Lotze and Marburg neo-Kantianism, Herrmann makes an explicit distinction between nature and history, *Natur* and *Geschichte*, the natural Jesus and the historical Christ, the basis of faith, *der geschichtliche Christus der Grund unseres Glaubens*. On the basis of this distinction, Herrmann's assertion in its simplest form is that the Christ of faith, encountered by the individual as a personal experience, is not to be reduced to a biological datum. Rather, the Christ of faith, the genuinely historical (*geschichtliche*) Christ, is somehow more than the natural Jesus, where 'more' is not a quantitative distinction, but a confession of the decisive significance of a lived, experiential encounter with God *in the present moment*. This is the foundation of Herrmann's entire theology, that the personal encounter with God in Christ is not a material event but a private and spiritual experience, and that therefore the Christ event itself must not be reduced to material or natural concerns.

This understanding of Christology is of such vital importance for Rudolf Bultmann precisely because it seems to cut across Bultmann's own position as both New Testament exegete and New Testament theologian. That is, by making a distinction between the biological datum of Jesus' life on earth, and the historical life of the risen Christ within the encounter between God and the individual, Herrmann seemed to have made it impossible for anyone to be both exegete and theologian. His condemnation of contemporary liberal theologians who attempted to reconstruct the life of Jesus on earth as the basis of faith, which preceded Albert Schweitzer's, illustrates precisely this tendency in Herrmann's thought, at once its strength and its weakness. If Bultmann's own work as a theologian was in any sense a continuation of that of his teacher, it was to a great extent in the manner in which he wrestled with this problem, and overcame it.

Bultmann himself, however, did not hold to Herrmann's understanding of the distinction between the natural or material Jesus, and the historical Christ of faith. On the contrary, one does not find in Bultmann's thought any emphasis upon, or even mention of, the 'natural' Jesus. Bultmann's operative distinction is that between *Historie* and *Geschichte*, not *Natur* and *Geschichte*, that is, not two separate realities within one individual, but two ways of regarding that figure. *Historie* and *Geschichte* are not so much two 'levels' upon which the individual might encounter Jesus Christ, as two 'tools', each of which has a specific and clearly defined role to play in the articulation of Christology. To a great degree, the negative purpose of *Historie* – that is, to define what faith is *not* concerned with – is counterbalanced by the positive significance of *Geschichte* – the individual's story, in which her encounters with the risen Lord via the kerygma are revealed.

In this way, Bultmann redressed the balance of Herrmann's apparent neglect of biblical studies. But in so doing, Bultmann was not motivated simply by the desire to 'correct' the work of his teacher. On the contrary, it is possible at this point to recognise the emergence of that pedagogic intent within Bultmann's theology which forms one of its central themes. That is, the return to a sophisticated, historical-critical appreciation of the New Testament is part of Bultmann's concern to lead the individual away from culturally relative images of Jesus Christ, and towards the encounter with the risen Lord. Certainly, in that movement historical-criticism serves a negative purpose, that is, it serves to demonstrate to the individual what she is not to believe (see below). But this does not in turn negate the basic contention: that New Testament research for Bultmann has a crucial role to play in the education of the Christian believer.

It was this slide away from Herrmann's relatively unsophisticated position that helped to establish Bultmann's entire theological method. In large part, the development of Bultmann's understanding of this question can be traced to the influence of Martin Kähler's famous book, *The so-called historical Jesus and the historic, Biblical Christ* (Kähler, 1964). Here, Kähler is attacking precisely those individuals attacked by Herrmann: liberal theologians attempting to use historical-critical tools with which to establish their images of Jesus, as the basis of faith; the attempt, in other words, to find and secure the 'real' Jesus. He writes: 'How can Jesus be the authentic object of the faith of all Christians if the questions as to who and what he really was can be established only by ingenious investigation, and if it is solely the scholarship of our time which proves itself equal to the task?' (Kähler, 1964, p. 102). That is, rather than revealing the true Christ for the individual to encounter, life-of-Jesus Christology – the product of Liberal Protestantism in the nineteenth century – is, on the contrary, concealing him behind the appearance of scientific respectability. Kähler is not, it should be noted, questioning the importance of the natural Jesus for faith (and in this respect he disagrees with Herrmann). But he is attacking the mistaken belief that historical-critical tools can ever reveal to us the Christ of faith. He writes: 'The historical Jesus of modern authors conceals from us the living Christ' (Kähler, 1964, p. 43). The question for Kähler, then, is how one understands the relationship between the historical Jesus and the Christ of faith. Ignoring the historical Jesus, as Kähler thinks Herrmann does, is not an answer to that question, but rather its rejection. It simply avoids the matter of Christianity's existence as a historical religion, founded by the material life and death of a specific individual. On this point, Bultmann is influenced more by Kähler than by Herrmann, with lasting significance for Bultmann's appreciation of the role of eschatology in the individual's encounter with Jesus Christ.

One must be careful here not to distort Herrmann's Christology. He is not, by any means, rejecting the belief that Christianity as a revealed religion had its origins in the biological datum referred to as the life and death of Jesus of Nazareth. But he does come dangerously close to rejecting the historical or natural Jesus in the *narrative* of salvation. Irrespective of Herrmann's strictures against metaphysical speculation, it remains true that he reduces the *effective* plane of salvation to the emotional, or psychological; this is the specific experience with which he is concerned. There is very little in Herrmann's work that is directed explicitly towards the reality of the concrete, material world. On the contrary, his theological method carefully excludes this aspect of the historical dimension, in a way that implies that a satisfactory standard of ethical conduct will follow, necessarily, upon the prior, experiential or psychological encounter with Jesus Christ. In this sense, systematic theology can be nothing other than ethics, because the practical effect of such a theological understanding of religious existence is implicit within its theoretical foundations.

Bultmann's own rejection of *Historie* as a suitable starting-point

for theology, by contrast, influenced by Kähler, is not to be understood as a rejection of the concrete, material world, but rather its
affirmation in a sense radically different from that of *Historie*. That
is: by affirming the *meaning* or significance of the concrete world as
Geschichte, Bultmann is not abstracting away from *Historie*, but
establishing it in that which is ontologically prior. On this understanding, *Geschichte* is not so much an alternative to *Historie*, but
its complement and its fulfilment. Without it, Bultmann asserts,
genuine theology is an impossibility. This echoes the point
made earlier, that is, the danger in Herrmann's theology is so to
undermine the material – by a concentration upon the personal
relationship between God and the individual, in Christ – that it
effectively disappears, leaving behind not a theology, but rather an
imaginative description of one person's own relationship with
'God'. Certainly, Bultmann's move away from Herrmann's categories, towards his own understanding of reality in terms of
Historie and *Geschichte*, can be regarded as an attempt to safeguard
theology against this danger. In placing such a tense relationship at
the heart of his reflection, however, Bultmann is inviting disaster
(cf. Chapter 5).

Nevertheless, *Historie* is central to Bultmann's theology, and
therefore cannot be ignored in any consideration of his treatment
of the question of the historical Jesus. This point can be illustrated
by a simple reading of Bultmann's Christology. To understand the
meaning and significance of Jesus' historic (*historische*) life on earth,
one must first understand Christ's ontologically prior divine existence. This is a 'Bultmannian' reading of the Johannine claim that:
'In the beginning was the Word...and the Word became flesh'
(John 1.1; 1.14). The 'meaningfulness' (*Bedeutsamkeit*) of *Historie*,
therefore, is *Geschichte*. But that understanding of the relationship
between the theological motifs 'Jesus' and 'Christ' in Bultmann's
Christology is only open to the thinker concerned with historical
reflection. Once again, the influence of Kähler seems to be to the
fore, rather than Herrmann's more psychological reflection.

This, in turn, is precisely how Bultmann can maintain his role
both as exegete and theologian of the New Testament, irrespective
of the criticisms of Herrmann and Kähler. By emphasising the
importance of both *Historie* and *Geschichte*, not only in the work of
the theologian but also in the eschatological and faithful existence

of the individual, and by emphasising their mutual dependence, Bultmann challenges theology to regard itself always as *New Testament* theology, that is, as theology concerned with the question of the historical Jesus, and the proclamation of that figure in the kerygma of the earliest Christian communities. The task of the Christian, then, is to understand the life and death of Jesus of Nazareth in the light of the resurrection, from the perspective of faith. Only in faith, moreover, will the genuine purpose of Jesus' mission and message be revealed. This is the origin of Bultmann's conviction that New Testament theology begins with the earliest Christian communities, rather than Jesus of Nazareth. For faith is a consequence of the resurrection of Christ, encountered in faith, rather than in space and time.

With Kähler, therefore, Bultmann rejects historical-critical research of the New Testament as the starting-point of faith and theology. Against Kähler, though, Bultmann asserts the need for the believer to return to the historical Jesus for the sake of the kerygma. With Herrmann, Bultmann acknowledges the encounter with the risen Lord as the origin of faith. Against Herrmann, Bultmann rejects a psychological or emotional understanding of that encounter, in order to maintain the necessary historical relationship between Jesus of Nazareth and the risen Lord. Again, it is the *understanding* of that relationship, and its meaning for the individual from the perspective of faith, that concerns Bultmann. He does not question its existence.

From this, something of the subtlety and complexity of Bultmann's Christology may be deduced. His work as a New Testament exegete became overwhelmingly concentrated upon the theologies of Paul and John. But for Bultmann there was always implicit within this concern the question of the historical Jesus, how to envisage one's existence in relation to his, and how to understand his mission and message in relation to the faithful life of the individual, 'in Christ'. Faith within the mystery of the risen Christ must never turn its back upon the historical Jesus. But precisely how it must face that particular individual requires elucidation.

Bultmann's careful navigation of the myriad byways of the question of the historical Jesus in the first part of this century, then, cannot but be admired. And yet, here in his responses to the theology of his teacher Wilhelm Herrmann, one recognises the dangers that will return to haunt the contemporary reception of his thought. In this respect, this consideration of Bultmann's debt to Herrmann serves to raise the one question – of the almost solipsistic nature of any Christology that emphasises the individual's encounter and relationship with Christ – which remains constant in the secondary criticism of Bultmann's theology. That Bultmann was prepared always to insist upon its necessity, therefore, is indicative of the importance he attached to the pedagogic significance of that relationship. This point should not be forgotten. It means that the notion of an encounter with the risen Lord, by means of stories told about the historical Jesus, is of such importance for Bultmann that he is prepared to countenance the danger that his theology will sink into meaningless self-reflection. By placing this idea at the heart of his theology, therefore, Bultmann is not simply being true to that tradition of Liberal Protestantism and *Glaubenslehre* stretching back to Schleiermacher. He is also affirming a primary role and responsibility to theology as *education*. In response to faith as venture, consequently (cf. my Conclusion), a critical theology as education does not seek to tell people what to do. It seeks, rather, to show people how to be, *coram deo*. This is the ultimate goal of Bultmann's theology.

2   The Rediscovery of Eschatology

Both Herrmann and Kähler, therefore, raised the question of the historical Jesus in contemporary theology; and Bultmann learned from both of them. At the same time as he was being influenced by clashes upon the overtly theological wing of the Ritschlian movement, however, Bultmann was also being guided by the History of Religions School, which directed specific attention to the historical analysis of the traditions concerning Jesus of Nazareth and the earliest Christian communities. In particular, this meant individuals like Gunkel, Weiss, and Wrede. But as early as the first half of the nineteenth century, Strauss, Ghillany and Baldensperger had made attempts at a thorough examination of the eschatological importance of Jesus' message, and indeed his life. These attempts, however, despite their novelty and ground-breaking importance, were

insufficient to halt the growing trend in nineteenth-century dogmatics and systematics, which attempted to construct lives of Jesus
in order to establish some sort of historical and cultural basis to
Christian belief and religion. The full extent of this effort has been
documented in Albert Schweitzer's epochal study, *The Quest of the
Historical Jesus* (Schweitzer, 1954). Perhaps more revealing in the
short term, however, is Julius Kaftan's famous comment that: 'If
the kingdom of God is an eschatological matter, then it is a useless
concept as far as dogmatics is concerned' (cf. Weiss, 1971, p. xi).
This comment reveals the generally prevalent attitude towards
eschatology in the German tradition in the nineteenth century
before its final decade.

The significance of the rediscovery of eschatology, therefore,
was in its challenge to contemporary theologians, faced as they
were by the question: 'How does one relate the historical Jesus
of Nazareth to the contemporary situation, given that his mission
and message are rooted in an alien mentality, that is, that of
first-century Palestine?' Albert Schweitzer's own answer to this
question is famous, and unequivocal:

> The Jesus of Nazareth who came forward publicly as the
> Messiah, who preached the ethic of the Kingdom of God, who
> founded the Kingdom of Heaven on earth, and died to give
> his work its final consecration, never had any existence. He is
> a figure designed by rationalism, endowed with life by liberal-
> ism, and clothed by modern theology in an historical garb.
> (Schweitzer, 1954, p. 396)

Saying this, Schweitzer positioned himself at one extreme of the
theological spectrum, in so far as his attack upon liberal theology
led him to question the viability of historical-critical analysis as the
basis of theology or faith.

For Schweitzer, consequently, the fruits of historical-critical
research served to emphasise the alien nature of Jesus' mission and
message. It was impossible, Schweitzer argued, to rediscover the
historical Jesus. In the face of such historical-critical research, the
question of the historical Jesus recedes almost beyond sight. This
radical challenge to the work of such individuals as Herrmann and
Harnack in particular, serves to highlight the extent to which the

rediscovery of eschatology unsettled German theology at the beginning of the twentieth century.

Schweitzer's own work, however, great though its significance, was in fact preceded by two important monographs, both published in Leiden in 1891: *Die Lehre vom Reiche Gottes in den Schriften des NT*, by Otto Schmoller; and *Die Lehre vom Reiche Gottes im NT*, by Ernst Issel. Perhaps more so than Schweitzer's polemical work, these two studies indicated that a new appreciation of the eschatology of the New Testament was emerging. These monographs were succeeded by the more substantial, and more famous, works of Johannes Weiss, *Jesus' Proclamation of the Kingdom of God* (Weiss, 1971), and Wilhelm Wrede, *The Messianic Secret* (Wrede, 1971).

The coherent argument that these individuals, and other writers, presented is by now too well known to require much explanation. Weiss expressed the view that the message of the historical Jesus was apocalyptic, and concerned a kingdom of God that was to be realised in concrete, empirically verifiable terms in the imminent future. Wrede amplified this point, but because of his own metaphysical distinction between the supernatural and the natural (cf. Lotze and Herrmann), he argued that the natural life of Jesus served only to disguise his true, supernatural significance. Both men, however, were certain that the message of the historical Jesus was concerned with a kingdom of God that was expected imminently, but that did not occur as anticipated. There was, so to speak, a certain breakdown between expectation and fulfilment. Schweitzer expressed this same opinion more forcefully with this vision of Jesus' casting of himself upon the wheel of history, only to be broken by it.

As a New Testament exegete, Bultmann was undoubtedly and inevitably much influenced by the work of the figures mentioned above. Indeed, his 1921 text *The History of the Synoptic Tradition* (Bultmann, 1921) stands in a direct line of descent from the work of his predecessors in the History of Religions School. Rather than regarding the findings of men like Weiss, Wrede, and Schweitzer as causes for pessimism about the future of theology, however, Bultmann saw revealed therein the hidden secret of the New Testament message, and indeed, the figure of the historical Jesus. So when Schweitzer concludes that, 'The historical Jesus will be to our time a stranger and an enigma...he does not stay; he passes by our

time and returns to his own' (Schweitzer, 1954, p. 397), Bultmann
tentatively agrees. But for him this only means that the historical
Jesus points towards precisely that figure who *does* remain within
our time, in every moment, in every decision. That is, the historical
Jesus points away from himself, and towards the risen Lord. Or, at
least, that is how New Testament theology must present the relationship, as Bultmann understands it.

In many important respects, therefore, the rediscovery of eschatology reinforced precisely what Bultmann had learned from
Herrmann and Kähler, that is, that any identification between the
historical Jesus and the risen Lord encountered by the individual in
faith must be an identification of theological difference. This apparently difficult concept is in reality quite simple. It means that
though theology must make a distinction between the two motifs,
'Jesus' and 'Christ', for the sake of conceptual clarity, they are of
course one ontologically and therefore also from the perspective of
faithful, eschatological existence.

Theologically, then, for all intents and purposes there would
appear to be two 'Jesuses'. In Bultmann's Christology, however,
there are *three*:

1   the historical Jesus who lived and died on earth;
2   the Jesus who lives and dies in stories;
3   the risen Lord, the Christ of faith, the mystery of salvation.

The point of Christology, for Bultmann, was to elucidate the
necessary distinction between (1) and (2) above, so that subsequently the encounter with the risen Lord, (3) above, became a
genuine possibility for the individual. That is, the distinction made
between *Historie* and *Geschichte* is effectively the necessary distinction between the historical Jesus who lived and died on earth, (1)
above, and the Jesus who lives and dies in stories, that is, the
kerygmatic Christ, (2) above. The point of Christology, as part of
the teaching activity of theology, is to bring the individual to the
encounter with the risen Lord, in the power of the Holy Spirit, by
means of its consideration of the historical Jesus and the kerygmatic Christ. This threefold distinction may appear to be pedantic,
therefore, but it is in fact essential. Without it, and without the
necessary separation of the risen Lord from the more immediate

questions of Christology, it is impossible to appreciate the orthodoxy of Bultmann's doctrine of God. Without it, in other words,
'God' becomes a simile, evacuated of all ontological meaning.

What Bultmann's Christology does, in other words, is to assert a
continuity between these three 'Jesuses', on the basis of his understanding of eschatology. The historical Jesus points away from
himself, towards the kerygmatic Christ, the Jesus of stories. This is
his eschatological purpose, as God's event of grace. The kerygmatic
Christ, the Jesus of stories, announces the eschatological purpose of
the historical Jesus, at the same time – and here Bultmann's logic
is quite brilliant – fulfilling that purpose. In this sense, the first
theologians of the kerygma, Paul and John, are as essential to
God's soteriological purpose as was the historical Jesus, so tightly
drawn is the cord that connects them. Finally, in the authentic
understanding and acceptance of this eschatological event, the individual herself encounters the risen Lord. The point of Christology
is to make this encounter a distinct possibility, by proclaiming the
story and the individual in whom God spoke.

Bultmann, therefore, acknowledged the findings of Wrede,
Weiss, and Schweitzer. He acknowledged Herrmann and Kähler's
interpretations of the question of the historical Jesus. He also
believed what his own faithful reading of the New Testament told
him. And he knew that there was no inherent contradiction in
recognising the cultural relativity of the historical Jesus of Nazareth, the theologies of Paul and John, and the risen Lord, *so long as
one understood their identity in difference.* Jesus of Nazareth lived and
died; that much is taken to be a datum, the historical *Dass*, by
Bultmann. In the proclamation of the earliest Christian communities, and in contemporary proclamation, however, he lived again as
the kerygmatic Christ. So much is logically necessary, in the most
literal sense of the word: the stories about Jesus proclaim a different
individual from the one who actually lived and died, even when
those stories are true. And, finally, the risen Lord, in whom the historical Jesus and the kerygmatic Christ live and move and have
their being, is different again: he is nothing more nor less than the
mystery of faith. The three 'Jesuses' are necessary, in other words,
if theology is to be speech about God from the perspective of faith.

What remains to be seen is whether or not Bultmann can maintain this ingenious Christological structure as he manoeuvres it into

relationship with his theological heritage, as the necessary corrective to Liberal Protestantism.

3   The Historical Jesus I: *Historie*

In considering here Bultmann's understanding of the question of
the historical (*historische*) Jesus, my intention is to focus attention
on Bultmann's work as biblical exegete, employing the tools of historical-critical analysis. In so doing, I want to ask the question:
'What does Bultmann mean when he distinguishes between the historical Jesus and the kerygmatic Christ, between *Historie* and
Geschichte?' And, more importantly: 'What is the nature of the continuity between them, if such a continuity exists at all?' This section,
therefore, will proceed beyond the preliminary limits established by
Kähler, Herrmann, and the History of Religions School, towards
what Bultmann's own historical-critical research has to say about
the historical Jesus.

There are serious problems with any examination of Bultmann's
treatment of the historical Jesus, though, not the least of which is
the fact that the vast majority of his exegetical writings are not
directly concerned with this question at all. In so far as they are
concerned with the kerygmatic Christ, however, then the question
of the historical Jesus is implicit within that concern. Here, one
thing must be reiterated before any further progress can be made:
Rudolf Bultmann, without any doubt, believed in the concrete
existence of the Palestinian Jew Jesus of Nazareth, who lived and
died nearly 2,000 years ago. Moreover, Rudolf Bultmann the theologian makes this Jesus of Nazareth the basis and coping-stone of his
Christology, and therefore ultimately of his entire Christian theology. In this respect, Bultmann is entirely in agreement with
Wolfhart Pannenberg, when the latter writes: 'The central confession of Christians is that in dealing with Jesus of Nazareth we are
dealing with God himself' (Pannenberg, 1967, p. 101). The question that remains, of course, is *how* we should deal with Jesus of
Nazareth.

As was mentioned above, in many respects Bultmann's concern
with the historical Jesus focuses upon how that figure points away

from himself, towards the kerygmatic Christ, which figure in turn heralds the encounter with the risen Lord. That is, the historical Jesus directs attention towards his *purpose*: namely, to be the Redeemer, the eschatological event, and in so doing heralds the Word to be proclaimed by the apostles and evangelists. All three are one within the Christ event, but theologically this distinction between them can be made. This aspect of Bultmann's Christology has been recognised by secondary commentators, and heavily criticised. A. Barr, for example, writes:

> But if Bultmann thinks that he can win the allegiance of men of this generation, or of any other in our prospect, with his attenuated portrait of the historical Jesus, in which he leaves us with nothing but a pair of eyes peering intently and expectantly into the beyond, accompanied by a voice calling for decision for that which presses in from behind the veil – the rest in darkest shadow, I can only re-echo the oft-repeated comment of Karl Barth, 'I do not understand'. *Dass kann ich nicht verstehen.* (Barr, 1954, p. 352)

A similar point is made by M. S. Enslin in an article entitled 'The Meaning of the Historical Jesus for Faith'. Enslin writes:

> To me, this [Bultmann's Christology] simply does not make sense. It always reminds me of a man who ascends a very shaky ladder and, having managed to grab hold of the third-floor gutter, casually kicks the ladder away as being something dispensable. This action cannot annul the fact that the ladder is still very necessary. (Enslin, 1962, p. 221)

Enslin's metaphor is most apt, and seems to be justified by Bultmann's own writing. In a famous passage at the very beginning of his *Theology of the New Testament* (Bultmann, 1953), Bultmann states, that:

> The message of Jesus is a presupposition for the theology of the New Testament rather than a part of that theology itself. For New Testament theology consists in the unfolding of those ideas by means of which Christian faith makes sure of its own object, basis, and consequences. But Christian faith did not exist until

there was a Christian kerygma; i.e., a kerygma proclaiming Jesus
Christ – specifically Jesus Christ the Crucified and Risen One –
to be God's eschatological act of salvation. He was first so
proclaimed in the kerygma of the earliest Church, not in the
message of the historical Jesus, even though the Church frequently introduced its own account of Jesus' message, motifs of
its own proclamation. Thus, theological thinking – the theology
of the New Testament – begins with the kerygma of the earliest
Church and not before. (Bultmann, 1953, pp. 1–2)

The significant point here is Bultmann's reference to *eschatology*,
which, as indicated above, opens up the entire question of Bultmann's Christology, and indeed his theology proper.

Following the rediscovery of eschatology by Schweitzer and the
History of Religions School, theology was called upon to respond
to the claim that the eschatological nature of Jesus' mission and
message made it something alien to the contemporary world, and
therefore incomprehensible. Bultmann's response to this challenge
was radical. In affirming the role of eschatology at the very heart of
New Testament theology, he then went on to make a distinction
between what he referred to as 'apocalyptic' and 'eschatology'.
'Apocalyptic' becomes for Bultmann the external, objectivising
form of the historical Jesus' message. 'Eschatology', as has been
noted, becomes for Bultmann the purpose of that message. This
distinction serves to legitimise Bultmann's apparent relegation of
the historical Jesus, and his conscious self-understanding, to the
footnotes of New Testament theology, though not the New Testament *per se*.

In other words, the historical Jesus was for Bultmann an apocalyptic seer, incapable of grasping the genuine meaning of his
eschatological purpose. This, for Bultmann, was only possible from
a post-resurrection perspective, that is, the new beginning for
humanity (cf. 2 Cor. 5.17). In this way, Bultmann could conclude
with his notorious statement that:

The historical Jesus does not make any direct demand on us, nor
does he condemn us for any deed we have committed against
him....I must say bluntly: it is impossible to see what more was
done by the historical Jesus who goes to his death in obedient

love than was done by all those who, for example, in the world
war took the same road, also in obedient love....I calmly let
the fire burn, for I see that what are consumed are only the fanci-
ful portraits of life-of-Jesus theology, and that means nothing
other than 'Christ after the flesh'. But the 'Christ after the flesh'
is no concern of ours. How things looked in the heart of Jesus I
do not know and do not wish to know. (Bultmann, 1964, pp.
95–101)

This echoes so clearly Bultmann's remarks concerning the impact
of the First World War upon his own work.

Bultmann's response is of course not as dramatic as that. But this
declaration does go some way towards explaining the hostility
apparently motivating such secondary commentators as Barr and
Enslin. The reality is somewhat different. Following the History
of Religions School, Bultmann agreed that the historical Jesus'
mission and message was conditioned by the context in which it
originated. It is, as far as Bultmann is concerned, an apocalyptic
message, where for Bultmann 'apocalyptic' signifies the attempt to
describe, in objective terms, God's actions. Bultmann agreed that
Jesus' message was expressed in such objective terms, and was
therefore inadmissible for contemporary theology. He did not
agree, however, that this was the authentic meaning of Jesus' purpose. On the contrary, Jesus' purpose was to call individuals to the
encounter with God's will, which for theology is the only permiss-
ible way of speaking of God's soteriological and eschatological
action. By distinguishing between form and content, therefore,
Bultmann distinguishes between that which is apparently self-
referential in the historical Jesus, and that which points beyond
himself, towards the expression of God's will in the risen Lord.
In this sense, the message of the historical Jesus is indeed not a part
of the theology of the New Testament proper. But as its presupposition, as that in relation to which the theology of the New Testament is shaped, the eschatological purpose of his message affirms
Jesus of Nazareth as the historical basis of faith, understood from
the perspective of faithful existence. This is made clear in Bultmann's important little book, *Jesus* (Bultmann, 1926).

This brief examination of Bultmann's *Theology of the New Testa-*

ment (Bultmann, 1953) confirms the importance of the crucial issue of the role of eschatology in Bultmann's Christology and theology, an issue that will become philosophically dominant in the next chapter. At this point it is important to note that in relation to the question of the historical Jesus, that which is eschatological in Jesus' message is its purpose. Its purpose is to call individuals to the encounter with God in Christ, and therefore to a new life 'in Christ'. Eschatology for Bultmann, consequently, is that understanding of human existence which regards it as always *coram deo*. Eschatological existence is, in other words, faithful existence. It is from the perspective of faith that the eschatological purpose of Jesus' message can be distinguished from its apocalyptic form. Bultmann's exegetical concern with the New Testament, therefore, is guided by faith. This reiterates the point made earlier in this chapter: that the historical-critical study of the New Testament is part of the task of faithful existence, even though it can never be its basis.

In this way, certain features of Bultmann's theology become apparent and fall into place. Quite clearly, Bultmann is concerned to bring the individual to an encounter with God's will, as expressed in the Christ event. It is equally clear that he believes this encounter to be mediated by the kerygmatic Christ, a theological figure that in certain important respects is different from the historical Jesus. Bultmann asserts that faith is not to be established upon the basis of any historical-critical appreciation of the historical Jesus' mission and message. But in claiming that faithful existence is in reality eschatological existence, and that at bottom the meaning or purpose of Jesus' message is likewise eschatological, Bultmann raises an important relationship between the historical Jesus and the individual believer. In short, faith is called to consider the question of the historical Jesus, in order to discover Jesus' purpose. This purpose, in turn, informs the proclamation of the crucified and risen One, the kerygmatic Christ proper, who, hopefully, leads the individual to the encounter with the risen Lord. There is of course no certainty of such an encounter. There is no way in which Bultmann or any theologian can say: 'Do this and this and this, authentically', and the individual will then encounter the risen Lord. For that is the mystery of faith, and as such unintelligible. But as semantic devices, the theological expressions 'historical Jesus', 'kerygmatic

Christ', and 'faithful existence' are all joined by Bultmann's conviction that eschatology, as the non-objectifying expression of God's will to save the individual, is the key to the theologian's task.

Bultmann's theology, in other words, is nothing more nor less than the re-expression of what he means by 'eschatology', as found in the New Testament. As Chapter 3 will demonstrate, eschatology is a specifically *phenomenological* understanding of human existence; therefore, Bultmann's Christology is fundamentally phenomenological. This will become clear in the final section of the present chapter. For the time being, it is simply necessary to note that Bultmann is able to combine his work as New Testament exegete, Christian theologian, Lutheran preacher, and believing individual, because of his conviction that all of these aspects of human existence are defined by their recognition of the central significance of eschatology. In a word, Bultmann's theology is eschatological. Without that conviction, in faith, no sense can be made of Bultmann's concern with the purpose of Jesus' message. And without the eschatological purpose of Jesus' message – that purpose which the earliest Christian theologians, Paul and John, recognised and proclaimed – there could be no kerygmatic Christ, hence no encounter with the risen Lord, and therefore no faith or salvation. The historical Jesus, quite clearly, is by no means a dead issue in Bultmann's thought, but on the contrary a burning question.[1]

The *Dass* of the historical Jesus, therefore, is not the mere fact of his existence. It is, rather, his purpose: Jesus' existence *is* his purpose, from the perspective of faith and its understanding of eschatology. In this respect, Bultmann writes, in the introduction to his *Jesus*, that:

No attempt is here made to render Jesus as an historical phenomenon psychologically explicable, and nothing really biographical, apart from a brief introductory section, is included. . . . This book lacks all the phraseology which speaks of Jesus as great man, genius, or hero; he appears neither as inspired nor as inspiring, his sayings are not called profound, nor his faith mighty, nor his nature child-like. There is also no consideration of the eternal values of his message, of his discovery of the infinite depths of the human soul, or the like. *Attention is entirely limited to what he purposed, and hence to what in his purpose as a part of history makes a present demand on us.* (my italics; Bultmann, 1926, pp. 10–12)

Here one can see, quite clearly, the way in which eschatology forms the link between Christians in the contemporary situation, and the historical Jesus of Nazareth, who lived 2,000 years ago. It is Jesus' purpose, which 'makes a present demand on us'. It is entirely this principle of a continuity of intelligibility, based solely upon Bultmann's understanding of eschatology, which makes it possible to consider the question of the historical Jesus at all, with any hope of insight.

Bultmann explicitly condemns all aspects of life-of-Jesus theology, therefore. Yet he affirms the importance of the historical Jesus in his eschatological purpose. He writes:

However little we know of the life of Jesus, if we keep in mind that he was finally crucified as a messianic agitator, we shall be able *in the light of the eschatological message* to understand the fragmentary accounts of the end of his activity, overgrown though they are with legend. (my italics; Bultmann, 1926, p. 29)

Thus, the full fruits of Bultmann's emphasis upon eschatology as the foundation of intelligibility become apparent. Not only does it allow us to understand the historical Jesus' message, it is also the basis of his programme of demythologising, that is, existentialist interpretation. Hence, the entire question of hermeneutics, as it arises out of Bultmann's understanding of the role of eschatology in New Testament theology, begins with the question of the historical Jesus. This implication of Bultmann's thought was acknowledged by individuals like Ebeling, Fuchs, Bornkamm, and Käsemann (cf. Chapter 4).

It is possible to recognise, consequently, the fundamental framework of Bultmann's theology, how it involves the individual and her decision for faith, as well as the entire question of the contextual origins of Christianity as an historical religion. Given Bultmann's axiom, that to speak about God one must speak about the human individual, because God wills to come to that individual (as revealed in Jesus Christ), New Testament theology must first establish what it is that God in Jesus of Nazareth is saying about the individual. This is Jesus' purpose. And because it is that purpose which is the expression of God's eternal will, it is to be understood eschatologically, as that which is beyond the objective world and which cannot be reduced to spatio-temporal relations, but must rather be regarded as the decisive moment of the individual's existence. It is only in the appreciation of this fact, however, by the first Christian communities, that Christian faith, and hence Christian theology, became possible. One arrives, therefore, at the paradoxical heart of Bultmann's Christology. That is, Paul and John understood what Jesus did not, the latter's eschatological purpose. New Testament theology, consequently, begins with Paul and John. The kerygmatic Christ, therefore, as the creation of Paul and John, is nothing more nor less than the historical Jesus, reduced (phenomenologically) to his eschatological purpose. We only tell stories in the kerygma, in other words, about the side of the historical Jesus which directly concerns our salvation. On Bultmann's definition, that is the only side with any meaning.

In other words, theology for Bultmann – as the necessarily human attempt to speak meaningfully of God's divine and eternal will – must focus all attention upon the eschatological purpose of that will in the life, death, and resurrection of Jesus Christ. Almost by definition, this means that certain aspects of Jesus's mission and message, which cannot easily be defined in terms of eschatology, will be neglected. For Bultmann, this is perhaps unfortunate, but necessary. Or, rather, it is the result of the force and power of demythologising, that anything which is not eschatological is insignificant for Jesus' purpose, and therefore inauthentic. Theology's quest for the eternal, in this sense, leads it into a radical, almost eviscerating, interpretation of the New Testament.

Pedagogically, this is a dangerous move. By encouraging the premise that faith – and subsequently Christian theology – is concerned not with Jesus of Nazareth's mission and message in its entirety, but rather solely with its purpose, Bultmann introduces into individual reflection the question of personal judgement. Granted that the doctrines of the Church remain to guide the preacher in her presentation of the Christian kerygma, still the individual is left to interpret and evaluate the purpose of those doctrines and stories. That, as will be seen, is one part of the role of *Verstehen*, understanding, in faithful existence. There would seem to be no safeguard that Bultmann might introduce against the possibility that the individual's interpretation of Jesus' purpose is not simply the reflection of that individual's own presuppositions. Simply to state that the word of the preacher is authoritative, as it proclaims the eschatological Word, is insufficient. It still places an immense weight upon the shoulders of the individual believer. This may be no bad thing – Bultmann was, after all, a Lutheran – but it cannot be ignored.

In this respect, therefore, on might speak of a hermeneutic circle in Bultmann's theology. Individuals are authenticated by the eschatological purpose of Jesus Christ. Yet it is left to individuals to speak of that same purpose. In terms of the consistency of his theology, Bultmann's response to this concern will determine the success or failure of his attempt to identify that purpose.

What, then, *is* Jesus' purpose? The purpose of the historical Jesus is revealed in his words; in the light of Bultmann's understanding of eschatology, these words themselves have the character of eschatological actions. The historical Jesus, in this sense, teaches the human individual to come to God, in so far as Jesus' 'teaching' is the event of this demand. Bultmann writes: When we encounter the words of Jesus in history, *we* do not judge *them* by a philosophical system with reference to their rational validity; *they* meet *us* with the question of how we are to interpret our own existence' (Bultmann, 1926, p. 15). Questioning the individual's existence, from the perspective of faith, is the purpose of eschatology. Or, rather, questioning the individual's existence from the perspective of faith *is* an eschatological questioning, and those words of Jesus that conform to this understanding of eschatology are regarded by Bultmann, axiomatically it must be said, as genuine. The circularity of this argument is readily apparent: Bultmann is, essentially, judging the words of the historical Jesus by the rubric of the kerygmatic Christ, though by stating the reverse; that is, by stating that the historical Jesus 'points to' the kerygmatic Christ, thereby securing continuity between God's revelation in Jesus of Nazareth and the apostolic proclamation. As stated, therefore, a hermeneutic circle is introduced at the heart of Bultmann's theology, which will come to be regarded as the root of much difficulty for Bultmann's Christology, and therefore his entire theology (cf. Chapter 5). For the present, it is sufficient to recognise this problem, and the role it plays in Bultmann's understanding of the Christ event.

Bultmann, then, recognises as authentic words of Jesus those that refer to the kingdom of God, for this is what Jesus preached. The form of the kingdom of God in Jesus' proclamation, according to Bultmann, is apocalyptic; that is, following Weiss, Bultmann acknowledges that Jesus of Nazareth expected a kingdom that would come objectively, in empirically verifiable terms. But this is not what the expression 'the kingdom of God' signifies eschatologically. Eschatologically, writes Bultmann: 'The Kingdom of God is a power which, although it is entirely future, wholly determines the present' (Bultmann, 1926, p. 49). In so far as the kingdom of God wholly determines the present, the individual must decide whether she is going to make it her future. The kingdom, therefore, brings with its power the constraint of decision: 'Jesus sees man as standing here and now under the necessity of decision, with the possibility of decision through his own free act' (Bultmann, 1926, p. 52). If this decision in truth determines the individual's future, it must therefore be of ontological significance for that individual. Such is the weight of the eternal impinging upon the temporal. Bultmann continues:

> A man should think seriously before he decides to have anything to do with this invitation. A ready acceptance in words has no value; an act of will is required. . . . It is the eschatological deliverance which ends everything earthly. . . . Whoever seeks it must realise that he cuts himself off from the world, otherwise he belongs to those who are not fit, who put their hand to the plough and look back. (Bultmann, 1926, pp. 33–7)

Thus is Bultmann's understanding of encounter and decision deemed to be eschatological, in so far as it signifies the end of the old order, and a new beginning 'in Christ' (2 Cor. 5.17).

The challenge of encounter and decision is a call to radical obedience. Such, then, is the nature of faithful existence. So Bultmann can conclude that:

> Radical obedience exists only when a man inwardly assents to what is required of him, when the thing commanded is seen

as intrinsically God's command; when the whole man stands behind what he does; or better, when the whole man is *in* what he does, when he is not doing something obediently, but *is* essentially obedient. (Bultmann, 1926, p. 73)

The historical Jesus, therefore, has an essential role in Bultmann's Christology. Jesus proclaims the moment of decision as the reality of God's grace, and as the reality of God's grace Jesus *Christ* becomes the moment of decision – in the kerygma. For it remains certain that, despite his theological conviction that the historical Jesus proclaimed the near and far God in terms of his eschatological preaching, Bultmann dismisses the possibility of the contemporary individual encountering this proclamation *as it was given*. That is impossible because, quite simply, then and now are separated by nearly 2,000 years. The purpose of the historical Jesus, therefore, can only be encountered as purposiveness, in its soteriological potential, within the proclamation of the crucified and risen One; that is, through the theologies, for Bultmann, of Paul and John. Thus, Bultmann can write:

Jesus looks to the future and points his hearers to the *coming* Reign of God, which, to be sure, is coming even now, is already breaking in. Paul, on the other hand, looks back and points to what has already occurred. For him, the turn of the age has already taken place, the day of salvation is already present! (Bultmann, 1967, p. 224)

Bultmann's own solution to the problem of the hermeneutic circle, therefore, is to identify the kerygma of the early Church as the criterion of Jesus' eschatological purpose, since it is the theologians of the early Church – primarily Paul and John – who define Christian faith as overwhelmingly a response to a challenge met in encounter with the risen Lord. By emphasising this Pauline and Johannine definition, Bultmann is able to justify his own representation of the Christian gospel as essentially kerygmatic. He does not speak as an individual, therefore. Rather, he listens to what the New Testament says, and tells us what he hears. By focusing upon what Paul and John say about Jesus of Nazareth, Bultmann attempts to bypass the problem of his own subjective judgement of the mission and message of the historical Jesus.

Bultmann has established, therefore, the continuity between the historical Jesus and the kerygmatic Christ proclaimed by Paul and John. But he has not yet established the continuity between the kerygmatic Christ proclaimed by Paul and John and the risen Lord encountered spiritually – there is no other word for it – by the individual in the moment of decision. Nor will he. For the spiritual encounter with the risen Lord is the mystery of faith, a matter, in other words, for the individual and her God. As will be shown below, the only question of direct continuity that concerns Bultmann in his Christology is that between the historical (*historische*) Jesus who proclaims the kingdom of God, and the kerygmatic Christ who is proclaimed by Paul and John as the eschatological event of God's grace. This reinforces the threefold nature of the 'Jesus' motif in Bultmann's thought: the Jesus of Nazareth who lived and died in Palestine nearly 2,000 years ago; the kerygmatic Christ who is proclaimed by the Church; and the risen Lord of faith, Jesus Christ the event of grace, who is encountered in the eternal moment of decision. All three 'Jesuses' are linked by Bultmann's understanding of eschatology. But, in practice, for Bultmann it is correct to say that the moment of encounter with the risen Lord is mediated by the telling of the story of Jesus Christ by the Church, even though the existential encounter with the mystery of faith cannot be reduced to the telling of that story.

To this point, however, the precise theological meaning of the expression 'risen Lord of faith' remains obscure. Certainly, it might be just to Bultmann himself to acknowledge that it is not theology's task to say what the mystery of faith is. There can be, in other words, no absolute definition of the risen Lord. But this is not the point. If theology is to serve a pedagogic intent, it must be genuinely critical, that is, at the every least, lucid. And it is precisely the theological *expression* 'risen Lord' that requires more of a home than Bultmann seems prepared to provide (see below).

4   The Historical Jesus II: *Geschichte*

Following on from this treatment of the historical Jesus, it would now seem to be necessary to turn to a consideration of the so-called

'Christ of faith'. Certainly, the classic, perceived understanding of Bultmann's Christology is based upon the distinction between the historical Jesus and the Christ of faith, the implication being that Bultmann's theology in some way stands in close proximity to Kähler's (cf. Käsemann, 1964). It is not as simple as this, however. Undoubtedly, there is a difference within Bultmann's Christology. But there is also an identity. Identity and difference, therefore: this is the paradox addressed by the historical (*geschichtliche*) Jesus, Bultmann's 'second' Jesus (see above).

In an article entitled, crucially, 'The Significance of the Historical (*geschichtliche*) Jesus for the Theology of Paul' (1964), Bultmann writes: 'The historical (*geschichtliche*) Jesus makes the preaching of Paul into Gospel' (Bultmann, 1964, p. 202). What does this mean? First, it is necessary to identify what it does not mean. It does not mean that the *historische* Jesus makes the preaching of Paul into gospel. This would be an impossibility, for Jesus of Nazareth was crucified and therefore dead prior to Paul's involvement with the early Christian sect. No: it means, radically, that the story of Jesus somehow makes it possible for Paul's proclamation to become gospel. In some way, that is, the story of Jesus of Nazareth as the crucified and risen One so empowers Paul's words that they become, in the moment of decision, the decisive soteriological event of God's grace. They become Christ himself, so that those who meet Christ in the proclamation at the moment of decision are thereby one with Christ. This can mean nothing more nor less than that Bultmann is asserting some form of continuity between the kerygmatic Christ proclaimed by Paul, and the origins of God's action in Jesus of Nazareth, *in the geschichtliche Jesus*, so that the word of Paul becomes the Word of God. This continuity, for Bultmann, is ensured by the shared understanding of eschatology that he finds in Paul and in the *historische* Jesus.

This is the notion that is of radical significance. It is the *geschichtliche* Jesus himself, presented in the story of the crucified and risen One as the eschatological messenger, who *is* the very continuity with which Bultmann is concerned; that is, by telling the Jesus story solely in terms of its eschatological significance, the continuity between Jesus and Paul, and then Jesus and the individual, is maintained and insured. But this is more for Bultmann than a neat semantic trick. It is indicative of the necessary understanding that is the precondition of faith itself, as the human involvement within faith. The individual must first accept that the preaching Church which brings the message of the gospel as the event of salvation stands in continuity with the *historische* Jesus in whom God acted. Without this, there can be no step forward into faith; no turning towards God; indeed, no Christology. If the preaching Church does not have the *geschichtliche* Jesus in its midst – that is, if it does not tell the story of the crucified and risen One in terms of the eschatology that certifies the continuity between the historical Jesus and that Church – then it cannot be the preaching Church. Its Christology, then, cannot be Christology. Only if this one, unifying understanding of eschatology is preserved in the story of Jesus, so that Jesus is at once both 'story-teller' and 'story', can Paul's preaching become gospel.

Bultmann provides the evidence for this interpretation of his Christology in an essay entitled 'Das Verhältnis der urchristlichen Christusbotschaft zum historischen Jesus' (1967). He writes: 'Insofar as Jesus understood himself as an eschatological phenomenon, we can say that his proclamation implies a Christology' (Bultmann, 1967, p. 457). Here is a decisive point. For the Christology that it implies can only be a Christology that preserves that understanding of eschatology which is found in Jesus' purpose as an eschatological phenomenon. For Bultmann, it is simple but correct to say, this means only in the theologies of Paul and John, and those theologies that are dependent upon them. In a signal passage, Bultmann argues, that:

> From the discrepancy which I emphasise between the historical Jesus and the Christ of the kerygma it does not at all follow that I destroy continuity between the historical Jesus and the primitive Christian proclamation. I say expressly, between the historical Jesus and the primitive Christian proclamation, and not between the historical Jesus and the Christ. The Christ of the kerygma is not an historical figure which can enjoy continuity with the historical Jesus. The kerygma which proclaims him is an historical [*historisches*] phenomenon, however. Therefore it is only the continuity between the kerygma and the historical Jesus which is involved. (Bultmann, 1967, p. 448)

What Bultmann is saying is that the concrete utterance of the kerygma in the presence of an individual involves the representation of the story of the historical Jesus in both of his guises, that is, as both *Historie* and *Geschichte*. Indeed, the semantic presentation of the story of Jesus is only story (*geschichtliche*) if it preserves the original understanding of eschatology, which means if it preserves its continuity with the *historische* Jesus. The neatness of Bultmann's Christology cannot but be admired: the proclamation is not *Historie*, but nor is it *Geschichte* if it does not preserve its continuity with *Historie* through eschatology, which thereby validates the truth of the *Dass* of Jesus as his eschatological purpose.

This, however, does not mean that the Christ who is God's eschatological event can be encountered as the semantic occurrence of the story of Jesus, told in, through, and by the kerygma. On the contrary, the Christ who saves can only be encountered in decision. But one is only presented with the moment of decision as the possibility of salvation in, by, and through the kerygma. In this way, the Christ who saves is identical with the Christ who is proclaimed as story, but not to anyone who attempts to quantify that relationship. There can be no such quantifiable continuity. There must be room for the leap or, better, the decision of faith.

Bultmann writes: 'How far does all this take us? Actually, it makes intelligible the historical continuity between the activity of Jesus and the kerygma' (Bultmann, 1967, p. 458). That continuity is the necessary precursor of the encounter with the Christ of God's grace. But once that necessity has been understood, the historical Jesus fades. Bultmann writes that: 'The Christ of the kerygma has, as it were, displaced the historical Jesus and authoritatively addresses the hearer – every hearer' (Bultmann, 1967, p. 458). Displaced, but not replaced: like many things in Bultmann's theology, the historical Jesus in both of his guises serves his purpose and then makes way for the question mark which is placed above all human existence. Bultmann's theology in its entirety may be reduced to this one question mark, but only if one understands the absolute necessity of that which is displaced in the process of that reduction.

As early as 1917, Bultmann had identified this argument in the proclamation of his own Christian theology. In a sermon published under the title 'Concerning the hidden and the revealed God', Bultmann writes:

It frequently happens that in listening to a piece of music we at first do not hear the deep, fundamental tone, the sure stride of the melody, on which everything else is built, because we are deafened by the fullness of detail, the veritable sea of sounds and impressions which overwhelms us. It is only after we have accustomed our ear that we find law and order, and as with one magical stroke, a single unified world emerges from the confused welter of sounds. (Bultmann, 1960, p. 26)

Listening to the Word of God is a lot like this for Bultmann. One cannot but hear the voice of the historical Jesus, for he indeed is the very stuff of which the proclamation is made. But one must go deeper, into the heart of the proclamation, before one can hear its melody.

In fact, Bultmann's own theology is very similar to the analogue which he employs in that 1917 sermon. So far in this chapter we have considered its 'deep, fundamental tone...on which every-thing else is built': Bultmann's treatment of the question of the his-torical Jesus. In turn, we saw how Bultmann introduced his basic theological principles of faith, encounter, decision, and eschatology, into his treatment of this question. In this way, he established the necessary continuity between the historical Jesus and the keryg-matic Christ. Indeed, all of Bultmann's work as a New Testament exegete and scholar is directed towards the understanding of this continuity.

If this is the deep, fundamental tone, however, on which every-thing else is built, what is the 'everything else'? Where does Bultmann's treatment of this question lead us? It leads the individ-ual to the encounter with the risen Lord. In consideration of this encounter, Bultmann's theology is revealed in all its glory.

5 The Risen Lord

At this point, it is worth recalling the simile of the hour-glass that was employed earlier in this chapter. Bultmann's treatment of the question of the historical Jesus, beginning in the wide ranges of his theological teachers, Herrmann, the History of Religions School and the rediscovery of eschatology, encompasses every element of his intellectual activity, exegetical and theological. Implicit within his basic axiom, that to speak about God one must speak about humanity, because God has spoken about humanity in Jesus of Nazareth, this concern with the question of the historical Jesus channels the development of his central theological motifs. Themes of encounter, decision, faith, the eschatological nature of authentic existence: all are located in the purpose of the mission and message of Jesus of Nazareth. It is a small matter, in this sense, that Bultmann solely uses the notion of eschatological continuity between the historical Jesus and the kerygmatic Christ in order to distance faith and the encounter with the risen Lord from any direct dependence upon 'empirical evidence'. Even here – especially here – Bultmann is concerned with the question of the historical Jesus.

His emphasis upon the eschatological continuity between the figure of Jesus, and the figure of the kerygmatic Christ, because of their shared purpose, that is, calling people to the encounter with the risen Lord, means that Bultmann is secure from any accusation that his Christology reduces the Christ event to a mere symbol, used to express an essentially humanist claim for the good (i.e. authentic) life. In Bultmann's Christology, it is Christianity, not humanism, that is revealed to be an historical religion, founded, ironically to be sure, in the activity of a particular individual, which activity is open to our understanding because of our acknowledgement, in faith, of the eschatological nature of existence.

If the simile of the hour-glass is accepted, however, where does it lead? Given that Bultmann's thoughts, his theology, are directed by his treatment of the question of the historical Jesus, towards the kerygmatic Christ, and thereby explicitly to that individual whom God wills to encounter and call to faithful existence, what precisely happens in that encounter? It must certainly be more than simply the presentation of a proposition, the semantic advocacy of an alternative (albeit authentic) way of life. The entire point of Bultmann's insistence upon eschatology as the basis of faithful existence, and any genuine understanding of the question of the historical Jesus, is to refute the idea that the story of Jesus Christ can be accepted as a rather better alternative role model than those presently on offer. But where is the emphasis that raises this question to the soteriological, and therefore ontological, level upon which Bultmann locates it?

The direct answer is that Bultmann's entire theology ultimately comes to rest upon the shoulders of the *risen* Lord. It is the resurrection, in other words, that transforms Jesus Christ from being merely an excellent human being. In the same way, it is *dying and rising* with Christ, 'in Christ', which authenticates the individual's life as faithful existence. John 11.25, therefore – Jesus said, 'I am the resurrection and the life. He who believes in me, though he die, yet shall he live, and whoever lives and believes in me shall never die' – is a signal passage for Bultmann's theology. In his commentary upon this passage, Bultmann writes:

Jesus speaks as the Revealer. He is the Resurrection and the Life, since for those who believe in him; i.e., who acknowledge him as the Revealer of God, life and death as men know and call them are no longer realities. If the Revealer is described as the life and as the resurrection, the reason for that is not simply that the dialogue is directed against the primitive conception of resurrection and would affirm that whatever is significant in that idea finds its answer in Jesus; it also brings to expression that the life is an eschatological phenomenon; i.e., that it is accessible only in the resurrection.

'I am the life' is not a description of the metaphysical nature of Jesus; it speaks of his gift for the man who comes to faith and thereby 'rises'. That he is the life in his significance for faith is exactly what is meant by the linking together of resurrection and life.

The self-predication is unfolded in a couplet. The two lines say the same thing, positively and negatively; by a paradoxical mode of expression they remove the concepts of life and death into another sphere, for which human death and human life are only images and hints: the believer may suffer the earthly death, but he has 'life' in a higher, in an ultimate sense. And for the man who tarries in the earthly life and is a believer, there is no death in an ultimate sense; death for him has become unreal. Life and death in the human sense – the highest good and the deepest terror – have become unreal for him; in so far as he sees the Revealer with eyes of faith, he stands before God himself. *Nam mors animae abalienatio est a Deo.* (Bultmann, 1971, pp. 402–3)

'In so far as he sees the Revealer with the eyes of faith...': this means nothing more nor less than seeing the Revealer eschatologi-

cally. It follows, therefore, that if one sees Jesus Christ eschatologically, that is, in terms of his purpose, one automatically sees him
as the Revealer. And contrariwise: if one sees him as the Revealer,
then in faith one stands before God. Then is revealed the high-
point of Bultmann's theology. As the Revealer, Jesus Christ reveals
that he is the Revealer; that is, he does not 'reveal' anything further
in an objective sense. But in that he is the Revealer, he is the
eschatological event of God's grace, the will of God to save.
Encountered as such, via the story of Jesus Christ told and
perceived eschatologically, 'in Christ' the individual is one with
God.

This introduces the final theme of Bultmann's theology, explicitly formulated in the essay *New Testament and Mythology* (Bultmann, 1948), and commonly regarded as the *leitmotiv* of his mature
thought – that is, the question of demythologising, or existentialist
interpretation. On the basis of what has been said so far in this
chapter, the following definition of 'demythologising' can be
offered with confidence. 'Demythologising' – existentialist interpretation – as a hermeneutic principle means reading and thinking the
questions of faith, the kerygmatic Christ, and the historical Jesus,
solely in terms of the expressed understanding of eschatology
which Bultmann finds explicit in Paul and John, and implicit in the
purpose of Jesus' message.

In Chapter 3, it will be shown that thinking everything in terms
of eschatology means, philosophically, understanding everything
phenomenologically. Here, we can say that demythologising is not
at all the rejection of the objective, but rather the assertion of
its ontological significance in terms of its relationship with the
eschatological event. In this way, an existentialist interpretation of
the question of the historical Jesus is not a rejection of that figure's
soteriological significance *per se*, but is rather a rejection of its
significance in objective terms. As must be apparent by now, the
soteriological significance of the historical Jesus is revealed –
through existentialist interpretation – in terms of his eschatological
purpose, and therefore his role within the self-revelation of God's
will.

The manner in which demythologising works can be illustrated
with reference to the question of the resurrection. Contrary to
popular opinion, Bultmann does not argue that one cannot believe

in an *historische* resurrection (cf. Pannenberg, 1967, pp. 131–3). Rather, he is saying that there is simply no point to such a belief, because the eschatological nature of the resurrection means that it cannot be encountered objectively, but only existentially; that is, only in terms of its eschatological significance, where all faithful existence is by definition eschatological. It is this distinction that is so important for any understanding of Bultmann's interpretation of the resurrection, and indeed for his entire Christology. One can believe whatever one will – as long as one does not believe solely in objective terms, this does not matter, although Bultmann is adamant that the reduction of the Christian gospel to objective 'facts' is the very devil. To be saved, however, one must believe decisively; that is, one must decide for faith, in faith. Such is eschatological existence.

This understanding of demythologising as fundamentally eschatological interpretation informs Bultmann's understanding of the proclamation of the word, and subsequently the (possible) encounter with the Word, the risen Lord. It will be remembered how Bultmann asserted that the proclamation of the kerygma is a concrete, *historische* action. It must be so, because there can be no other way in which the Christian minister can preach the word of God, the story of Jesus Christ. For the kerygma to be proclamation, there must be a hearer for the word spoken. This symbiotic relationship between speaker and hearer of the word establishes the possibility of semantic comprehension concerning the story of Jesus Christ. It is, therefore, a linguistic event.

Bultmann's understanding of the task of Christology is in fact subordinated to his understanding of the task of ontological reflection. All such thought, in so far as it is pedagogic, is ultimately reflexive; that is, it returns to the concerns of the subject. Bultmann's God is a God who accepts, or better, ordains this state of affairs (cf. Chapter 3).

Although it is clear that in Bultmann's theology God's action in Christ as eschatological event cannot be reduced to a symbol, because the eschatological event affects human existence in its entirety, whereas a symbol only has meaning given to it in the act of cognition and judgement, the primary accusation against Bultmann of this line of thought – that is, that he makes Christology subservient to philosophy, to some form of humanist anthropology – remains. Indeed, it is a common accusation levelled against Bultmann that his entire theological activity was in fact simply an attempt to restore to theology the degree of rationality that it had lost, at least in Germany, through the advent of pietism. This raises, therefore, the question of the order in which theology and philosophy are to be taken in Bultmann's thought; that is, which has priority in his understanding of the Christian message. The answer – that the relationship between theology and philosophy in Bultmann's thought is entirely commutative – is of central importance for the next chapter. It means that theological statements are only meaningful in so far as they relate God's action to the human condition, and that philosophical statements are only meaningful if they understand God as the ontological foundation of every possibility of human existence. This principle is found most clearly in Bultmann's Christology, which is why, ultimately, his treatment of the question of the historical Jesus is the key to understanding his entire theology. On this, Jüngel writes, that:

> For Bultmann, the anthropological relevance of theological statements is the criterion of their truth, because for him revelation is constantly an eschatological happening which as such becomes event in an historical 'that'. It amounts to the 'paradoxical identity', that an historical 'that' becomes historically significant as eschatological event. (Jüngel, 1976, p. 59)

As with his understanding of the continuity between the *historische* Jesus and the kerygmatic Christ, the principle upon which the continuity between philosophy and theology is founded is the principle of the eschatological event. That is, for Bultmann 'eschatology' functions as both a philosophical and a theological principle of interpretation. Theology, therefore, like faith, is a hermeneutics of eschatological interpretation. The individual can never take this for granted, however; it cannot be treated simply as a symbol waiting to be cognised. So Bultmann can conclude that: 'The Word of God never becomes our property. The test of whether or not we have heard it correctly is whether we are prepared always to hear it anew, to ask for it in every decision of every life' (Bultmann, 1960, p. 169). Such is Bultmann's understanding of the Christian life as eschatological faith. In so saying, he is entirely loyal to Luther's principle that:

> et ita Deus per suum exire nos facit ad nos ipsos introire et per sui cognitionem infert nobis et nostri cognitionem.
>
> Thus, in going out of himself, God brings it about that we go into ourselves; and through knowledge of him he brings us to knowledge of ourselves. (cf. Bultmann, 1965b, p. 29)

For Bultmann, therefore, the concept of revelation, which means in effect his understanding of the eschatological event of God's grace, expresses as much about humanity as it does about God. How is this possible? It must centre upon the original dialectical nature of the relationship between God and humanity which Bultmann accepts in the 1920s, and which Barth had expounded as the basis of dialectical theology; that is, the 'infinite qualitative distinction' between God and humanity. This distinction – or ontological difference, to employ an expression that will become crucial in Chapter 3 – is not to be understood in a static sense, but as the active principle for interpreting the relationship between God and humanity. In other words, in so far as God wills to be the One to overcome the infinite qualitative distinction between God and humanity, God acts in the eschatological event of the Christ to preserve the ontological difference as that process or movement of revelation which constitutes the pathway by which the individual comes to God and God comes to the individual. God, therefore, must at one and the same time be hidden and revealed, as the individual must at the same time be hidden and revealed: only in this way can Christ be God's eschatological event in eternity. Bultmann writes: 'God the mysterious and hidden must at the same time be the God who is revealed' (Bultmann, 1960, p. 30). This for Bultmann is simply the distillation of the story of Jesus Christ which he finds proclaimed in the New Testament. He states that:

> We may very well say that the paradox, that is, the eschatological event as the event of the Christian message, in which the historical Jesus becomes present – that this paradox finds expression in the Gospel of Mark in a primitive way, in that theory of the

'messianic secret' which does, in fact, answer the question why
Jesus' messiahship remains hidden during his lifetime. It was,
in fact, because he would not have it disclosed; because he
concealed it. In John's Gospel this theory is developed or
transformed in a very remarkable way – Jesus' messiahship here
is not hidden because he concealed it but because he revealed it.
(Bultmann, 1965a, p. 260)

For Bultmann, as for the Fourth Evangelist, the paradox of the
eschatological event is that it is both hidden as it is revealed, and
revealed as the hiddenness of God is understood. For only when
the individual understands God as the God who wills to act in self-
revelation, through sheer love of humanity, can that individual
encounter the Christ of faith in the moment of decision. Revelation,
therefore, is identical with concealment. Only in that identity can
the individual encounter God in Christ as the truly eschatological
Word.

Bultmann writes, therefore, that, 'Revelation consists in nothing
other than the fact of Jesus Christ' (Bultmann, 1965b, p. 18) because Jesus Christ is the eschatological event. That this revelation is
of ontological importance for the individual, Bultmann attests
when he writes that: 'Revelation is an occurrence that places me in a
new situation as a self. . .' (Bultmann, 1965b, p. 2), and that in the
process of revelation this event conquers death: '. . . what can be
called revelation can only be what actually abolishes death. . .'
(Bultmann, 1965b, p. 15), thereby fulfilling the eschatological
meaning of 2 Corinthians 5.17, that 'in Christ' the individual
becomes a new creation. So Bultmann can conclude that:

> If the primary meaning of revelation in any case is that God *does*
> something, then the meaning of this deed or occurrence as some-
> thing wrought by *God* is strictly maintained, in that it is asserted
> not that this occurrence is a fact within the world – even one of
> the greatest possible cosmic dimensions – but rather that it is
> precisely an 'eschatological' fact; that is, the kind of fact in which
> the world comes to an end. (Bultmann, 1965b, p. 22)

At the very bottom of the first bell of the hour-glass, therefore,
returning to the simile previously cited, one finds in Bultmann's
Christology the narrowest possible definition of what it is to

encounter the Christ of faith as God's Word of salvation: Christ becomes a question mark. Bultmann's entire theology leads (cf. Gal. 3.24) the individual to this one, single, narrow path to God. It is, in fact, a tightrope that only God can walk, in Christ. It is certainly clear that for Bultmann, God could walk other paths, if they were chosen, but that God has chosen this narrowest of paths for the event of God's self-revelation. 'Why?' remains a mystery not to be questioned by the individual. It is certain, however, that Bultmann concentrates all of his efforts, most notably in his programme of demythologising or existentialist interpretation – that is, the eschatological interpretation of the story of Jesus Christ – upon keeping clear this narrow path. This is indicated by his interpretation of the 'I am' saying of John 14.6 – 'I am the way, the truth, and the life' – concerning which Bultmann writes:

> According to John the redemption is an event which takes place in human existence through the encounter with the Revealer, with the result that the believer's present is already based on his future; his existence is eschatological existence; his way is at the same time his goal.
>
> 'I am the way': this is pure expression of the idea of revelation. The Revealer is the access to God which man is looking for, and what is more – as is implied in the phrase 'I am' – the only access. Not, however, in the sense that he mediated the access and then became superfluous; i.e., not in the sense of a mystagogue, who brings doctrines and celebrations that are the means to the vision of God. On the contrary, he is the way in such a manner as to be at the same time the goal. (Bultmann, 1971, pp. 605–6)

This is the clearest possible definition of the pedagogic intent of Bultmann's theology.

The path is the path of preaching, of proclamation, the kerygma that makes known to the individual the grace of God, as the eschatological story of Jesus Christ. Bultmann states that: 'Demythologising will make clear this function of preaching as a personal message' (Bultmann, 1958, p. 36). Bultmann's programme of demythologising, therefore, like his eschatological understanding of God's action in Christ as event, is at the disposal of the risen Lord. But not solely the risen Lord. For in so far as the risen Lord is encountered in the eternal moment of decision, this presupposes the encounter with the semantic moment of the story of Jesus of Nazareth (cf. Ricoeur, 1980). Bultmann can write, therefore, that: 'The preaching of the New Testament proclaims Jesus Christ, not only in his preaching of the Kingdom of God, but first of all his person' (Bultmann, 1958, p. 16). In this respect, the contemporary proclamation of the word of God is one with the biblical proclamation of the word of God, in so far as both are unified by this particular understanding of eschatology. Demythologising recognises this principle. For mythology objectivises eschatology so that it no longer confronts that which is truly future for the individual in her historical existence – that is, salvation or condemnation. In other words, eschatology in Bultmann's understanding deals with a future that is not temporal but ontological, as the plane of possibility, in decision. Bultmann writes:

> Eschatological preaching views the present time in the light of the future, and it says to men that this present world, the world of nature and history [*Historie*], the world in which we live our lives and make our plans is not the only world: that this world is temporal and transitory, yes, but ultimately empty and unreal in the face of eternity. (Bultmann, 1958, p. 23)

And it is face to face with eternity that Bultmann's Christology intends to bring the individual. One recognises once again, though here in a more explicitly philosophical sense, his pedagogic intent.

In pursuit of this goal, Bultmann does some odd things to the historical Jesus, and many of the claims that he reduces this figure to a simple shadow have justification. In one respect, however, Bultmann is always clear: the key to all Christological reflection is a right understanding of eschatology. And in a right understanding of eschatology, the purpose of the historical Jesus' mission and message is revealed. Bultmann writes: 'Jesus proclaims the will of God and the responsibility of man, pointing towards the eschatological event, but it is not because he is an eschatologist that he proclaims the will of God. On the contrary, he is an eschatologist because he proclaims the will of God' (Bultmann, 1958, p. 26).

This is how Bultmann distinguishes between the apocalyptic form of Jesus' message, and its eschatological purpose, which distinction was elaborated and explained above. In like manner, each individual who accepts the will of God in the moment of decision becomes an eschatologist, and thereby rises with Christ. In this resurrection the believer becomes a new creation, and must therefore abandon the old creation. This is the essence of faithful existence: that one takes up one's new creation. Faith means positively abandoning the past, and leaving the dead to bury their dead (Matt. 8.22; cf. Chapter 5):

> The Word of God addresses man in his personal existence and thereby it gives him freedom from the world and from the sorrow and anxiety which overwhelms him when he forgets the beyond.... To believe in the Word of God means to abandon all merely human security and thus to overcome the despair which arises from the attempt to find security, an attempt which is always vain.... Faith is the answer to the message. Faith is the abandonment of man's own security and the readiness to find security only in the unseen beyond, in God. (Bultmann, 1957, p. 40)

Faith, therefore, is keeping open the path between God and the individual, and as such is the gift of God which the individual receives in the moment of decision, and in which the same individual actively participates. It is this pathway as God's action that is the mystery of God's love, of which faith is the witness. For Bultmann, therefore, God is not to be thought of in terms of essence at all, but only in terms of action 'in Christ'. And in so far as God's action 'in Christ' is the perfect manifestation of God's Will, and Christ is one with God, God is to be thought of as Will – that is, as Christ. The unknown God is therefore 'known', that is, encountered, in Christ, *as* Christ. This encounter with Christ is ultimately an encounter with the individual's real possibility *coram deo*. In the final analysis, this is what Bultmann hears in the Bible as the Word of God: 'I think our interest is really to hear what the Bible has to say for our actual present, to hear what is the truth about our life and about our soul' (Bultmann, 1957, p. 52). That is: to speak about God, one must speak about humanity, because God has spoken about humanity in the Word.

Thus, Bultmann's theology comes full circle, and returns to that axiom from which it began, an axiom that is founded in the question of the historical Jesus, as this chapter has attempted to demonstrate. The next stage of this examination is to consider the philosophical basis and implications of Bultmann's theology. This means considering not only what Bultmann actually wants to say about the individual's existence, given that it is an eschatological existence *coram deo*. It also means considering *how* he says it. Unavoidably, this latter question concerns Bultmann's intellectual relationship with the German phenomenologist, Martin Heidegger.

2

The Human Question

In the previous chapter, I attempted to demonstrate the structural development of Bultmann's theology in terms of his treatment of the *question* of the historical Jesus. Motifs and expressions such as faith, decision, encounter, existence, and history itself, were all discussed in the light of Bultmann's Christology. In turn, I argued that it was his understanding of the role and significance of eschatology that formed the basis of his Christology, so that a continuity was maintained between the historical Jesus, the kerygmatic Christ, and the Christian believer 'in Christ', on the strength of their participation in the event of salvation. For Bultmann, eschatology is everything, because within the eschatological moment, everything is; that is, the moment of decision as eschatological event 'in Christ' is of ontological significance. The purpose of the next two chapters is to demonstrate that Bultmann's ontological understanding of eschatology must itself be understood phenomenologically, in the Heideggerian sense of that expression. The goal of this present study, with respect to Bultmann's relationship with Heidegger, can therefore be summarised quite straightforwardly. I want to show that Bultmann's is not an existentialist theology, but rather a phenomenological one.

Bultmann the theologian is not an existentialist, therefore; he is a phenomenologist. And yet he writes, almost ceaselessly, of existence: human, faithful, authentic, inauthentic, but always existence. This would appear to contradict the claim that Bultmann is not an existentialist. That, however, is not the case. Rather, the juxtaposition of existentialism and phenomenology helps to clarify, once and for all, the nature of Bultmann's debt to Heidegger, and indeed Heidegger's debt to Bultmann.

There are in Bultmann's thought two clear and distinct questions, these being the two sides of his ontological reflection. These we can designate the human question, and the God question; that is, the precursor to theology, and then theology proper. The human question concerns not the nature, but rather the meaning of human existence as fundamentally being-towards-God, either accepted or rejected by the individual will (see below; cf. Heidegger, 1962, p. 30). For Bultmann, this is not so much an essential, as an hermeneutic question, in the broadest sense of that term; that is, the meaning of human existence is to be understood and interpreted historically. In this sense, we might call the human question in Bultmann's thought, the existential question.

The human question, in turn, points towards the God question, as per Bultmann's famous axiom that to speak about God, one must speak about humanity. The God question itself, by definition, cannot be answered directly, but must rather be approached tangentially. That is, for Bultmann it is God who by an active revelation of Will comes to the individual in the encounter. Without this divine initiative, there can be no expression of the individual's own will. In this fashion, one might speak of God's 'journey' in Bultmann's theology, whereby God's coming to the individual in encounter – and thereby addressing the human question – is revealed as the meaning and purpose of the incarnation, God's action in Jesus Christ. The God question, therefore, is the question of the ontological difference, where 'difference' is understood in a dynamic sense, as something that differentiates but at the same time is always being overcome (cf. Chapter 3). The human question, by contrast, concerns Bultmann's attempts to discover that pre-theological understanding of human existence as being-towards-God, either accepted or rejected, which in turn will inform his own, subsequent theological proclamation. On this point, Bultmann is clearly in agreement with Heidegger, when the latter writes, in *Being and Time*, that '*Theology* is seeking a more primordial interpretation of man's being towards God, prescribed by the meaning of faith itself and remaining within it' (Heidegger, 1962, p. 30). To seek 'a more primordial interpretation': this is the purpose of Bultmann's ontological reflection in terms of his answer to the human question.

Bultmann, though, is by no means concerned to delve as deeply as Heidegger does into questions of 'primordial interpretation'. As Heidegger rightly remarks (and in many respects, Heidegger has always been Bultmann's best commentator), because of the positive nature of theology – and indeed the positive nature of the *religionsgeschichtliche* analysis that precedes it – theology's 'primordial interpretation' is always prescribed by faith, where 'faith' for Bultmann is fundamentally determined by the attitude of the individual towards human existence as being-towards-God. There is nothing in Bultmann's thought, consequently, of the complexity of Heidegger's analysis of *Dasein*. The question of faith is itself only concerned with certain aspects of being and time, which aspects, to be sure, it regards as primary. This will become clear as this chapter develops.

It has been traditional, nevertheless, for the secondary literature to locate Heidegger's influence solely upon the side of the human question. In this process, Bultmann's reflections upon the meaning of human existence are raised to the level of a full-blown anthropology, which is then, with reference to Heidegger's *Being and Time*, turned into ontology *per se*; that is, the human question becomes, erroneously, the sole ontological question, which in fact it can never be for Christianity. In this fashion, the way is cleared for certain commentators to describe Bultmann's as a fundamentally atheistic clarification of what occurs in human existence.

The mistake here is obvious. By locating Heidegger's influence solely upon the human question, a false premise is established; namely, that the God question is somehow separable from Bultmann's relationship with Heidegger. It is not. Heidegger's primary influence upon Bultmann's theology is an influence upon the God question, that is, *the* ontological question. As such, it is a phenomenological rather than an existential or anthropological influence. Indeed, anthropology, understood as the objective analysis of human existence, is explicitly excluded by both Bultmann and Heidegger.

regarded, erroneously and disastrously, as solely an analysis of human existence, is far less important for Bultmann than many people realise. What is important for Bultmann in *Being and Time*, and which Heidegger subsequently spent his entire life elucidating, is the embryonic understanding of the ontological difference between *Sein* and *Dasein* as an event (*Ereignis*) of revelation which may be recognised as such. It is this understanding that informs Bultmann's answer to the God question. Chapter 3, in so far as it considers Bultmann's relationship with Heidegger, will be concerned with the event of revelation as the answer to the God question in Bultmann's theology.

The next two chapters, therefore, are concerned with the human question and the God question respectively. Although the God question is by far the most important, however, the human question must not be neglected. For it is the question of Bultmann's own tradition, the Lutheran. What I will attempt to show in this chapter, consequently, is that Bultmann arrived at a basic understanding of human existence not because of his reading of *Being and Time* (although *Being and Time* certainly helped to clarify aspects of Bultman's thought – see below), but because of his own positive *religionsgeschichtliche* concerns. In other words, Bultmann is guided by the *positum*, the 'given', of earliest Christianity. He is not free to commence elsewhere, and he is certainly not free to attempt the kind of 'fundamental ontology' that Heidegger moves towards in *Being and Time*. In this respect, Bultmann's analysis of the *positum* of the Christian religion is informed by the tradition in which he stands; that is, what might be called the Lutheran tradition.

With this acknowledgement of the question of faith's influence upon Bultmann's 'primordial interpretation', it is justified to speak of a distinction within Bultmann's thought between the *fides qua creditur*, 'the faith by which one believes', which is in fact Bultmann's 'primordial interpretation' (prescribed by faith, as Heidegger insisted); and the *fides quae creditur*, 'the faith which is believed', which is nothing more or less than the revelation of God in Christ. In this way, the human and God questions can be seen for what they are; that is, two sides of the one coin, Christian faith. This means that any *a priori* rejection of the *question* of faith is tantamount to a rejection of the human question. As will be seen in Chapter 3, this is of great importance for both Bultmann and Heidegger.

In a famous statement in his *Jesus*, Bultmann writes:

> Man has departed from God; he does not see God's activity in the everyday events of the world; the thought of omnipotence is to him an empty speculation which gains meaning only if he sees God's miracles. And when he takes refuge in prayer to God, he abandons the idea of an omnipotent God and confesses that he cannot perceive God. God is the distant God; that means, man stands in the world alone, without God, given over to fate and death like the prodigal son in the strange land. God is the near God; that can only mean, the very sense of insecurity which characterises the life of man separated from God arises from the fact that God is seeking man. And that God is seeking man can only mean that God imposes his claim upon him. That man is separated from God, then, evidently means that man does not fulfil the demand of God upon him. The distance of God from man has the same cause as the nearness of God, namely, that man belongs to God, that God imposes a claim upon him. When man fails to hear this demand, he himself transforms God's nearness into remoteness. (Bultmann, 1926, pp. 179–80)

'God is seeking man': the awareness of that fact, be it almost subconsciously or in the most tangential manner or fashion, is fundamentally the prior disposition or pre-understanding (*Vorverständnis*) concerning human being, through which the individual realises the parlous and isolated nature of existence without God. It is, one might say, the awareness that human existence, in all of its finitude, is meaningless without reference to the divine. In this sense, Bultmann's conviction that 'God is seeking man' can be recognised as one part of a tradition reaching back to Augustine, via Barth, Herrmann, Ritschl, Kierkegaard, Schleiermacher, Luther, and the German mystical tradition. Here, one may speak of the *positive philosophy of Bultmann's Christian religion*, which is informed by the ontological reflection of his own predecessors in this particular tradition, as well, of course, as his own 'primordial interpretation'.

This is certainly not to deny the importance of Bultmann's own ontological reflection in addressing the human question. Rather, it is to deny that it should be regarded as in any sense novel. In other words, to recognise and to preserve the special character of Bultmann's answer to the God question, with Heidegger's assistance, it is necessary to acknowledge the essentially derivative nature of Bultmann's answer to the human question. That is, in Heidegger's terms, Bultmann stands in a tradition which regards human being as being-towards-God, prescribed by faith. Thus, the basic themes that establish Bultmann's understanding of such motifs as existence, encounter, and decision – that is, his ontological reflection upon or 'primordial interpretation' of being and time – are to be seen in relation to the tradition in which he stands. Bultmann's real significance for contemporary thought – as an event theorist of revelation (cf. Chapter 3) – stands in sharp relief to the apparently profound existential tradition with which he is normally associated, but which is in fact of secondary importance within his theology.

1   Ontological Reflection

(a)   Being

What is 'being'? In many respects, it is simply a useful expression by which a thinker speaks about human existence. Bultmann, as a theologian, speaks about human being as being-towards-God in terms of faith: there is faithful existence, and faithless existence; two ways of being human which are in fact antitheses. 'Faith' here is the theological motif established by reflection upon the meaning of being. 'Faith', therefore, signifies the authentic recognition of being as being-towards-God. It is this recognition of being as being-towards-God that the Christian kerygma must stimulate. The kerygma, therefore, as the vehicle of Christology, is intimately related to Bultmann's 'primordial interpretation'. This is something that will be developed throughout this chapter.

This analysis, however, will not suffice for very long. For there is indeed human being, and then there is the divine Being. These cannot, obviously (and even simply as signs or symbols), be alternative modes of being, alternative possibilities for the individual. On the contrary, they must be completely distinguished one from the other. There is, in this sense, an 'ontological difference' between divine Being and the human being (cf. Chapter 3) as being-towards-God; that is, being-toward-Being. In theology, this idea has grown up with the twentieth century: Barth employed it in his *Commentary on Romans* (Barth, 1963), but in fact within philosophy it goes back to Kierkegaard's 'infinite qualitative distinction', and before that to Trendelenburg's 'infinite specific distinction'. Bultmann writes:

> But I think I always saw one thing clearly, namely, that the decisive thing is to make it clear with what concept of reality, of being and events, we really operate in theology, and how this relates to the concepts in which not only other people think and speak of reality, being and events, but in which we theologians also think and speak in our everyday lives. Ontological reflection is thus needed. (Jaspert and Bromiley, 1982, p. 87)

Here he is quite clearly referring to a reflection upon human existence, in terms of this ontological difference between human being and divine Being.

One of the implications of Bultmann's ontological reflection as a theologian, therefore, is that human being is not the same thing as human existence. On the contrary, human existence is clearly to be regarded as human being as being-towards-God either accepted or rejected. That is, divine Being is normative for the theologian's understanding and judgement of reality, being, and events. The implications of this discovery for our understanding of Bultmann's method are very clear. The theme 'being' in his positive philosophy establishes the theological motif 'existence' only in so far as that theology takes seriously the idea of an ontological *difference*. Descriptions of human being in Bultmann's work, consequently, belong to his positive philosophy, which in turn belongs to his work as an historian of the primitive Christian religion. As such, they are clearly influenced by the fundamentally pietistic Lutheran tradition in which he stands. Such descriptions of human being – part of the human question – only become theologically pertinent – part of the God question – when understood in the light of the event of the ontological difference.

There is a danger that this idea will appear more complex than in fact it is. Bultmann is not arguing that human and divine being are connected by something akin to a 'great chain of Being'. He writes: 'Man is not regarded as an instance of universal human Being, which in its turn is seen to be an instance of cosmic Being in general' (Bultmann, 1956, p. 180). Rather, Bultmann is simply arguing that since human being must always *be* human existence *coram deo*, accepted or rejected, then that *being* cannot in itself be identical with human existence. Instead, human existence is somehow 'more' than human being.

What precisely 'more' means here remains to be seen, but this point can be confirmed quite easily. Bultmann writes that: 'Man's essential being is not Logos, reason or spirit. If we ask . . . where the essential being of man resides, there can be only one answer: the will' (Bultmann, 1956, p. 180). Human being as Bultmann understands it, is, therefore, will. This must be correct for Bultmann, for human existence, interpreted theologically and functioning therefore as a theological motif, is will operated either with or against God's Will. For Bultmann, consequently, the ontological difference is not, as with Heidegger, one of Being and being, *Sein* and *Dasein*, but one of Will and will; that is, divine Will and human will. When confronted by the divine Will in Christ, the human will can either accept or reject God (cf. the quotation from Bultmann's *Jesus* above). This of course is the meaning of the infinite qualitative distinction, that God's Will is separated from the individual's will until God destroys that distinction by breaking the bounds of death and raising up Christ. It is this act of God's Will that confronts the individual's being as will and that in turn determines that being as authentic or inauthentic existence. This is of the essence of Christianity, as Karl Rahner has observed: 'The ultimate, the eternal is surely that to which man must stand in a relation of freedom, able to say YES or NO, if he is to work out his own salvation and not merely be saved passively, or be rewarded for one kind of salvation with a totally different kind' (Rahner, 1972, p. 66).

A preliminary understanding of Bultmann's reflection upon being, therefore, would be that it brings the individual into a radically questioned stance *coram deo*. This, fundamentally, is the position in which the individual always finds herself, wittingly or unwittingly. The first step on the pathway to the encounter with God, for Bultmann, is clearly that understanding or *Verstehen* which recognises this. By definition, that recognition must be open to a pre-Christian interpretation. In this respect, it is not difficult to see how Bultmann's ontological reflection, at least with respect to being, can be mistaken for a secular discipline. That this is not the case, however, is determined by its role within the overall relationship between the human and God questions, as outlined above.

The purpose of Bultmann's theology as *Glaubenslehre*, that is, pedagogics, is to elucidate this understanding of the relationship between God and the individual. The extent to which that theology as pedagogics is a critical theology, however, depends entirely upon how successfully it reflects, and reflects upon, the context or predicament in which that individual finds herself. As will be demonstrated, it is this question that any meaningful appreciation of Bultmann's thought must consider.

One can quite easily see, consequently, how Bultmann's positive philosophy relates to his theology; that is, how the human question relates to the God question. In this instance, theological motifs such as existence, faith, and decision, are given meaning, are animated, by Bultmann's ontological reflection upon the theme, being. The fact that he refers to this question of being as being-towards-God in terms of the individual's will, however, is very revealing, for it marks a significant departure from Heidegger's own understanding of the ontological difference, as one between *Sein* and *Dasein*. Although the question of Bultmann's relationship with Heidegger will be considered exhaustively in Chapter 3, it is worth pausing to consider this point here. For it confirms the present study's claim that Bultmann's debt to Heidegger, such as it is, is not to be located primarily in the former's answer to the human question.

As early as the 1926 lectures on the basic problems of phenomenology, Heidegger was confronting the question of the ontological difference, there via the work of scholastic writers. He, like Bultmann, refused to regard the ontological difference solely in terms of human being. On the contrary, it must be a difference between human being and something that transcends human being. In Bultmann's theology this is the divine Will, active in Christ. For Heidegger, it is *Sein*. Heidegger argues that the scholastic writers he is concerned with failed to appreciate this point, and that instead they spoke of the ontological difference in terms of two constituents of human being, then going on to discuss an identity between human and divine being on the basis of their analysis of these constituents. Thus, rather than understanding the ontological difference as one between human being and something that transcends it, according to Heidegger the scholastics interpreted the ontological difference as somehow 'within' human being. On this, Heidegger writes, in his *Basic Problems of Phenomenology:*

> Thus the distinction between *realitas* – that is, *essentia* – and *existentia* does not coincide with the ontological difference; it belongs, rather, on the side of one member of the ontological difference. This means that neither *realitas* nor *existentia* is a being; rather, it is the two of them which makes up the structure of being. (Heidegger, 1976b, p. 109)

This can only mean for Heidegger that any speech about the essence of human *existence* is in fact doomed to failure if it is an attempt to make that existence intelligible to individuals; for it can have nothing to do with their historical being. On this aspect of Heidegger's work on scholastic thought, John D. Caputo writes, in his *Heidegger and Aquinas*: 'Essence and existence are then taken to mean objective structures of being which have nothing to do with the conscious subject out of whose concrete life they are born' (Caputo, 1985, p. 78). As one part of a philosophy of identity, the abstract distinction between essence and existence is meaningless in relation to that positive philosophy which is the genuine and necessary precursor of ontological reflection.

The importance of this point for Bultmann's own positive philosophy can be easily illustrated. The greatest temptation is to follow convention and to describe human existence in terms of its essence, being. Or: the greatest temptation is to follow convention and to identify divine Being with its 'image', human being. Both cases are simply wrong, argues Heidegger (and Bultmann), when human existence is acknowledged to be historical. As Heidegger demonstrates, the old scholastic distinction between essence and existence is merely an arbitrary abstraction from the human condition, and one that is fundamentally meaningless. In other words, it is pointless for a theologian such as Bultmann to speak about the 'essence' of either human being or human existence, if by 'essence' is understood something which determines that being as existence, or that existence as being. It is meaningless, therefore, for any student of Bultmann's work to search for the 'essence' of human existence in term of his understanding of human being. For there simply is no such 'essence'. Instead, what is found at the heart of Bultmann's theology is the aforementioned ontological difference between God's Will and the individual's will, as the fundamental expression of his positive philosophy and its ontological reflection.

This last point is crucial, for it is here that Heidegger's own analogy breaks down, and the gulf separating it from Bultmann's becomes most clear. For in Heidegger's thought it is precisely his conception of Being as *Sein* which cannot be established convincingly in historical existence, despite his brilliant efforts (i.e. everything written after *Being and Time*). It remains always tantalisingly adrift from the individual's understanding. Bultmann cannot be confronted by this problem. For Bultmann, the revelation of God's Being as Will begins with the most positive and historical of events, that is, the event of Jesus of Nazareth's crucifixion, which occurs as the origin of primitive Christianity. It is the notion of will, therefore, which forms the link between Bultmann's positive philosophy and its theological expression in terms of the ontological difference, and which, consequently, establishes the relationship between God and the individual.

The specifics of Bultmann's positive philosophy, thus, cannot derive from Heidegger's transcendental analysis, for that analysis by its very nature cannot confront the question of will which is at the centre of Bultmann's thought. There is, in other words, good reason to look elsewhere for the antecedents to Bultmann's ontological reflection.

In the *Philosophical Fragments*, Kierkegaard writes: 'But the moment I speak of being in the ideal sense I no longer speak of being, but of essence' (Kierkegaard, 1985, p. 32). That is, it was Kierkegaard who recognised the limitations of the essence-existence distinction, rejected it, and replaced it with the infinite qualitative distinction as an ontological difference, thereby grounding Bultmann's positive philosophy, rather than Heidegger's transcendental *Daseinsanalyse*. The human question in Bultmann's thought, in other words, is influenced decisively by his antecedents in the Lutheran tradition. It can be demonstrated, therefore, that Bultmann, like Kierkegarrd before him, concentrated upon the will of the individual, and that any consideration of that will must be established in historical events before it can be considered conceptually.

In his lucid study, *Kierkegaard and Heidegger: The Ontology of Existence*, Michael Wyschogrod writes: 'Where previously the essence-existence distinction was applied in a completely objective way to all kinds of beings, among which the thinker had no preeminence, the Kierkegaardian existence is that of the subjective thinker whose thinking proceeds from his personal involvement in his thought' (Wyschogrod, 1954, p. 9). Kierkegaard, in other words, understands human being in terms of the expression of the will of the individual subject or self within that individual's personal existence. There can be little argument that Bultmann follows him at this point, even if inadvertently, so that, when Kierkegaard writes, 'The only reality that exists for an existing individual is his own... reality' (Kierkegaard, 1941, p. 280), he writes also for Bultmann. As it is for Kierkegaard, then, so it is for Bultmann, that: 'The task of the existential thinker is to understand himself, and he accomplishes this not by understanding the concrete abstractly, but, on the contrary, by understanding the abstract concretely' (Elrod, 1975, p. 23). In so far as Bultmann believes this to be a possibility for the individual, it is also possible for that individual to encounter God in Christ.

Kierkegaard's own positive philosophy of the Christian religion is indeed far more complex than Bultmann's. In *Stages on Life's Way*, he writes:

> There are three existence-spheres: the aesthetic, the ethical, the religious. The metaphysical is abstraction; there is no man who exists metaphysically. The metaphysical, ontology, is but does not exist; for when it exists it is in the aesthetic, in the ethical, in the religious, and when it is it is the abstraction of or the prius for the aesthetic, the ethical, the religious. (Kierkegaard, 1940, p. 430)

Bultmann knows nothing of these 'existence-spheres': he speaks only of authentic and inauthentic existence, and he does not narrate stages on life's way, but proclaims the moment of decision.

Nevertheless, on this question of Bultmann's ontological reflection, as it informs his positive philosophy, it is important to acknowledge Bultmann's debt to Kierkegaard. And it is doubly important to recognise that which many of Bultmann's followers and supporters are reluctant to recognise. That is, that Bultmann does indeed refer his theology – on the basis of his positive philosophy – to the individual subject or self, after Kierkegaard, and that in this reference he is 'guilty', if that is the correct term to use, of perpetuating the reflexive or self-referential nature of modern Western philosophy and theology.

At this stage, it would be crude to claim that Kierkegaard's influence upon Bultmann on this question of the role of the will in human existence is necessarily direct. Indeed, Bultmann was always coy about precisely how much Kierkegaard he had ever actually read.[2] But that, of course, is not the point. The mediation of these ideas did not begin with Kiekegaard. On the contrary, they predate Kierkegaard, as part of that tradition to which he himself belonged. What this comparison should make clear, rather, is that at this stage of his consideration of the human question, Bultmann is far from Heidegger's *Daseinsanalyse*. He remains, so to speak, in the heartlands of his own Lutheran world.

On this question of the individual's self or subjectivity, however, there is an important difference between Bultmann and a thinker such as Kant. Whereas Kant perpetuates and refines a logical subject–object dichotomy, Bultmann advocates an historical subject–subject diastasis, which can only be overcome in that ontological difference as encounter which is God's Will to save the individual, active in Jesus Christ, the eschatological event. Bultmann does this for explicitly faithful reasons, because for Bultmann being as being-towards-God, prescribed by faith, always concerns the individual's own will. The synthetic outcome of the original diastasis – dying and rising 'in Christ' – can only be accomplished by God. There is no way, therefore, that the individual's subjectivity can be understood in any absolute or logical sense. On the contrary, the individual's subjectivity – if it can so be described at all – is only meaningful in the light of God's grace. The individual participates in this event, if at all, solely as a covenant partner, and then solely because it is God's Will.

The way in which we have been speaking about Bultmann's positive philosophy reveals the fact that his ontological reflection – his answer to the human question – is established in his consideration of concrete events. Overwhelmingly, this begins with his work as a historian of primitive Christianity. It should come as no surprise, therefore, to discover that Bultmann locates the conviction that human existence is human being as being-towards-God, either accepted or rejected, in the New Testament, specifically in the theology of Paul.

Here, however, because of the prevailing objectifying anthropology of the historical context within which the New Testament texts were written, Bultmann finds being described as *soma*, body. This is not problematic for Bultmann's own ontological reflection, for the expression *soma* simply emphasises the fact that being is not an abstract concept, but a way of referring to the ontic reality of humanity prior to the encounter with God in Christ. Being is body, therefore; that is, being is will, where will is expressed bodily by the individual. So Bultmann writes, in his *Theology of the New Testament* (Bultmann, 1953):

> That *soma* belongs inseparably, constitutively, to human existence is most clearly evident from the fact that Paul cannot conceive even of a future human existence after death 'when that which is perfect is come' as an existence without *soma* – in contrast to the view of those in Corinth who deny the resurrection (I Cor. 15, esp. vv35ff.). (Bultmann, 1953, p. 192)

Bultmann's appropriation of Paul's understanding of the body as in part constitutive of human existence emphasises the point that underlying his entire ontological reflection is the concrete situation of the individual. The essence of this existence, according to Bultmann, in so far as 'essence' here signifies the eternal moment of decision which is always present for the individual, is found within Bultmann's understanding of human being, as being-towards-God. So Bultmann can write, with great clarity, that: 'Man is called *soma* in respect to his being able to make himself the object of his own action or to experience himself as the subject to whom something happens. He can be called *soma*, that is, as having a relationship to himself – as being able in a certain sense to distinguish himself from himself' (Bultmann, 1953, pp. 195–6). In this way, *soma* or body cannot be limited to any corporeal definition, but rather must be understood as signifying the meaning of human existence. Here, Bultmann's claim that the individual may be called body in that she has a relationship to herself, illustrates his constant concern that the individual understands herself as God understands her, that is, as open to the encounter.

Being is, therefore, one of the *a priori* aspects of humanity before it is realised as either authentic or inauthentic existence. In this respect, the manifestation of the will of the individual is clearly of decisive importance for Bultmann's understanding of being as being-towards-God. Here, Bultmann writes that: 'The attitude of man in which he receives the gift of "God's righteousness" and in which the divine deed of salvation accomplishes itself with him is faith' (Bultmann, 1953, p. 310). For Bultmann, consequently: 'Man must make an absolute surrender to the grace of God' (Bultmann, 1956, p. 183). If the individual does not make such a surrender, then she bars her way to God. Paradoxically, therefore, the individual who as being is open to the future is often cut off from that future because of the manner in which she expresses her being, her will. Bultmann writes: 'While humanity is essentially openness for the future, the fact is that man bars his own way to the future by wanting to live unto himself' (Bultmann, 1953, p. 184). It is only by the grace of God, quite literally, that this wilfulness on the part of the individual does not prove fatal. God comes to the individual. And it is the certainty of this possibility that is the future opened up in the name of Christ. So Bultmann can conclude:

> For the Christian understanding, God is always the hidden one and the coming one. God's beyond is his constant futurity, his constant being-out-before. With this transcendent God man has communion only in openness to the future, which is not at man's disposal or under his control. He has communion only in readiness to enter the darkness of the future hopefully and confidently, as Luther often has said. This readiness to enter the darkness of the future confidently is nothing else but readiness for my transcendent self which stands before me. (Bultmann, 1953, p. 83)

With this, it becomes necessary to consider the question of time.

(b) Time

Certain things, hopefully, will now have become clear. As a theologian, Rudolf Bultmann is not an existentialist, but rather a

phenomenologist. This is my contention. As what I refer to as a
'positive philosopher of the Christian religion', however – what
others might erroneously call an anthropologist – Bultmann is certainly concerned with those themes that one might say 'belong' to
that nebulous school, existentialism. The nature of the relationship
between Bultmann's positive philosophy and his theology proper,
was clarified by the above examination of the theme, being. Thus,
Bultmann's ontological consideration of the theme being becomes
theological when being is regarded as being-towards-God, *accepted
or rejected*. In this way, the motifs 'authentic existence' and 'inauthentic existence' are always theological motifs because their role in
Bultmann's thought is always informed by the axiomatic role of the
expression of the individual's will, as being-towards-God accepted
or rejected. Paradoxically, therefore, we find that that which by all
accounts should be part of Bultmann's so-called existentialism –
that is, his use of the motif 'existence' – is not. On the contrary, it
belongs to his theology. Bultmann is not an existentialist, consequently, when he uses the expression, 'existence'.

This is a very illuminating idea. Correctly understood, it means
that even the practice of referring to Bultmann's positive philosophy as existentialism, makes very little sense. The entire point of
Bultmann's ontological reflection upon being and time, originating
in the positive history of earliest Christianity, seems to be to identify those very conditions that transcend that positive history. This,
of course, was also Heidegger's concern: an analysis of *Dasein's* very
concreteness, its *in-der-Welt-sein*, so as to identify its transcendental conditions. As was shown above, Bultmann's own emphasis
upon will and the subjective individual takes him far closer to
Kierkegaard than to Heidegger at this point. Nevertheless, they are
all concerned with transcendental conditions, reducing phenomenologically to those conditions from an original analysis of historical
existence.

Existentialism, by contrast, with its emphasis upon the psychological disposition of the individual, seems never to make this
necessary reduction, in a phenomenological sense, to the level of
transcendental conditions. It remains upon the level of the psychological, and therefore stands not as part of Bultmann's positive
philosophy, *but as an alternative to his theology*. As will be demon-

strated in Chapter 3, this is the reason why both Bultmann and Heidegger were so careful to reject any claim that their thought was tantamount to an atheistic existentialism (Bultmann *contra* Buri) or even a form of humanism (Heidegger *contra* Sartre). On the contrary: these are the specific enemies they fought against. And one of their primary weapons in this struggle was the necessary reduction from the positive to the level of transcendental conditions. In this sense, it is of course correct to say that Kierkegaard too was a phenomenologist.[3]

This is why 'being' is a logical condition rather than a specifically theological motif, such as 'existence'. The primary quality of such a condition is its transcendental status. As such, therefore, it does not exist. Only when it is informed by the considerations of a specific religious proclamation, does it become raised to theological significance as existence. To speak about God, therefore, is to speak about the individual in terms of this ontological reflection, but returned to the arena or plane of human, historical experience, and then confronted by the eschatological event, Jesus Christ. This is the nature of the shift in Bultmann's thought from positive philosophy, and its inherent phenomenological reduction to transcendental conditions, to a genuine theology. It is one of reduction to conditions, in order to realise the meaning of existence.[4]

In his concentration upon will and the individual subject as the central concern of his own ontological reflection, Bultmann's stance is distanced from that of Martin Heidegger's analysis of *Dasein* (despite the former's use of this expression after 1928; see below), and indeed has far greater affinity with Kierkegaard. Both ultimately stand in that pervasive tradition that might be designated the Pauline–Augustinian–Lutheran. It is Kierkegaard rather than Heidegger, therefore, and the entire Lutheran tradition of which Kierkegaard is the greatest nineteenth-century exemplar, to whom Bultmann owes the greater intellectual debt in the exposition of his 'primordial interpretation'. For, as James D. Collins writes in *The Mind of Kierkegaard*: 'Kierkegaard sought to clarify the common tradition by showing, first, that the image of God is present in men only as individuals and in proportion to their spiritual awareness of their individual existence and, second, that this highest form of individuality is fully attained only in Christian religious existence'

(Collins, 1983, pp. 203–4). Kierkegaard's influence upon Bultmann, however, is most clear in the latter's employment of the theme or condition, *time*.

In an essay entitled 'Humanism and Christianity', Bultmann writes: 'Knowledge of God is meant rather in an existential sense as knowledge of the "moment"' (Bultmann, 1955, p. 154). Clearly, therefore, Bultmann is not using 'knowledge' in the sense of experiential cognition. What, however, is the 'moment', upon which knowledge of God seems to depend? Bultmann continues: 'The encounter of the "moment" seeks always to make man afresh and to free himself from himself' (Bultmann, 1955, p. 158). The 'moment', therefore, is of ontological significance; that is, like being, it is a transcendental condition. 'Knowledge of the "moment"', as 'knowledge *of God*', consequently, must mean the theological realisation of this transcendental condition in a positive religious context. This is what one sees in Bultmann's understanding of the kerygma as positive proclamation (cf. Chapter 1). As condition, however, time as moment, like being, transcends the positive or historical.

It would be wrong, therefore, to understand the ontological significance of time as moment in terms of causal efficiency, after, for example, the meaning employed by Reichenbach in *The Philosophy of Space and Time*, where he writes: 'We shall finally recognise that time order represents the prototype of causal propagation and thus discover time-space order as the schema of causal connection' (Reichenbach, 1958, p. 113).

As Robin Collingwood correctly observes, *that* way of understanding time has everything to do with mechanical causality (which may indeed be part of the natural world), but nothing to do with the ontological possibilities of human existence. On this problem, Collingwood writes, in a paper entitled *Some Perplexities about Time: With an Attempted Solution*, that: 'The first condition of cleaning up our conception of time is to stop thinking of it as a special kind of one-dimensional space and to think of it as what it is – a perpetually changing present, having somehow bound up with it a future which does not exist and a past which does not exist' (Collingwood, 1926, p. 145).

Collingwood's 'first condition' leads us further into our consideration of Bultmann on time. If Collingwood's 'first condition' is accepted as axiomatic for our consideration of Bultmann's understanding of 'time' or 'temporality' as in some sense a transcendental condition, it is necessary to distinguish between Bultmann's ontological understanding of the moment, and a causal comprehension of time as past, present, and future. Whatever the nature of the states that the 'moment' stands 'between', they are not, and cannot be, causally connected. In other words, it is impossible to proceed from a state of inauthentic existence to a state of authentic existence by any action which can be quantified causally. There can be no such action, and therefore no such event. This is important, because it is a common mistake to suppose that when Kierkegaard writes about the three existential-spheres of aesthetic, ethical, and religious, he believes it is possible to proceed from one to another by means of causal action. On the contrary, for Kierkegaard, temporality cannot be reduced to any metaphysical schema or system of life 'stages' if those stages are in any way thought to exist in what we like to think of as 'space and time'. Such life stages are ontological possibilities, ways of realising being, and as such are not to be sacrificed to the individual's purposive activity.

Heidegger himself has acknowledged Kierkegaard's attempt to understand temporality in this fashion, but customarily he has also attempted to undermine the latter's position by means of his own philosophical concerns. Heidegger writes, in *Being and Time*:

> Kierkegaard is probably the one who has seen the ontic [*existentiell*] phenomenon of the moment of perception with the most penetration; but this does not mean that he has been correspondingly successful in interpreting it ontologically. He clings to the ordinary conception of time, and defines the 'moment of perception' with the help of 'now' and 'eternity'. When Kierkegaard speaks of 'temporality', what he has in mind is man's 'being-in-time'. Time as within-time-ness knows only the 'now'; it never knows a moment of vision. If, however, such a moment is experienced ontically, then a more primordial temporality has been presupposed, although ontologically it has not been made explicit. (Heidegger, 1962, p. 497)

Bluntly stated, Heidegger's criticism is that Kierkegaard has reflected solely upon the individual's ontic situation as 'being-in-time', and has become bound by the constraints of that situation. Thus, although Kierkegaard must, logically, presuppose the onto-logical possibility of his understanding of temporality if he can speak of the 'being-in-time' of the life of the individual, Kier-kegaard has not reflected upon the origin of this possibility as a moment of vision. He has not, that is, reflected ontologically.

Heidegger's criticism, however, is somewhat disingenuous, for Kierkegaard, like Bultmann, clearly *has* reflected ontologically. Heidegger's main complaint, quite simply, is that Kierkegaard has arrived at an ontological understanding that establishes the ontic or historical existence of the individual in the eternity of God's revel-ation in Christ. Far from failing to 'know a moment of vision', therefore, which in Heideggerian terms would be tantamount to a failure to think phenomenologically, Kierkegaard has recognised a moment of vision, as revelation, as the meaning of eternity, and therefore understands the meaning of human temporal exist-ence eschatologically. So Kierkegaard writes, in the *Philosophical Fragments*:

> And now the moment. Such a moment has a peculiar character. It is brief and temporal indeed, like every other moment; it is transient as all moments are; it is past, like every moment in the next moment. And yet it is decisive, and filled with the Eternal. Such a moment ought to have a distinctive name; let us call it the Fullness of Time. (Kierkegaard, 1985, p. 22)

John Heywood Thomas, one of Kierkegaard's best English interpreters, acknowledges that it is this eternity within the moment that is fundamental to human existence: 'To be human is to be that strange creature which awkwardly but marvellously synthesises time and eternity' (Thomas, 1973, p. 34). The diastatic character of the moment within human existence, therefore, gives way to syn-thesis as its purposiveness before God's revelation is recognised; that is, as ontological reflection is realised explicitly in theology.

Kierkegaard writes:

> It is only *momentarily* that the particular individual is able to realise existentially a unity of the infinite and the finite which

transcends existence. This unity is realised in a moment of passion. In passion, the existing subject is rendered infinite in the eternity of the imaginative representation, and yet he is at the same time most definitely himself. (cf. Elrod, 1975, p. 35)

Quite simply, therefore, the moment cannot be understood as temporal in anything like the normal, causal understanding of that word. It is, rather, a process, as Kierkegaard acknowledges: 'But precisely because every moment, like the sum of moments, is a process (a going by), no moment is a present, and in the same sense there is neither past, present, nor future' (Kierkegaard, 1980, p. 77).

Kierkegaard's expression of the moment as a process is of course not accidental, and it is utterly unsurprising that this agrees with Heidegger's understanding of the ontological difference as process. For in both cases they are events of revelation, given some form of conceptual status, either theologically or philosophically. The difference lies in their respective beliefs as to what it is that is revealed, although both would insist that what is revealed is of ontological significance as the relationship which gives meaning to human existence. For Kierkegaard it is the meaning of human existence *coram deo*. For Heidegger it is the relationship between *Dasein* and *Sein*. Clearly, Bultmann follows Kierkegaard's lead at this point.

For Kierkegaard, therefore:

> The instant is that ambiguous moment in which time and eternity touch one another, thereby positing the temporal, where time is constantly intersecting eternity and eternity constantly permeating time. Only now does that division we talked about acquire significance: the present, the past, and the future. (Kierkegaard, 1980, p. 80)

Following Kierkegaard to this end point, any speech about before and after the moment must only be ontological, that is, in terms of the realisation of the possibilities of being. 'Being' and 'time', therefore, are for Bultmann effectively one and the same thing (cf. Heidegger, 1962: Division II, Part III, 'temporality as the ontological meaning of care', gives this sense to Division I, Part VI, 'care as the being of *Dasein*'; see below), in the sense that they represent the

purposive status of being prior to its realisation as authentic or
inauthentic existence. The moment, in this sense, is indeed a 'space'
to be filled by the individual's decision. It is no wonder, therefore,
that in this respect Bultmann can conclude, in his 'History and
Eschatology in the New Testament', that: 'The time between the
resurrection of Christ and his expected Parousia has not only
chronological but also essential [ontological] meaning. It is this
meaning which gives to the Christian life its character as Christian'
(Bultmann, 1954, p. 14). Effectively, Christian existence can be
expressed as this spatialisation towards the purposiveness of the
moment as temporality, where of course 'spatialisation' has nothing
whatever to do with causality, but everything to do with a phenomenological understanding of being and time. For Bultmann, the
spatialisation of time means perceiving the possibility of tem(porality as the moment of decision, as the 'between' or *Unterschied* or
vitality of the ontological difference or relationship between God
and the individual in which the individual, through the grace of
God, can somehow have this 'space' filled by God's love. The present, therefore, is not 'now', but 'future': it is the eschatological
reality of salvation.

In other words, in the encounter with the risen Lord in the
kerygmatic Christ, there is a 'space' into which the individual can
step, with God, or fall, alone. Bultmann finds this point being made
by the Fourth Evangelist, in passages such as 12.23, 12.31, 13.1,
13.31, 17.1, and 17.13. Of John 17.1, Bultmann writes in his *Commentary* that:

> The decisive hour has come. To fulfil its purpose, it must be-
> come the hour of glorification (12.23); this is the first petition
> of the prayer, and is in fact its whole contents. Thus it becomes
> the eschatological hour, which marks the turning-point of the
> ages. . . . But in what does the Son's glorification consist? . . . .
> What does Jesus' exaltation into the heavenly mode of existence
> mean in the context of the Gospel? What is the significance of
> his work, and of his honour? His work consists – such is the
> interpretation give in v.2 – in his being able to give eternal life
> to his own; thus he who is *doxastheis* is at work in his com-
> munity. And he is at work there as the Revealer; for according to
> v.3, the life which he bestows is nothing other than the *knowledge*
> of God and of himself as the Revealer. He is therefore at work

where he is recognised and honoured as the Revealer.... This means however: Jesus' *doxa* is not something already existent, a metaphysical quality which could be seen apart from revelation and faith, such as could be acknowledged theoretically in a Christological dogma; no, it is brought about in his work as Revealer and in men's response to that work within history. (Bultmann, 1971, pp. 490–2)

With the attention now turning to history, it is time to examine precisely how being and time are realised as human existence.

2   The Problem of History

Turning to the problem of history, and how Bultmann understands and tackles that problem, we return directly to the subject matter of Chapter 1, leaving behind the transcendental reduction of Bult-mann's analysis of being and time. In other words, we return to the question of the historical Jesus: how one is to regard that particular individual; how one encounters the kerygmatic Christ as the story of the historical Jesus, told as eschatological event; how one decides for the risen Lord, in faith. Here, in considering the prob-lem of history and its role in Bultmann's thought, we stop at the boundary of the human question, and behold the God question, as from afar. We stop, so to speak, at that point where Bultmann moves to realise his work on the human question in theological terms (see above). Aspects of this process have already been con-sidered. For example, the way in which Bultmann's discussion of the question of 'existence' *coram deo* is based upon his reduction of human being to will. Or, how the transcendental condition time becomes 'theologised' as the moment of decision. It is only with the consideration of history, however, that this process becomes entirely intelligible.

At this point, it is worth pausing for a moment to reconsider fully the moves that Bultmann makes in his approaches to the human question.

We began with what I referred to as Bultmann's 'positive philosophy of the Christian religion', which I specified as his consideration of the origins of earliest Christianity. Bultmann's

Christology comes under this rubric: the distinction he makes
between the historical Jesus and the kerygmatic Christ is part of
Bultmann's 'positive philosophy of the Christian religion', which
only then takes on theological meaning on the basis of his ontological reflection. In this sense, Chapter 1 can be seen to be intimately
related to Bultmann's consideration of the human question, which
has been examined in the present chapter.

From those investigations into positive philosophy, Bultmann
reduced back to its transcendental conditions; that is, he moved
to consider the questions of being and time. The notion of a
transcendental reduction belongs without argument to the realm
of phenomenology proper; both Heidegger and Husserl speak
explicitly of its necessity. 'Where', however, does one reduce the
positive 'to'? At this point, the clearest thing we can say is that the
transcendental conditions of possibility constitute a negative philosophy, the possible theoretical corrective to any examination of the
positive. For Bultmann, this so-called negative philosophy consists
of his consideration of being and time. And here, as we have seen,
Bultmann has been more heavily influenced by Kierkegaard and
that predominantly Lutheran tradition which originated in a very
particular interpretation of Paul and John.

It is no surprise, therefore, that Bultmann can state, quite categorically, that on this point Heidegger is saying nothing new, but
simply 'secularising' what is already found in the New Testament;
that is, the reduction of the positive to the level of transcendental
conditions, or the negative. As will be seen in Chapter 3, Bultmann
is entirely correct in one sense: Heidegger's preliminary consideration of *Dasein*, and its transcendental conditions – even before he
began to use those expressions – had its origins in an examination
of the eschatological passages of certain of the Pauline epistles (see
below). Even when he starts using the expression *Dasein* himself,
ostensibly following Heidegger's lead, Bultmann is in fact far closer
to Kierkegaard's understanding of being as will, and time or temporality as the intersection of the present with the eternal. Indeed,
Dasein for Bultmann always means being-towards-God, and therefore his usage of Heidegger's key term is in fact informed by
religious concerns that predate his relationship with the latter's
phenomenology.

To this point, one can see how Bultmann has managed to

combine his work as a New Testament exegete, examining the *religionsgeschichtliche* background to the earliest Church, and what one refers to as his ontological reflection; that is, his reflection upon being and time. It is also possible to see how, theoretically or conceptually, Bultmann can 'theologise' his ontological reflection, by returning it to the level of the positive within a specific religious proclamation. In this fashion, we can understand Bultmann's claim that he is simply doing *now* what Paul and John did *then*. That is, reflecting upon the ontology of human existence in order to understand the eschatological event, Jesus of Nazareth, God's Christ.

Terms like existence, decision, and encounter, therefore, are theological motifs based upon Bultmann's ontological reflection. This is all obvious conceptually, and semantically one can see the structure of Bultmann's emerging position quite clearly. How, though, does the story of God's action in Jesus Christ, understood against the backcloth of an ontological reflection that sees human existence in terms of the transcendental conditions, being and time, once again become relevant in the positive circumstances of present life? How, in other words, is Bultmann's work on the human question made pertinent for the present life of the individual? The answer lies in Bultmann's treatment of the problem of history. Here one sees the realisation of Bultmann's reduction to the level of transcendental conditions. And here, in his understanding of history and eschatology, one sees finally not only Bultmann's understanding of the most fundamental connections between the various Christian believers, but also his understanding of the relationship between the individual and Jesus of Nazareth. The history question, therefore, is the coping-stone of the human question. And in so far as it addresses the question of Christology, it provides the foundations for Bultmann's answer to the God question, and his relationship with Martin Heidegger.

Undoubtedly, on the question of history Rudolf Bultmann was heavily influenced by the work of Martin Kähler, most notably Kähler's famous study, *The so-called historical Jesus and the historic, Biblical Christ* (Kähler, 1964), which was first published in 1892. The subject of this present discussion is to examine the significance of the concepts *Historie* and *Geschichte* for Bultmann, and their relevance to his theological objectives. With this in mind, it is perhaps easier to commence with Bultmann's understanding of

Historie, and his arguments against its theological importance, than with his understanding of *Geschichte*, which becomes clear once it is understood what Bultmann means by *Historie*.

Certainly, aspects of this discussion were introduced in the previous chapter. Where the present chapter differs from Chapter 1, however, is in its consideration of the philosophical role of these expressions in Bultmann's thought. In other words, *Historie* and *Geschichte* are here to be considered as they form part of Bultmann's answer to the human question. The present consideration, therefore, anchors the Christological concerns of Chapter 1, while simultaneously anticipating Bultmann's answer to the God question, and his intellectual relationship with Martin Heidegger.

Basically, Bultmann has (via Kähler) taken over the term *Historie* from the mainstream of German historiography, as typified by Burckhardt and von Ranke. It is in fact precisely this historiography, and the use made of it by theologians such as Troeltsch in Liberal Protestantism, that Bultmann explicitly attacks in his writings on the question of history. In *History and Eschatology*, for example, Bultmann writes:

> Historicism is perfectly right in seeing that every present situation grows out of the past; but it misunderstands the determination by the past as purely causal determination. . . . It does not understand the present situation as the situation of decision – a decision which, as our decision over against the future, is at the same time our decision over against the past concerning the way in which it is to determine the future. (Bultmann, 1957, p. 141)

Here, by 'Historicism' Bultmann means the historiography typified by von Ranke and Burckhardt, as this passage in *History and Eschatology* makes clear. Bultmann's argument is that this form of historical (*historische*) analysis is concerned solely with the historical process as a succession of causally connected events, and that consequently Historicism becomes obsessed with the historical process itself as the goal of analysis. Bultmann writes: 'The goal of history [*Historie*] is not an eschatological future but is the historical process itself' (Bultmann, 1957, p. 68). This tendency can be illustrated quite simply, by reference to those lives-of-Jesus in Liberal Protestant theology which attempt to regard the historical Jesus as the pivotal moment in the history of salvation (*Heilsgeschichte*). In this respect, Historicism came to resemble that type of natural scientific enquiry which was concerned solely with physical laws and causal connections and which, through neo-Kantianism, came to dominate German theology from 1870 onwards. Thus was created the environment in which Liberal Protestantism could turn to the question of the historical Jesus, armed with weapons of recreation. This is precisely the attitude towards Christology which Bultmann's theology, in its entirety, is intended to destroy.

In Bultmann's thought, therefore, *Historie* can never be a means to theological expression. If theology, then, is to concern itself with God's revelation in Christ as addressed to the individual in her historical existence – which is understood, transcendentally, as being and time in an explicit non-*historische* sense – then one cannot speak about that existence in terms of *Historie*, for God's revelation cannot be conceptualised as a 'fact' amongst other causally related facts. One cannot speak, therefore, of a causal connection between God's revelation and the individual's salvation, for the very suggestion of causality means the encroachment upon theology of the natural sciences.

This does not mean, of course, that Bultmann rejects Historicism out of hand. There are sufficient of his writings to show that he himself was adept at employing the methods of Historicism at times in his analyses of the context within which primitive Christianity developed, as per his understanding of the positive philosophy of the Christian religion. But he made a strict distinction between these analyses, and theology proper. Theology has to do with the individual's historical existence, because God has to do with the individual's historical existence. And one speaks about that historical existence in terms of *Geschichte*, because only a *geschichtliche* (i.e. phenomenological – see below) analysis can conceptualise the call to decision concerning human existence, which confronts the individual in the shadow of the cross.

What then does Bultmann mean by *Geschichte*? He writes: 'The history [*Geschichte*] of the human person comes into being in the encounters which man experiences' (Bultmann, 1957, p. 43). *Geschichte*, therefore, is that history of the individual within which it is possible to speak of events and experiences in such a way that they are not reduced to psychological considerations or merely causal connections within a larger, unique historical (*historische*) process. In other words, it is a way of understanding the history of the individual which is true to those transcendental conditions – being and time – as Bultmann has described them. In this way, being and time are realised as *Geschichte*. *Geschichte*, therefore, is the individual's *story* understood in terms of being and time, or will and decision, as Bultmann perceives them, whereas *Historie* is the individual's story measured objectively.

Bultmann is able to go one stage further, however. He writes: 'At all events the Pauline conception of history and its unfolding of the dialectic of Christian experience contains the solution of the problem of history and eschatology' (Bultmann, 1957, p. 47). Clearly, therefore, for Bultmann historical existence *coram deo* is eschatological in nature. We can see, consequently, how Bultmann's move from his positive philosophy and its reduction to the transcendental conditions, being and time, back to theology proper, in fact meshes with his Christology, and the possibility of the individual encountering the risen Lord via the kerygmatic Christ. When history as *Geschichte* is regarded as the authentic realisation of being and time, and when history as *Geschichte* is understood eschatologically, then the history of the individual becomes the history of Jesus Christ. Then the individual is 'in Christ'. Thus, Bultmann can write:

> The man who understands his historicity [*Geschichtlichkeit*] radically, that is, the man who radically understands himself as someone future, or in other words, who understands his genuine self as an ever future one, has to know that his genuine self can only be offered to him as a gift by the future. (Bultmann, 1957, p. 150)

That is, authentic existence as the individual's *Geschichte* is to be understood eschatologically. This realisation on the part of the individual confronts her as an ever-present question mark. Bultmann writes: 'For every Now, every moment, in its historical-relatedness of course, has within itself a full meaning' (Bultmann, 1957, p. 135). That meaning can only be the meaning of existence itself, which can be identified as the question: 'What is truth?' (John 18.38; see below). So Bultmann must write: 'The history [*Geschichte*] in which we live is conditioned by the "Krisis" in Jesus Christ' (Bultmann, 1969, p. 140), and therefore John O'Neill is entirely correct, when he states that: 'True historical existence is attained only in the act of submission to revelation' (O'Neill, 1970, p. 391).

This returns the entire question of history, of existence understood authentically, to the realm of Christology, and therefore primarily eschatology. So Bultmann can write, famously, that: 'To exist means to exist eschatologically' (Bultmann, 1948, p. 31), for authentic existence can only be the gift of God in Christ. Bultmann characterises this authentic historical existence as *Geschichte*. It follows, therefore, that inauthentic existence is somehow intimately bound up with *Historie* (cf. Chapters 3 and 5).

Briefly, this does not mean that the individual's *Geschichte* is some form of existence which can be divorced from the positive reality of earthly life. Such a belief would be nonsensical, and Bultmann acknowledges as such when he writes: 'History (*Geschichte*) as the field of human actions cannot, however, be cut off from nature and natural events' (Bultmann, 1957, p. 139). In other words, *Geschichte* must never be divorced from positive reality. But to reduce existence to something that can merely be measured, objectively, is to turn away from the light of revelation. Thus, Bultmann can conclude:

> The historicity (*Geschichtlichkeit*) of the human being is completely understood when the human being is understood as living in responsibility over against the future, and therefore in decision. And, furthermore, it must be said that historicity in its fullest sense is not a self-evident natural quality of the individual, but a possibility which must be grasped and realised. (Bultmann, 1957, p. 136)

When the individual's story or history (*Geschichte*) is understood as the realisation of being and time, and both history and the ontological reflection upon being and time are established by eschatology, in so far as faith is always eschatological and faith prescribes the theologian's 'primordial interpretation', then it becomes possible for Bultmann to deploy theological motifs such as existence, decision, encounter, and authenticity/inauthenticity, in a fashion intelligible to the individual. Then Bultmann's Christology, with its threefold division, becomes operative, theoretically at least, on a pedagogic level in the life of the believer. By being true to his conviction that it is necessary for the theologian to reflect ontologically (see above), Bultmann has bridged the gap between Jesus of Nazareth and the contemporary individual.

He has not demonstrated, however, that his theological motifs – used to speak about human existence *coram deo* – genuinely speak *of God*. To do that, he must answer the God question.

3

Through Phenomenology to Faith

We have seen how the human question is to be regarded as the necessary preparation for the God question, which in turn is to be the subject of the present chapter. There have also been sufficient hints in Chapter 2 to reveal my conviction that the God question is for Bultmann to be answered phenomenologically. Indeed, this was admitted in so many words at several points. What, however, is 'phenomenology'? And how valid is it to speak of Bultmann as a 'phenomenologist', rather than as an 'existentialist'? To a certain extent, I have tried to answer this latter question in Chapter 2. A reader might reasonably argue, however, that although I have demonstrated the unsuitability of referring to Bultmann's theology as existentialist, because of the overtly psychological nature of existentialism – which is anathema to Bultmann – I have not shown how Bultmann is genuinely a phenomenologist. The questions still stand, therefore: 'Why, and how, phenomenology?'

Briefly, I would argue that Bultmann's explicitly transcendental and ontological reduction of the positive question of existence in primitive Christianity to being and time, as considered above in Chapter 2, is phenomenological. I would also wish to say that, in this respect, Bultmann is as influenced by Kierkegaard as by Heidegger, and that in retrospect one might well wish to think in terms of Kierkegaard's own phenomenology, as has been intimated (see above).

This, however, is of limited interest. Even if Bultmann's onto-logical reflection upon the positive philosophy of the Christian religion is phenomenological, it is not here that we should locate Heidegger's primary influence. On the contrary, and as stated above, this primary influence is upon Bultmann's answer to the God question. My contention here is that when Heidegger moves beyond his transcendental analysis of *Dasein* in *Being and Time*, and begins to speak of the event (*Ereignis*) of the ontological difference, he has a massive and lasting influence upon Bultmann's understanding of the event (*Ereignis*) of God's eschatological action in Jesus Christ, as the decisive moment of ontological importance for the individual. Clearly, therefore, if this insight is correct, Bultmann's understanding of eschatology must be phenomenological, given that, following Heidegger, all ontological reflection is explicitly phenomenological. The remainder of this chapter is devoted to demonstrating the significance of this insight for our understanding of Bultmann's theology.

Chapter 3 will be divided into a number of different sections. First, as part of our answer to the question, 'What is "phenomenology"?', we will consider the development of Heidegger's own understanding of this term, explicitly in relation to earliest Christianity. Second, we will examine how Heidegger regards this understanding in relation to theology, by a consideration of his 1928 lecture in Marburg, dedicated to Rudolf Bultmann, and entitled 'Phenomenology and Theology'. This will lead us to, third, a final look at *Being and Time* before, fourth, the main section of Chapter 3, which will consider the question 'What is truth?' (John 18.38). Finally, fifth and sixth, Heidegger's mature reflection upon *Time and Being* places his work on *event theory* in the context of his entire career, casting invaluable light on Bultmann's own work as an event theorist, and in the process answering the God question to the best of Bultmann's ability.

1   Heidegger as Hermeneutic Phenomenologist

In Volume I of his *The Phenomenological Movement: A Historical Introduction*, Herbert Spiegelberg quotes Paul Ricoeur to the effect, that: 'Fundamentally, phenomenology is born as soon as we treat the manner of appearing of things as a separate problem by "bracketing" the question of existence, either temporarily or permanently' (Spiegelberg, 1960, p. 7). This in itself is sufficient to describe Bultmann as a phenomenologist. For as was revealed in Chapter 2, it is precisely Bultmann's 'bracketing' off of the question of existence, and its analysis in terms of its conditions, being and time, which marks Bultmann's primary response to his *religionsgeschichtliche* consideration of primitive Christianity, and its positive philosophy.

In itself, however, this does not take us too far. There are many different types of phenomenology. And as has been seen, Bultmann's debt to the phenomenology of Kierkegaard is at least as great as his debt to Heidegger, certainly at this stage in his consideration of the human question. Here, though, one runs across direct literary evidence for bringing Heidegger and Bultmann together.

In an unpublished letter to the late Canon C. H. Duncan, Rudolf Bultmann writes:

> Später lernte ich dann die Phänomenologie kennen, und als ich in Marburg (etwa 1924) Martin Heidegger kennen lernte, wurde ich von ihm entscheidend beeinflusst. Wir standen in lebhaftem Austausch, sowohl in vielen Gesprächen, als auch dadurch, dass ich an seinem philosophischen Seminar teilnahm und er an meinem neutestamentlichen.[5]

Here is explicit evidence that Bultmann learned not existentialism but phenomenology from Heidegger, and that it had a 'decisive' (*entscheidend*) influence upon him. Bultmann also writes that not only did he attend Heidegger's seminar, but that Heidegger also attended his own New Testament seminar. It is this latter point that proves to be a way into our fullest understanding of Bultmann's relationship with Heidegger, his phenomenology, and ultimately his event theory.

No one will discover for sure why Heidegger attended Bultmann's New Testament seminar, not at least until the former's personal papers and letters are released from embargo, an event that seems to be many years hence. There seems to be no argument, however, that Heidegger himself was deeply interested in theology, and learned much from it. In an important letter to Karl Barth,

dated 11–15 November 1952, Bultmann writes: 'Aber eben, weil ich
bei Herrmann gelernt habe, war ich für Heidegger vorbereitet.
Dieser hat übrigens auch von Herrmann gelernt und schätze ihn
hoch' (Jaspert, 1977, p. 188). Of greater interest, however, is a
letter written by Bultmann to Hans von Soden in December
1923, a few months after Heidegger's arrival in Marburg, in which
he states:

> Concerning the number and motivation of students, we have had
> another fine winter. In my exegesis course, I am discussing Barth
> again. His *Epistle to the Romans* is certainly an amazing work, and
> though I find its exegesis artificial and allegorising, I find its
> questions most fruitful for any effort of interpretation. My sem-
> inar confirms this; under the debatable title 'The Ethics of Paul',
> I treat the position of the justified in the world. This seminar is
> especially instructive because our new philosopher, Heidegger, a
> student of Husserl, participates in it. He comes from Catho-
> licism, but he is totally a Protestant....I...noticed with
> interest that Heidegger is familiar with contemporary theology.
> He is especially an admirer of Herrmann, and knows Gogarten
> and Barth. (Hobbs, 1985, pp. 9–10)

In fact, Bultmann's observation concerning Heidegger's 'Protestantism' is confirmed by a letter written by Edmund Husserl to
Rudolf Otto on 5 March 1919, after Otto had written to Husserl
about the possibility of Heidegger's elevation to a full professorship
in Marburg. Husserl describes the change that has overtaken
Heidegger, from his Catholic origins towards Protestantism, and
adds: 'I have not exercised the least influence on Heidegger's...
migration over to the ground of Protestantism' (cf. Sheehan, 1979,
p. 313). This letter is important, because it explicitly separates
Husserl, and therefore the world of Husserl's transcendental phenomenology, from Heidegger's movement towards the thought
world of Protestantism. This in itself is significant, because it means
that Heidegger is hereby indicating, implicitly if not explicitly, his
dissatisfaction with any notion of a transcendental ego or psyche,
as the foundation of an understanding of human experience and
cognition. (This move, prior to Heidegger's relationship with
Bultmann, is important because it keeps the latter away from
Husserl, and strengthens the argument that by 'phenomenology',

Bultmann always understood Heidegger's historical, hermeneutic phenomenology.)

In fact, Heidegger had already indicated this dissatisfaction in his very early paper, 'The Problem of Reality in Modern Philosophy' (Heidegger, 1973). But its coincidence with a move towards Protestantism is very illuminating, especially given Bultmann's explicit statement that Heidegger was influenced by Herrmann. Granted Heidegger's rejection of a transcendental ego or psyche, it seems likely that he would have found Herrmann's own description of the inner life of the individual equally unsatisfactory. What would have interested the Heidegger of the period 1919–21 in Herrmann's work, instead, would seem to be the latter's concern with the nature of experience. There is little direct evidence to support this view. There is, however, a tantalising glimpse into Heidegger's state of mind during this period in the series of lectures he gave, in Freiburg during the winter semester 1920–1, under the title 'Introduction to the Phenomenology of Religion'.

In examining these lectures, it is not my intention to claim any direct correlation between either Herrmann and Heidegger, or Heidegger and Bultmann. The extent of influence cannot be ascertained with anything like that degree of certainty at this early date. What can be demonstrated, though, is the way in which Heidegger *wrestles with the human question on the basis of the positive philosophy of the Christian religion*, and how, therefore, he moves closer not only to his own mature analysis of *Dasein* in *Being and Time*, but also to Bultmann's work as exegete and phenomenologist. In the process of this lecture course, Heidegger identifies, over two years before his arrival in Marburg, the point at which *his* phenomenology will agree with Bultmann's. That is, their mutual recognition of eschatology as the foundation of the Christian understanding of human existence interpreted as generated temporality; that is, in terms of being and time. This concern with what is fundamentally the historical meaning of human existence marks out, as with Bultmann, the point at which Heidegger's phenomenological reduction to the conditions of existence effectively ends, to be replaced by his turn to an understanding of the event of revelation.

For Heidegger, the place where this struggle takes place, the first discernible location of his so-called *Kehre* (which should be characterised as a return to a primary goal, rather than any alteration in direction or purpose), is the world of the New Testament.

Heidegger's lecture course, 'Introduction to the Phenomenology of Religion', met twice weekly on Tuesdays and Fridays from noon to one o'clock, from the beginning of November 1920 through to 25 February 1921, with a month's recess for Christmas (cf. Sheehan, 1979). Part 1, consisting of eight lectures, was devoted to an 'Introduction to the Phenomenon of Factical Life-Experience'. Part 2, consisting of sixteen lectures, was devoted to 'A Phenomenological Interpretation of Original Christianity in St. Paul's Epistles to the Galatians and Thessalonians'. Part 2 comprises two sections: (a) how original Christianity is a factical life-experience; and (b) how original Christianity, as factical life-experience, is primordial temporality. Together, Parts 1 and 2 illuminate not only the origins of Heidegger's *Being and Time* in primitive Christianity's understanding of historical existence, rather than Husserl's transcendental phenomenology, but also the origins of Bultmann's own ontological reflection upon the positive philosophy of primitive Christianity.

In Part 1, Heidegger establishes the basic phenomenon with which his historical phenomenology is concerned: 'factical life-experience', or *faktische Lebenserfahrung, das faktische Leben*. This experience is pre-theoretical and pre-rational, in an ontological sense; that is, it is immediate. Already, therefore, Heidegger is attempting to establish his methodology upon a more primordial plane than that of the cognition of sense data. Although it is not so described in these lectures, it is clear that *die faktische Lebenserfahrung* will, by 1927, be clarified as *Dasein*. Here, however, Heidegger's thought is still in embryonic form. Concerning this, in his important article 'Heidegger's "Introduction to the Phenomenology of Religion", 1920–1921', Thomas Sheehan writes: 'Philosophy as universal phenomenological ontology takes its departure from the hermeneutic of *Dasein* which ties all philosophical inquiry down to the point where it arises and to which it returns: existence' (Sheehan, 1979, p. 316). On this, Sheehan agrees with Ricoeur's definition of phenomenology, given above. Judged by both definitions, Heidegger's analysis of primitive Christianity can be seen to be phenomenological, and in agreement with Bultmann's ontological reflection as elucidated in Chapter 2.

Die faktische Lebenserfahrung means for Heidegger the individual's general 'coming-to-grips' (Sheehan) with the world, in such a way that the individual understands her existence in terms of her generated temporality; that is, in terms of being and time. This constitutes a move by Heidegger away from Husserl's cognitive categories or conditions, towards his own understanding of the conditions of human existence. This has been designated the shift from transcendental to historical or hermeneutic phenomenology. Heidegger then classifies the unifying characteristic of everything experienced in *die faktische Lebenserfahrung* as 'meaningfulness', *Bedeutsamkeit*. Lived-through *Bedeutsamkeit* as the reality of human existence is designated by Heidegger as primordial temporality or *history*.

It is in his affirmation of history, in its primordial sense, that is, in terms of generated temporality, being and time, which precisely agrees with Bultmann's understanding of history, that Heidegger signals his shift away from theories of cognition such as neo-Kantianism and Husserl's transcendental phenomenology. For Heidegger has recognised the validity of (for example) Herrmann's rejection of the material as the only basis of any analysis of human existence. He himself rejects, however, any abstraction to an a-historical plane of 'reality' which can be characterised as the 'inner life of the individual' or as the 'transcendental ego'. On the contrary, Heidegger asserts the concreteness of human experience and existence – as does Bultmann's positive philosophy – and attempts to formalise the method by which one can understand that experience and existence.

Although the terminology is awkward at this stage, it is clear that what is found in Heidegger's lectures of 1920–1 constitutes one of the first attempts to work out the complex but essentially simple terminology to be found in *Being and Time* by 1927. What cannot be denied, moreover, is that in 1920–1 Heidegger is wrestling with this problem by engaging with the eschatological passages of certain of the earliest Christian writings, and not with the ethics or religious belief of the inner individual. Heidegger has left behind the neo-Kantianism of Herrmann's understanding of religious experience in his Part 1, therefore. In his Part 2, he will identify that which he finds to be the foundation of a Christian understanding of primordial history: eschatology.

Sheehan writes: 'For Heidegger, religious phenomena are to

be approached in terms of factical life-experience and specifically in terms of the temporality and historicity of that experience' (Sheehan, 1979, p. 319). For the Christians of the communities in Galatia and Thessalonia, their temporality and historicity is characterised eschatologically. Thus, Heidegger's ontological reflection agrees with Bultmann's, as outlined above. This is the essence of the Christian gospel, argues Heidegger, and he characterises the situation of the epistle as 'preaching' (Sheehan, 1979, p. 320). This understanding of the foundations of human existence is found in the epistles in question, argues Heidegger. *He merely reveals what is already there* (Bultmann!). Sheehan writes:

> *Genesthai* in all its forms points to the basic state of Being of St. Paul and of the Thessalonians, namely, their 'already having become' or 'already having been' (*Gewordensein* – cf. 2 Cor. 5.17). This is not to be taken in the sense of some past and by-gone event (*das Vergangene*), but rather as the whole of what is already operative and determinative of the Thessalonians present 'Now'. Their *Gewordensein* is their *jetziges Sein*. (Sheehan, 1979, p. 320)

On this understanding, eschatology as generated temporality or primordial historicity, as the meaningfulness of human existence, understood as being-towards-God, must, as the expression of God's grace, become the foundation of the Now or moment of present existence; that is, eschatology as generated temporality or primordial historicity is the foundation of the human question, which in turn is the precursor to the God question. This means that for Heidegger, the Christian doctrine of eschatology articulates not a 'future' in any time-indexical sense, but rather the meaningfulness or *Bedeutsamkeit* of human existence. So Sheehan can conclude, paraphrasing Heidegger's lectures, that:

> The Christian – or Pauline – meaning of eschatology has shifted from the expectation of a future event to a presence before God, what Heidegger calls a *Vollzugszusammenhang mit Gott*, a context of enacting one's life in uncertainty before the unseen God. The weight has shifted to the 'how' of existence. Yes, the parousia seems to St. Paul to be imminent, but for Heidegger that imminence serves only to characterise the 'how' of factical life: its essential uncertainty. (Sheehan, 1979, p. 322)

One could not wish for a more 'Bultmannian' conceptualisation of the Christian doctrine of eschatology than that given by Heidegger in the winter of 1921.

2   Phenomenology and Theology

Despite the 'Bultmannian' style and content of Heidegger's reading of Galatians and Thessalonians, however, these 1920–1 lectures must be treated with great care. Certainly Heidegger appears to be conducting the same sort of analysis as that later attempted by Bultmann. And yet his interests and concerns are at once far more extensive than Bultmann's. Bultmann, influenced directly or indirectly by the Kierkegaardian quest for the subjective individual and its background in the Lutheran tradition, considers the twin questions of being and time because of their significance for his theology. Heidegger, by contrast, is at this stage still groping towards that mature phenomenological analysis of *Dasein* which will reach a preliminary statement in *Being and Time*. For all their points of contact, therefore, Bultmann and Heidegger stand far apart on one vital question, that is, the nature of the relationship between theology phenomenology. For Bultmann, phenomenology is a necessary stage in the expression of the theological conviction that salvation comes through Jesus Christ. For Heidegger, 'theology' is a productive way of working out his fundamental analysis of human existence. In this respect, one should note the manner in which Heidegger's terminology was refined during the years 1921–7, overwhelmingly through the influence of a secular source, the correspondence between Yorck and Dilthey (Dilthey and Yorck, 1923).

Heidegger's understanding of this relationship is made explicit in his lecture, 'Phenomenology and Theology'. This text provides the climax to our understanding of Heidegger's contribution to the human question. It also leads Bultmann forward directly to the God question, away from a reductive phenomenology (which has now served its limited purpose), and towards an event theory proper, as the fullest expression of the meaning of eschatology and, therefore, historical phenomenology.

On 14 February 1928, after he had been appointed Professor of Philosophy at Freiburg, in succession to Husserl, Martin Heidegger returned to Marburg to give a guest lecture at the Theology Faculty. That lecture was entitled 'Phenomenology and Theology', and immediately after Heidegger had delivered it he made extensive corrections, while remaining in Marburg. There is no direct evidence to support the conjecture, but it seems obvious that Heidegger made these corrections with the aid of Rudolf Bultmann. In any case, when the lecture was published in the collection entitled *Wegmarken*, it carried a dedication to Bultmann (cf. Heidegger, 1976a, p. 45). It seems certain, therefore, that the lecture 'Phenomenology and Theology' can be regarded as the definitive statement of both Heidegger's and Bultmann's understanding of the nature of their intellectual relationship during the decisive years of their friendship in Marburg during the 1920s. As such, this text illustrates the crucial significance of the notion of *Verstehen* for Bultmann's thought concerning the human question (see above), and the way in which Heidegger interpreted that significance in terms of his own hermeneutic or historical phenomenology.

After a few preliminary observations, Heidegger moves into his stride, making the claim that both phenomenology and theology are sciences, and that it is upon the basis of this understanding of their nature that one should attempt to examine the relationship between them. This does not, of course, mean that theology and phenomenology share the metaphysical presuppositions of the so-called 'scientific' world-view; that is, the belief in objectivity and the preeminence of empirical verification as axioms of cognition and judgement. On the contrary, it simply means for Heidegger that both phenomenology and theology proceed in a critical manner. In this sense, theology is still, for Heidegger, a science in the same way that Aquinas was able to define theology as a science (cf. *Summa Theologiae* I la 1.2). With this in mind, Heidegger is able to offer the following definition of 'science': 'Science is the founding disclosure, for the sheer sake of disclosure, of the self-contained regions of being or, as the case may be, of Being' (Heidegger, 1976a, p. 48).

There is an important difference, however, between philosophy (by which in this lecture Heidegger always understands phenomenology) and theology. For whereas phenomenology is a deductive science, because it proceeds from a critical analysis of human existence, theology is a positive science, because its subject matter appears to be that which is not given in this world; that is, God. In the first instance, therefore, Heidegger can write: 'Theology is a positive science and as such, therefore, is absolutely different from philosophy' (Heidegger, 1976a, p. 49). In Heidegger's own words, theology is the positive science of the self-contained region of God. Phenomenology is the deductive science of Being (see the quotation above).

On a first examination, therefore, Heidegger makes a clear and definite distinction between theology and phenomenology. In its crudity, however – essentially it is founded upon a distinction between the religious and the secular – it serves a simple pedagogic purpose. That is, it serves to demonstrate to his readers that Heidegger is not prepared to rest his analysis upon objective criteria of judgement. This first definition of the relationship between theology and phenomenology, in other words, is raised in order to be dismissed.

Heidegger, therefore, is not satisfied with this preliminary conclusion. On the contrary, there is, he insists, far more to the relationship between phenomenology and theology than merely an absolute qualitative distinction. Rather, phenomenology and theology must be related in such a way that their independence is secured, but their relationship recognised. This apparent paradox leads Heidegger to the conclusion that although theology is indeed a positive science, as he had stated, the subject of that positive science cannot be what he first thought it to be, that is, God, for that would maintain a rigid and inviolable distinction between philosophy and theology (the previously cited religious/secular distinction). In a very important passage, Heidegger writes:

> Proper to the positive character of a science is: first, that a being which in some way is already disclosed is to a certain extent come upon as a possible theme of theoretical objectification and enquiry; second, that this given positum is come upon in a definite prescientific manner of approaching and proceeding with that which it is; third, it is proper to the positive character that this prescientific behaviour toward whatever is given is also already illuminated and guided by an understanding of Being – even if it is nonconceptual. (Heidegger, 1976a, p. 50)

The positum of theology as a positive science is the religion of primitive Christianity; its history in the biblical texts, and Bultmann's *religionsgeschichtliche* study of those texts, satisfies Heidegger's first criterion. The 'understanding of Being' which illuminates and guides is that understanding of God's action which regards it as the revelation of God in Christ (for Bultmann, the Revealer) which is given only to faith. This satisfies Heidegger's third criterion.

If these two points are true, however, it must mean that the positum of theology as a positive science is not God, but rather human existence in primitive Christianity as illuminated and guided by God's revelation in Jesus Christ. In other words, the positum of theology as a positive science is existence from the perspective of faith, which in turn will direct theology's 'primordial interpretation' (see above). One sees, therefore, how Heidegger's understanding of the positum of theology as a positive science points towards 'primordial interpretation', ontological reflection, in phenomenological form. As yet, however, one cannot see the precise nature of the relationship between theology and philosophy.

Heidegger's second criterion provides the solution to this riddle, in so far as it looks back towards his first criterion, and the possible theoretical objectification and enquiry into the positum of theology. In other words, the prescientific nature of the positum of theology as a positive science must by definition be open to enquiry. It must, that is, be open to 'primordial interpretation', as its deductive analysis. So Heidegger can state that: 'If faith would totally oppose a conceptual interpretation, then theology would be a thoroughly inappropriate means of grasping its object, faith' (Heidegger, 1976a, p. 54). At this stage, therefore, Heidegger concludes that: 'Theology is the science of faith' (Heidegger, 1976a, p. 55).

Faith, however, can not be regarded as solely a supernatural occurrence. As Heidegger stipulates, in so far as faith as the object of theology as a positive science must be open to theoretical conceptualisation and analysis, there is involved with faith the entire question of what he refers to as 'primordial interpretation', what in Bultmann finds expression as ontological reflection or understanding, *Verstehen*. In so far as faith informs and directs ontological reflection, faith is more than simply belief. It is also understanding (one might almost speak of *fides quaerens intellectum*). In answer to the question, 'What is faith?', therefore, Heidegger writes: 'Faith is the believing-understanding mode of existing in history (*Geschichte*) revealed; i.e., occurring in the Crucified' (Heidegger, 1976a, p. 54). This statement is almost too perfect. It contains absolutely everything, in the most balanced of summary forms, that this study has been trying to demonstrate. The role of phenomenology and ontological reflection in theology; faith as that which informs and characterises 'primordial reflection'; *Geschichte* as the story of faith, so understood; revelation as the guiding principle of the move from the human to the God question, and the point of ontological reflection; and, above all, the relating of all of these themes to the historical Jesus of Nazareth, the Crucified: in this one sentence, Heidegger reveals himself to be Bultmann's finest commentator. It is also an important statement because Heidegger's use of the expression 'believing-understanding' is clearly not accidental. In the context of this lecture, it is a very precise and definite reference to the concept of *Glauben und Verstehen* which is crucial to any appreciation of Bultmann's theology.

But Heidegger has more to say about the relationship between phenomenology and theology. He writes: 'Formally considered, then, faith as the existing relation to the Crucified is a mode of historical, human existence, of historically being in a history which discloses itself only through and for faith' (Heidegger, 1976a, p. 55).

For Heidegger, if faith is to be understood as a form of historical existence, then it must be open to scientific analysis, which for Heidegger can only mean that faith as an historical form of existence must be open, in some way, to phenomenological analysis. That is why Heidegger describes faith as the 'believing-understanding' mode of historical existence. For Heidegger requires the two-fold nature of faith to enable faith, in theological terms, to be both a mode of existence *coram deo*, and therefore open only to the eschatological revelation of God in Christ, and for faith to be a form of historical existence, in the world, and therefore open to phenomenological analysis. It is faith as 'understanding', argues Heidegger, which is open to phenomenology, as that necessary 'primordial interpretation' which is informed by faith and which in turn informs positive theology. Heidegger writes, therefore, that: 'The positive science of faith needs philosophy only in regard to its scientific character' (Heidegger, 1976a, p. 61). The scientific character of faith is an understanding of humanity's historical existence. Heidegger concludes, therefore, that: 'Philosophy is the possible ontological corrective which can formally point out the ontic and, in particular, the pre-Christian content of basic theological concepts. But philosophy can be what it is without functioning factually as this corrective' (Heidegger, 1976a, p. 66). That is, phenomenology may achieve for the positive science of theology that 'primordial interpretation' of its positive origins in primitive Christianity which faith demands. Heidegger, the reader may notice, is speaking about demythologising (see below).

Excursus I: *Being and Time*

There is one quite significant implication in Heidegger's lecture that Bultmann was at pains to point out, again and again. That is, that the task of 'primordial interpretation' or ontological reflection does not have to be carried out explicitly by historical or hermeneutic phenomenology. The faith by which one believes, the *fides qua creditur*, is itself phenomenological, and does not require description as in any sense Heideggerian. In this way, Bultmann can claim, again and again, that Heidegger is simply secularising what theology finds in the New Testament; that is, ontological reflection upon the conditions of human existence.

Whatever Bultmann's reasons for saying this, it cannot be denied that he was heavily influenced by Heidegger in Marburg in the 1920s. Granted that Bultmann's own understanding of being and time owes more to Kierkegaard and the Lutheran tradition in which they both shared; that one should reduce phenomenologically to the level of transcendental analysis, to the level of 'primordial interpretation': this is the extent of Bultmann's debt to Heidegger with respect to the human question in theology. Bultmann himself makes this debt clear in his important, and previously cited, letter to Karl Barth of 1952, where he writes:

But I think I always saw one thing clearly, namely, that the decisive thing is to make it clear with what concept of reality, of being and events, we really operate in theology, and how this relates to the concepts in which not only other people think and speak of reality, being and events, but in which we theologians also think and speak in our everyday lives. Ontological reflection is thus needed. . . . If such ontological reflection is part of the business of theology – and your questions have not made me doubtful but simply confirmed me in the belief that it is so – it follows that theology must concern itself with philosophy, and today the philosophy which has posed the ontological question afresh; it must clarify its relationship to this. (Jaspert and Bromiley, 1982, p. 87)

Here, Bultmann is clearly referring to Heidegger and historical phenomenology. Given the nature and extent of their relationship in Marburg during the 1920s, as documented in Bultmann's letter to the late Canon Duncan, it is clear that Bultmann must have had an intimate knowledge of Heidegger's major work of that period, *Being and Time*.

The extent to which Bultmann knew and understood *Being and Time*, however, has been greatly underestimated. In a most revealing passage in his *Notizen zu Martin Heidegger*, Karl Jaspers reminisces that: 'Meine Reaktion oder vielmehr Nichtreaktion auf *Sein und Zeit* hat er (Heidegger) nie vorgeworfen. Als das Werk erschien, sagte er, pessimistisch in bezug auf den Widerhall wie beiläufig: Bultmann und ich würden es verstehen' (Jaspers, 1978, note 210 on p. 226). 'Bultmann and I would understand it. . .': this statement should not be underestimated.

The above examination of 'Phenomenology and Theology' brings to a conclusion our consideration of Bultmann's answer to the human question in theology, and the limits of Heidegger's influence upon that answer. Given Jaspers's comment about Heidegger's estimate of Bultmann's understanding of *Being and Time*, however, what I want to do in this first excursus is to look a little more closely at one particular aspect of Heidegger's text; that is, its sometimes cryptic references and allusions to the ontological difference proper, which came to dominate Heidegger's thought and work after 1927. If Bultmann knew *Being and Time* as well as Jaspers's note intimates, then I want to see what there is in that text which looks forward to Bultmann's answer to the God question, and Heidegger's pivotal role in that answer. This development is not incompatible with the phenomenological reduction proper which has been the subject of this chapter so far. On the contrary, the turn towards an event theory of the revelation of the ontological difference as process, which we see in Heidegger after 1927, is the necessary development of that phenomenological reduction. It is, in other words, not only a legitimate step to take, but a necessary one.

We turn, therefore, towards Heidegger's thinking of Being, *Sein*, and away from the phenomenological analysis of *Dasein*. Here we may see the basis of Heidegger's influence upon Bultmann's answer to the God question, his theology proper. One at least of the main protagonists has accepted the validity of this proposal:

> Heidegger himself, when he addressed a group of Bultmann's former students at Marburg in 1960, suggested that if his effort had any relevance at all, it might be considered in terms of analogy: as philosophical thinking is to Being, so theological thinking (the thinking of faith) is to the self-revealing God. (Richardson, 1965, p. 87)

Once again, theology stands to benefit from Heidegger's insight. Before we can elaborate upon that insight in the next section of the present chapter, however, we must take one last look at *Being and Time*.

In his quite magnificent essay, 'Being as Appropriation' (*Sein als Ereignis*), Otto Pöggeler points out that Heidegger first explicitly broaches the subject of the ontological difference, the way forward from the phenomenological analysis of *Dasein*, in his analysis of guilt and the problem of the ontological origin of Non-Being (*das Nichts*) (cf. Heidegger, 1962, pp. 325ff; cf. Pöggeler, 1978, p. 100 –1). Heidegger then developed this idea quickly and efficiently, in the lecture 'What is Metaphysics?' and the essay 'The Essence of Reasons'. The reference to the problem of the ontological origin of Non-Being, though, betrays the fact that Heidegger's entire concern with the question of Being itself is the starting-point for his consideration of the ontological difference as process of revelation; that is, that which overcomes Non-Being by giving meaning.

This is implicit in his choice of Leibniz's question – 'Why is there something rather than nothing? – as the opening shot in his lecture,

'What is Metaphysics?' But it is found also in *Being and Time*. In his introduction to that text, concerned explicitly with the question of Being itself, Heidegger states:

> ...even the ontological task of constructing a non-deductive genealogy of the different possible ways of Being requires that we first come to an understanding of 'what we really mean by this expression "Being"'.... Basically, all ontology, no matter how rich and firmly compacted a system of categories it has at its disposal, remains blind and perverted from its ownmost aim, if it has not adequately clarified the meaning of Being, and conceived this clarification as its fundamental task. (Heidegger, 1962, p. 31)

The paradox of this statement of Heidegger's, of course, is that he himself never adequately clarified the meaning of Being, until he understood and explained Being as event (*Ereignis*); that is, that process of revelation, as truth (*aletheia*) and language (*logos*), which itself gives meaning through illumination.

Bultmann's thought is analogous to Heidegger's at this point because he too, as a Christian, wishes to assert an ultimate Reality, in this case the Creator God, as the Being which overcomes Non-Being in the creative act of self-revelation, the eschatological event of grace, Jesus Christ. In this sense, Bultmann too begins with Leibniz's question, 'Why is there something rather than nothing?' But whereas Heidegger makes this explicit, Bultmann does not. It remains one of the necessary implications of his stance as a positive theologian. That is, the claim that what Heidegger knows as 'Being' is for Bultmann known as 'God', is the necessary implication of faith's prescription of theology's 'primordial interpretation'. (Of course, *Sein* for Heidegger never indicates divinity in any religious or theological sense.) One should never imagine, however, that this question of Being as the question, 'Why is there something rather than nothing?', is ever missing from Bultmann's thought. It is not.

It is only with the turn to the matter of revelation, though, and its understanding as event, that this question is given any sort of clear definition in either Heidegger or Bultmann. When turning to the God question, therefore, we are turning to *the* ontological question (see above). All subsequent theology must be informed by this understanding of revelation as eschatological event, *if* it is to be genuinely theological, argues Bultmann. With this in mind, we can now turn to that question in its biblical form: 'What is truth?' (John 18.38).

3   What Is Truth?

(a)   *Aletheia* and *logos*

In an unpublished letter, written to Friedrich Gogarten on 19 October 1924, Bultmann states 'Moreover, during an afternoon each week I am now reading with Heidegger the *Gospel according to St. John.* I hope to learn all sorts of things from these meetings' (cf. Barash, 1988, note 40, p. 190). This confession frames the ensuing consideration of the question, 'What is truth?', as it elaborates and informs Heidegger's understanding of the event of the ontological difference, understood as a process of revelation, and Bultmann's understanding of the eschatological event of God's self-revelation, Jesus Christ. *Aletheia*, therefore, is the key to any appreciation of Bultmann and Heidegger as event theorists, and ultimately to Bultmann's answer to the God question.

Because in Bultmann's theology the risen Lord is always encountered in the kerygma, the remainder of this chapter will concentrate upon Bultmann's programmatic text, 'New Testament and Mythology' (Bultmann, 1948, pp. 15–53). It will be examined in relation to those writings of Martin Heidegger's which convey most clearly his understanding of the process of revelation as the question of truth, *aletheia*, understood phenomenologically. These are: Section 44, 'Dasein, Disclosedness, and Truth', in *Being and Time* (Heidegger, 1962, pp. 256–73); 'Vom Wesen der Wahrheit' (Heidegger, 1976a, pp. 171–202); *'aletheia* (Heraklit Fragment 16)' (Heidegger, 1954b, pp. 257–82); '*logos* (Heraklit Fragment 50)' (Heidegger, 1954b, pp. 207–29); 'Platons Lehre von der Wahrheit' (Heidegger, 1976a, pp. 203–38); and 'Vom Wesen und Begriff der physis. Aristoteles, Physik B,1' (Heidegger, 1976a, pp. 239–301). This analysis will hopefully establish, once and for all, the genuine nature and extent of Heidegger's influence upon Bultmann's answer to the God question, his theology proper.

In an essay entitled 'Untersuchungen zum Johannesevangelium

A: aletheia', Bultmann writes: 'The final and deepest meaning of the Greek *aletheia*-concept, insofar as *aletheia* means "revealedness", is the revealedness of my essential existence (*Dasein*)...which is offered to me in language, and in which I can and should come to the essentiality of my existence' (Bultmann, 1967, pp. 152–3). As will be demonstrated, this understanding of the relationship between the act or process of revelation (*aletheia*) and language (*logos*) is shared by Martin Heidegger. But in addition, Heidegger is concerned, in his writings on early Greek thinking, with the gradual deterioration of the understanding of *aletheia* in terms of *logos*, language, towards its understanding in terms of *glossa*, discourse or objectifying speech. This, for Heidegger, is a movement away from understanding, towards misunderstanding. It is this development that is at the heart of Bultmann's interpretation of the 'mythology' which came, in his estimation, to surround humanity's eschatological expectation. In other words, 'language' and 'discourse' in Heidegger's writings mean the same as 'language' and 'myth' in Bultmann's writings.

In terms of Greek thought, however, Heidegger regards it as a *gradual* development from language to discourse, and he traces this development from Heraclitus to Aristotle, via Parmenides and Plato. He begins with Heraclitus, Fragment 16: 'to me dunon an tis lathoi' – 'How can one conceal oneself before that which never sets?' (Diels, 1951, p. 155).

It is very significant that Heidegger should begin his consideration of *aletheia* as the process of revelation, of revealing the truth, with a study of a fragment from Heraclitus that contains no reference to revelation in any explicit form, but a very clear reference to concealment, as Heidegger acknowledges (cf. Heidegger, 1954b, p. 260). For concealment before that which never sets (i.e. Being) is the necessary presupposition for any consideration of revelation *by* that which never sets. In other words: 'Self-concealing guarantees self-revealing its essentiality' (Heidegger, 1954b, p. 271). This only makes sense because Heidegger always considers the ontological difference as a process, a coming-to-pass, of revelation. This process of revelation must then include within itself a moment of concealment, so that Heidegger can write: 'Unconcealment is the essential quality of that which has come to light, and has left behind concealment' (Heidegger, 1954b, p. 259).

Heidegger notes that Heraclitus, in Fragment 16, is prepared to designate the essential quality of that which has come to light by this process of concealment–unconcealment, as the *physis* or essence of a being in that which has come to light. In other words, in discussing the *physis* of a being in terms of its relationship with *Sein*, Being (that which never sets), Heraclitus, argues Heidegger, is not concerned with describing metaphysically the constitution of the being in question, but rather is concerned with relating to the essence of that being as something that is revealed out of concealment. This clarifies Heidegger's otherwise cryptic statement that: '*Physis* is not the essence of things, but the essence of things (as process) as *physis* thinks the saying (i.e., Fragment 16)' (Heidegger, 1954b, p. 271). The meaning of existence, in other words, is revealed before that which never sets – what one might refer to, theologically, as the light of the world.

In pre-Socratic thought, therefore, Heidegger finds an awareness of the ontological difference between beings and Being (that which never sets) as a process or event of revealing-that-which-was-concealed in such a way that the being in question is not reified into a 'thing', but remains open to the encounter as it is revealed before that which never sets, Being. *Aletheia*, as truth, means therefore the process of revelation of the 'essence' of the being in question. The essence of truth, then, is revelation. Truth is the revelation of the 'essence' of a being, before that which never sets. If this process is recognised, then it is possible to understand – that is, to encounter authentically – the meaning of the being in question.

For Heidegger, understanding in the sense of encountering the meaning of the being in question can only be true if it understands the process of revelation as process; that is, dynamically. In other words, one can only come to understand by acknowledging the conditions of existence, before that which never sets. (This is found in Bultmann too: one can only understand, and therefore encounter, the Christ of God, when one understands the meaning of human existence *coram deo* as eschatological; see below.) Once this understanding of truth is subordinated to the notion that the 'truth' of a being is the correspondence of its description with its appearance, argues Heidegger, then the meaning of the being in question is concealed, and Being itself is forgotten. Then, for Heidegger,

Wahrheit becomes *Richtigkeit*. This 'forgetting' of Being is the beginning of misunderstanding the meaning of human existence.

At this stage, it is important to note that for Heidegger, *logos* is the language of understanding the process of revelation as *aletheia*. When this process is forgotten, however, language becomes mere discourse, *glossa*. Discourse is the medium of misunderstanding, of forgetting. Bultmann demonstrates that he is completely aware of this argument when he states that: 'Man speaks of the "truth" of things. . . . Aristotle made this basic definition clear, when he equated *aletheia* with *pragma* and *phainomena*' (Bultmann, 1967, p. 145). Discourse (*Reden*) has no alternative but to discuss 'things' as reified objects, when it talks 'about'. The only alternative is one that is ontologically prior to discourse; that is, for a language, *logos*, to be thought as *aletheia*, as the process of revelation as Heidegger finds it in Heraclitus Fragment 16. It is this language as the fundamental articulation of *aletheia* as the process of revelation that allows the *physis* of a being to realise itself as being before that which never sets; that is, in terms of the event of the ontological difference. Thus, Bultmann can write: '*Aletheia* means: letting a matter (*Sache*) be seen as it really is' (Bultmann, 1967, p. 147). In this way, Bultmann argues that: 'Language should be characterised as *aletheia*' (Bultmann, 1967, p. 148).

Quite clearly, therefore, there is a definite affinity between Bultmann and Heidegger at this point. Bultmann writes: 'The character of language is *apophanis*, letting-be-seen. . . it does not produce *aletheia*, but it lets it be seen' (Bultmann, 1967, pp. 147–8). This echoes precisely Heidegger's thinking at two points. In *Being and Time*, Heidegger writes of how Aristotle could equate *aletheia* with *apophainesthai*: 'as exhibiting something and letting it be seen with regard to the "truth" and within the range of the "truth"' (Heidegger, 1962, p. 256). And in the *logos* paper, Heidegger asks: 'Will thinking finally learn to catch a glimpse of what it means that Aristotle could characterise *legein* as *apophainesthai*? The *logos* by itself brings that which appears and comes forward in its lying before us to appearance, to its luminous self-showing' (Heidegger, 1954b, p. 213).

In a fundamental sense, consequently, language is for both Bultmann and Heidegger identical with truth as the process of revealing that which was concealed, of understanding, and language therefore is capable of articulating the essence or *physis* of a being which, as process, transcends its merely ontic appearance or characteristics. Language, then, arises from this process of revelation, and must consequently be distinct from discourse, which attempts to describe that process precisely in terms of its ontic characteristics, thereby reifing it (cf. Heidegger, 1954b, pp. 262f). It is, argues Heidegger, the reification of a being into a 'thing' that is the clearest indication that the process or event of revelation has been misunderstood, and thereby forgotten. As will be shown, this has profound implications for Bultmann's programme of demythologising, and therefore for his Christology and theology proper.

It is this understanding of language as a word capable of articulating the event of revelation of the meaning of a being that Heidegger is concerned to examine in his paper '*logos* ('Heraklit Fragment 50)'. The fragment reads: 'ouk emou alla tou logou akousantas homologein sophon estin hen panta einai' – 'When you have listened not to me but to the logos, it is wise within the same logos to say: one is all' (Diels, 1951, p. 161). Heidegger interprets the fragment in the following way: '*Hen panta* is not what the *logos* pronounces, but *hen panta* reveals the way in which the *logos* meaningfully occurs (as process)' (Heidegger, 1954b, pp. 219–20). In other words, for Heidegger it is axiomatic that a thoughtful audition of the word or *logos* will allow one to articulate, in the same language, the fact that 'one is all'; that is, that Being is the light which reveals the meaning of each and every being. For Heidegger, this fragment means nothing more nor less than that for anyone who thinks all is one, he or she can participate in the process of language or authentic revelation, without resorting to discourse. In this way, *logos* is *aletheia*; that is, a process of revealing that which was concealed. This means that it is possible for one to think the language which reveals the meaning of beings which are otherwise concealed. So Heidegger can conclude at this stage that: 'When mortal *legein* is assigned to the *logos*, *homologein* occurs' (Heidegger, 1954b, p. 221). If this is forgotten, then language becomes atrophied into discourse. Heidegger recognises that adverse development in the work of Plato and Aristotle.

Agreeing with Heidegger, Bultmann states that: 'Language

should be characterised as *aletheia*' (Bultmann, 1967, p. 148), thereby adopting at an important stage in his thinking Heidegger's distinction between language and discourse, and the distinction which underlies it, that between understanding and misunderstanding. In this sense, Bultmann is concerned to pursue the same line of thinking as Heidegger in his (Bultmann's) conception of the role of understanding as the *fides qua creditur*, the faith by which one believes. Bultmann does this by echoing Heidegger's understanding of truth and language, as the phenomenological understanding of revelation as the process or event of coming-to-light.

Bultmann does not continue to articulate the nature of discourse in his 1928 paper (as will be shown, this was achieved in 'New Testament and Mythology'). Rather, at this stage it is Heidegger alone who thinks through the 'forgetting' of Being in the works of Plato and Aristotle, and thereby the birth of misunderstanding.

In effect, Heidegger argues, Plato achieves a transformation of the essential character of the ontological difference as process into the notion of the supreme *Idea*, from which the *ideas* derive their own powers of illumination. In so doing, according to Heidegger, Plato forgot the meaning of the ontological difference as *difference*; that is, process, and instead described objectively the system of *ideas*. For Heidegger, Plato turns his attention upon the 'whatness' of the ontological difference, and it is for Heidegger this concentration upon the 'whatness' of the ontological difference, rather than its 'howness', which leads to misunderstanding, and thereby objectifying discourse, the inability of humanity to think the word of authentic language. So Heidegger writes: 'Out of the precedence of the *Idea* and the *ideas* over *aletheia* there occurs a change in the meaning of truth, which now becomes *opthates*, the "correspondence" of auditions and statements' (Heidegger, 1976a, p. 231).

As will be shown, it is theologically important for Bultmann that the individual has the choice to take this Platonic route. He writes: 'The question of Greece or Christianity is one which always confronts man' (Bultmann, 1968, p. 77). That is, the individual can decide for this alternative when confronted by the kerygma, and so can choose misunderstanding before understanding, discourse before language. It is called inauthentic existence, the turning away from God's revelation in Christ, God's eschatological event.

When Bultmann comes to work out this understanding in detail, however, he refers not to 'discourse', but to 'myth', no doubt because of his background in the History of Religions School. Bultmann's 'myth' is entirely consistent, however, with Heidegger's understanding of 'discourse'. So Bultmann can write, that: 'The struggle between *mythos* and *logos* must appear in a completely different form when it is seen as a struggle between two possibilities for the understanding of being' (Bultmann, 1942, pp. 146–7).

The final devolution (according to Heidegger) of pre-Socratic thought was the achievement of Aristotle, towards whom Heidegger turns his attention in 'Vom Wesen und Begriff der physis. Aristoteles Physik B,1' (Heidegger, 1976a). Once Heidegger has identified *physis* with *aletheia*, Aristotle's contrary understanding of *physis* as devolved from the original *noein* becomes a crucial devolution of *aletheia* itself:

Because *physis* in the meaning of the *Physics* is a type of *ousia*, and because *ousia* itself in its meaning derives from the original sense of *physis*, therefore *aletheia* pertains to Being, and therefore the presencing in the open of the *idea* (Plato) and of the *eidos kata ton logon* (Aristotle) discloses itself as one character of *ousia*. (Heidegger, 1976a, p. 301)

But this 'visibility' is itself only an appearance of the being as *ousia*, argues Heidegger, and therefore is nothing more than the 'visibility' of its form (*morphe*) for Aristotle. In this case, 'truth' now resides in the correspondence of the 'whatness' of a thing or object and its expression or description in discourse, as the articulation of its form. Of Heidegger's interpretation of this development, Father Richardson writes, in his *Through Phenomenology to Thought*, that:

In this case, the decision about what is true depends upon distinguishing authentic utterance from mere hearsay. This means that the place where truth resides is not, as originally, in the being-that-is-rendered-open, but in the expression. The place of the truth has changed from being to expression: with it the essence of truth has changed once more from non-concealment to correctness. (Richardson, 1963, p. 301)

It is now possible to discern the basic thesis of Heidegger's work on early Greek thought concerning *aletheia* and *logos*. For understanding to be possible, that is, for the ontological difference as the process of revealing that which was concealed to be encountered as event (*Ereignis*), the individual must think that difference before that which never sets, that is, before Being, or the light of revelation. Where this does not take place, as in the thought of Plato and Aristotle, misunderstanding occurs, and there then develops a tradition of speculative metaphysics which, according to Heidegger, has dominated Western philosophy until this day. Understanding is only possible, argues Heidegger, in the light of revelation as the ontological foundation of existence – most notably, human existence.

As has been demonstrated, it is with the ability to discern this truth, and to make it intelligible to the individual believer, that phenomenology, argues Heidegger, can furnish theology. Bultmann takes up this assistance in his understanding of the *fides qua creditur*, the faith by which one believes, which has been identified as the foundation of Bultmann's notion of *Verstehen und Glauben*. Bultmann makes his dependence upon Heidegger for this assistance clear when he writes: '*Aletheia* is the divine Being, the essential Being, which is also my essential being, and which is closed to me and remains closed to me, unless through the divine revelation the border is opened and I become raised up' (Bultmann, 1967, p. 159). Here, Bultmann transforms Heidegger's purely philosophical thought into a theological understanding of God's revelation in Christ. That is, the event of revelation, which for Heidegger can take place whenever the meaning of a being is understood and articulated authentically in the light of Being, is turned by Bultmann into the unique, eschatological event of God's grace in the risen Lord. By linking the notion of event to Jesus Christ, therefore, Bultmann establishes Heidegger's fundamental event theory in the theoretical presentation of one specific event. This is of course inevitable. For Rudolf Bultmann does not share Martin Heidegger's interest in rethinking the ontological difference for solely philosophical purposes. Bultmann is, though, committed to rethinking the significance for the Christian faith of the historical Jesus and the kerygmatic Christ, and it is because of this commitment that Bultmann echoes Heidegger's event theory. For it is only the kergyma, as the authentic word spoken by believers, which can articulate the Word of God as eschatological event. And it is only the eschatological event as the process of revelation involving both the historical Jesus and the kerygmatic Christ that leads the individual to the encounter with the risen Lord.

(b)   New Testament and Mythology

As was shown in our examination of Heidegger's treatment of the process of revelation, the ontological difference that 'irrupts' into the world through specific events, there must be in the ontic world something concealed which can be revealed by the engagement with that which transcends the ontic world. And in Bultmann's theology, it is true to say that in the earthly life of Jesus, the eschatological significance of the Christ event is concealed until Easter Sunday. This point is made clear in Bultmann's paper, 'History and Eschatology in the New Testament' (Bultmann, 1954). It is only in the process of revelation as the event of the (eschatological) engagement of the historical Jesus with the kerygmatic Christ, that both realise their true significance and importance. Only an interpretation of the story of Jesus that hears the Word of God as the language of the Christian kerygma, therefore, can articulate Jesus' eschatological purpose. To those who can only grasp discourse, however (and therefore misunderstand the language of revelation), everything is in riddles, and the messianic secret remains concealed.

The kerygma, therefore, is not merely a spoken utterance that in some fashion announces a doctrine about what is best for the way in which the individual should live. On the contrary, the kerygma challenges the individual on the basis of that individual's active conduct in the world, for good or evil, for God or against God. There is no escape from these two alternatives (Greece or Christianity, *logos* or *mythos*). Any action is an action before God, and therefore any action is taken in the light of Christ, in the light of the world. These two alternatives, in Heideggerian terminology, are authentic and inauthentic existence. They are, for Bultmann, necessarily alternative responses to God's demand in Christ.

It is in the essay 'Neues Testament und Mythologie' that

Bultmann examines this problem in the greatest depth. Here, he writes that: 'The world-perspective (Weltbild) of the New Testament is mythical' (Bultmann, 1948, p. 15). For Bultmann, 'mythical' here means the world-perspective that is contingent upon the social context in which the gospel was first proclaimed, understands the Word of God in terms of objectifying discourse, and therefore expects an objective realisation of the kingdom of God. It is the same definition, the reader will recognise, that Bultmann gives to 'apocalyptic'. In this way, the mythical world-perspective objectifies the transcendent divine Reality within this earthly world, describing it as such.

Myth, then, is a human perspective, and therefore an option, so to speak, for each and every individual. This perspective is not a particular epistemological viewpoint, but rather the comportment of the individual in the world. According to Bultmann, however, this mythical world-perspective is incapable of hearing or articulating the Word of God as the eschatological event. Instead, the eschatological event as the process of revealing Christ's soteriological significance in the kerygma of the story of Jesus of Nazareth is conceptualised as the objective incarnation of a pre-existing being. In Heidegger's terms, the mythical world-perspective is one that has 'forgotten' the meaning of the question which is placed before men and women in God's self-revelation. This means that when answers are articulated from the mythical world-perspective, they are inevitably based upon false premises. Bultmann writes: 'The mythical world-perspective forms the presentation of the salvation event as it corresponds to the essential content of the New Testament proclamation' (Bultmann, 1948, p. 23). In this way, Bultmann can distinguish between *mythische* and *mythologische*. For the *mythische* perspective is the prior basis for any *mythologische* description of the salvation event in speech. So it can be said that any adoption of a mythical perspective upon the process of revelation automatically disposes the individual to speak about God in the terminology of objective discourse, and thereby to 'forget', according to Bultmann, the Word of God. In this sense, the fundamental meaning of myth is a human self-understanding which corresponds to the 'misunderstanding' discourse in the Heideggerian terminology, and which conceals the eschatological significance of the kerygmatic Christ.

The mythical perspective always employs mythological images to describe what it understands as the transcendent divine Reality. But in attempting to describe that Reality, the mythical perspective is pursuing a false idol. The dichotomy of language/myth, as it represents the two basic possibilities of understanding and mis-understanding, is therefore fundamental to Bultmann's perception of the human situation *coram deo*, which always means in the light of the revelation event. Bultmann states, therefore, that:

> Myth provides the motive for the essential critique of its ob-jectifying representations, insofar as the essential purpose, to speak about a transcendent power to which the world and men are subject, is hampered and obscured through the objectifying character of its statements. (Bultmann, 1948, p. 23)

For Bultmann, then, any consideration of the individual's situ-ation *coram deo* must speak the same language as the Word of God, which for Bultmann means that the kerygma must address the individual's historical situation, because Christ as God's question addresses the individual's historical situation. It is this determi-nation to understand the individual's historical situation apart from its objective description that causes Bultmann to make his effort of ontological reflection. But the theological significance of that onto-logical reflection is revealed by Bultmann's methodological use of Heidegger's language/myth dichotomy. This in itself, of course, is simply the logical working-out of the implications for the God question found in Heidegger's paper, 'Phenomenology and The-ology' (Heidegger, 1976a), as considered above.

Two tasks, therefore, confront Rudolf Bultmann the theologian. First, he must, as a historian of religious ideas, retrieve from the mythological expression of the Christian faith in the New Tes-tament anything that might be of help in understanding the in-dividual's historical predicament. Second, and most important, Bultmann must hear the Word of God and proclaim it anew in its own language. In reality, these are two parts of the one task.

Bultmann writes: 'It is of course entirely possible that in a past mythical world-perspective "truths" may again be discovered which had been forgotten in a time of "enlightenment"' (Bult-mann, 1948, p. 17). This, then, is the basic point of demythologising: 'By demythologising, I understand a hermeneutic methodology for enquiring about the reality-content of mythological statements and/or texts' (Bultmann, 1975, p. 128).

In itself, this hermeneutic methodology is an attempt to retrieve something of value from texts purveying an inherently dangerous world-perspective, and it is a retrieval that must be applied exhaustively, so that no mythology remains to conceal the Word of God. It is a retrieval, moreover, which can only be successfully attempted from a position of understanding, that is, the position which in itself is open to encountering God's event of grace, Jesus Christ. Hence the radical nature of Bultmann's programme. All of the imagery of the New Testament story of Jesus of Nazareth must be interpreted eschatologically by this hermeneutic methodology, from a position of understanding, which ultimately means by believers. For only believers are capable of understanding the reality of human existence, thereby discerning that which 'forgets' the meaning of that reality as revelation. It is only in the light of revelation that human existence can be understood, or misunderstood. But it is only those who recognise the light of revelation as the light of revelation, who are able to turn towards God. In other words, let those who have ears to hear, hear.

But this retrieval cannot, ultimately, describe the Word of God in such a way that it might be heard. For the Word of God simply cannot be described at all. Consequently, Bultmann's hermeneutic programme is emphatically not merely an attempt to make the gospel story intelligible in the terminology and thought forms of modern humanity, because the gospel story, and the individual's encounter with it in the kerygma, must transcend any such terminology and thought forms. Because the believer who is born again 'in Christ' is a 'new creation' (2 Cor. 5.17), the discourse of the old creation cannot be of any soteriological significance at all. Thus, Bultmann can write that: 'An authentic human life would be one in which one lived out of the invisible and causally-unattainable and, consequently, abandoned all self-contrived security' (Bultmann, 1948, p. 30). This 'authentic human life' is granted by the grace of God, through faith in Jesus Christ, encountered by the individual via the kerygma. This is what Bultmann means when he states that: 'To exist means to exist eschatologically' (Bultmann, 1948, p. 31).

This examination of Heidegger's analysis of the meaning of

understanding and misunderstanding has revealed the fundamental structure of Bultmann's thought, a structure that Bultmann himself believed to be biblical, and that he finds acknowledged in Jesus' answer to Pilate: 'My kingship is not of this world; if my kingship were of this world, my servants would fight, that I might not be handed over to the Jews; but my kingship is not of this world' (John 18.36). For Bultmann, it is axiomatic that if Jesus' kingdom is not of this world, it must not be described as if it were of this world. Thus he writes: 'Eschatological existence has become a possibility for man because God has acted and made an end to the world as "this" world' (Bultmann, 1948, p. 42). Bultmann makes it clear that this action takes place in Christ as Truth and Word; that is, as revelation and kerygma. It is, finally, with the meaning of this event that Bultmann's Christology is concerned. For if salvation cannot by definition be mediated objectively, in terms of the historical Jesus alone, then it must be mediated eschatologically, by the kerygmatic Christ. So, writes Bultmann: 'As the salvation event the cross of Christ is not a mythical occurrence, but an historical (*geschichtliche*) event, which springs from the historic (*historische*) crucifixion of Jesus of Nazareth' (Bultmann, 1948, p. 47).

With that, we return to the question of the historical Jesus, by a long and circuitous route. It is here, once again, that we must begin our next consideration, of the critical reception of Bultmann's thought.

Prior to that, however, there are one or two loose ends to tie up.

Excursus II: *Time and Being*

In this second excursus, prior to our conclusion concerning Bultmann's answer to the God question, it is useful to say a few words about how the notion of Heidegger as event theorist helps to cast light not only upon his work in its entirety, but also its relationship with theology.

In his aforementioned essay, Pöggeler makes the very fair point that Heidegger's *Being and Time* patently failed in its task in one important respect; that is, it failed to elucidate time as the transcendental horizon for the question of Being (cf. Pöggeler, 1978,

p. 94). This failure on the part of the 1927 text was effectively corrected during the rest of Heidegger's life, culminating in Heidegger's essay, 'Time and Being' (Heidegger, 1972, pp. 1–24). What we find here is that Heidegger's elucidation of time as the transcendental horizon for the question of Being, as an event theory, is in fact a form of historical interpretation. When Heidegger speaks of the event of Being, therefore, as that process of revelation which as the ontological difference and the overcoming of non-Being gives meaning to *Dasein* as authentic existence, he is speaking, in Bultmannian terms, of the immediacy of history and eschatology, of time and eternity, in the moment of encounter, as the genuine opening-up, revealing, of meaning. In this moment of encounter, as event, therefore, we find an answer to the question, 'Why is there something rather than nothing?' – Leibniz's question, the ontological question, Pilate's question, the God question. Heidegger writes:

> In the sending of the destiny of Being, in the extending of time, there becomes manifest a dedication, a delivering over into what is their own, namely of Being as presence and of time as the realm of the open. What determines both, time and Being, in their own, that is, in their belonging together, we shall call: *Ereignis*, event. One should bear in mind, however, that "event" is not simply an occurrence, but that which makes any occurrence possible. What this word names can be thought now only in the light of what becomes manifest in our looking ahead towards Being and towards time as destiny and as extending, to which time and Being belong. (Heidegger, 1972, p. 19)

Here, as Pöggeler insists (cf. Pöggeler, 1978, p. 102), *Ereignis* is a *singulare tantum*; it is the culmination of everything that Heidegger thought, and everything that he tried to think. Finally, therefore, Heidegger was no longer simply a phenomenologist, but an event theorist. Everything was subsumed in that final task.

The same applies to Bultmann when we call him an event theorist, although here we now know we are not referring to the event of the ontological difference in Heidegger's sense, but using Heidegger's understanding as an analogy to illuminate Bultmann's thinking of the eschatological event, as Heidegger suggested (see above). Bultmann, therefore, never remains simply the exegete of primitive Christianity and its texts; the phenomenologist of being and time; the theologian of the kerygma. Rather, he is all of these things, at different stages. But it is only as the thinker of the eschatological event that each of those other tasks finds its rightful place in the scheme of Bultmann's thought. Without the eschatological event, there is Non-Being rather than theology. In his recognition of this as the meaning of human being as being-towards-God, Bultmann reasserted the primary role of Christology with a degree of philosophical rigour and theological insight unparalleled in the story of twentieth-century theology.

Conclusion: The God Question Answered

It is of the essence of the paradox of the Christian faith that God incarnate walked the earth; that is, that Jesus Christ as Saviour lived and died here on earth. Jesus' eschatological and soteriological significance, however, cannot be deduced from that objective life and death. This is of course the scandal or stumbling-block of faith; that is, the temptation to justify it, to describe the relationship between God and the individual as somehow accessible to scientific methods of enquiry. Christianity, argues Bultmann, must rediscover itself ever anew in the language of the story of Jesus of Nazareth. This is the only answer that can be given to Pilate's question. And by now, the reader will realise that for Bultmann, Pilate's question is indeed the God question itself.

What all of this means for the God question, the question of positive theology proper, is indeed quite simple. It means that the use of specific theological terminology – that is, words and expressions such as existence, death, life, authenticity/inauthenticity, encounter, decision, and explicitly biblical terminology such as cross, resurrection, miracle, and Word – must at all points and at all times be informed by Bultmann's understanding of the eschatological event. Only in this way can the complexity of Bultmann's consideration of the human question as the precursor to the God question, and the God question itself, be justified and maintained. In short, everything that Bultmann ever said 'about' God must be judged by this rubric of the eschatological event.

Bultmann would have it no other way, for he admitted of no other way of actually doing theology.

It is the strength with which this knot is drawn tight that poses the problems which must now be confronted in Chapters 4 and 5. Given that the hermeneutic heritage in contemporary theology draws its inspiration from Bultmann: to what extent is it true to his understanding of the eschatological event? Moreover, if there can be only one way of understanding the eschatological event, and therefore only one genuine theology, to what extent is this theology itself genuinely critical of the myriad complexities of the social and political environments in which theologians must live and work? These are the questions to which we must now turn.

4

The Hermeneutic Heritage

In the following two chapters, this examination of Bultmann's thought will become more explicitly critical. Whereas Chapters 1–3 were overwhelmingly an exposition of the major themes of Bultmann's theology, and their philosophical foundations, Chapters 4 and 5 will attempt to build on this work by considering the areas in which Bultmann's thought has exerted the most influence. This will be achieved by looking at two specific questions. First, 'How successfully does hermeneutic theology realise the goals that it sets itself?' (Chapter 4.) Second, 'How may such a theology as Bultmann's, and any subsequent hermeneutic theology, address the socio-political challenges that face Christianity today?' (Chapter 5.) The first question, quite clearly, considers the internal consistency of Bultmann's thought and the way in which it has been developed by his advocates and followers. The second must consider its fundamentally philosophical credibility with respect to external pressures. Only then, in the conclusion to Chapter 5, will it be possible to arrive at a consideration of Bultmann's work in the light of contemporary theology.

In other words, Chapters 4 and 5 seek to lead the reader, via the explicit heritage that Bultmann left to modern theology, to a preliminary consideration of its promise for the contemporary situation. Granted that to a great extent Bultmann's theology has today all but lost its original vitality, yet there remains the possibility of learning from his approach to the fundamental question of theology as education – that is, *Glaubenslehre*. Hence, Chapter 5's move towards a critical theology.

Despite their provocative nature, however, these two questions do not represent an attempt to destroy Bultmann's legacy. On the contrary, and in the words of Paul Ricoeur: 'I am not formulating these questions against Bultmann but with the aim of thinking more adequately what remains unthought in Bultmann' (Ricoeur, 1980, p. 67). One might add: for better or for worse.

Chapter 4 considers the hermeneutic heritage to Bultmann's theology. Chapter 5 will then examine the work of T. W. Adorno and Dorothee Sölle, and its significance for the reception of Bultmann's thought. This will be followed by a preliminary conclusion, pointing towards the scope of Bultmann's thought in contemporary theology. Before the argument of the present chapter really begins, however, it might prove worth while reconsidering what has been discovered hitherto.

Reprise

At the very outset, Chapter 1 attempted to demonstrate that the single most important problem in Bultmann's theology is his handling of the question of the historical (*historische*) Jesus. Of course, it was recognised that Bultmann had no desire to look into the heart of Jesus, or to attempt to reconstruct Jesus' own understanding of his mission and message. Nor was Bultmann under any illusion concerning the possibility of identifying a so-called 'bedrock' of 'facts' to do with the life of Jesus. On the contrary, his historical-critical work as an exegete attempted to reveal the precise nature of the New Testament tradition, a very different matter. Nevertheless, and even in the negative, Bultmann addressed the question of the historical Jesus. Certainly, his entire Christology was an attempt to understand the proclamation of the kerygmatic Christ by the first Christian communities as the medium through which the individual would encounter – in the moment of decision – the risen Lord, the Revealer and Saviour, God's eschatological event of grace. But in so far as those communities told stories about the historical Jesus, and in so far as Christians today must still tell stories about that particular individual, Bultmann realised the importance of the question of the historical Jesus.

One finds in Bultmann's theology, therefore, a curious tension. On the one hand, his basic theological vocabulary – encounter, decision, event, authentic existence, radical obedience – is clearly defined by how he regards the fundamental situation in which the kerygma is uttered and heard; that is, the one-to-one relationship of minister with individual believer, and the pedagogic intent of such a situation. Here, it is not difficult to see the influence of the Lutheran tradition to which Bultmann belonged. This tradition, moreover, helped to shape Bultmann's impressions of the kerygmatic Christ, the story Jesus who lies at the heart of the Christian proclamation. While acknowledging that Bultmann has something of importance to say about the nature and style of Paul's mission to the Gentiles, in which great emphasis was indeed laid upon the proclamation of the Christ, one must also recognise the manner in which Bultmann's own theological presuppositions have delineated a specific interpretation of kerygma, which leaves out far more than it takes in.

One should recognise, therefore, Bultmann's genuine concern that the individual realise her relationship with God in Christ by addressing her historical predicament, and that this takes place via the encounter with the kerygma of Jesus Christ. On the other hand, however, Bultmann realised only too well that the matter could not rest there. For despite its ability to speak of both the individual's situation in the world and God's commitment to an act of salvation – that is, despite its genuinely theological nature – such an understanding of the relationship between God and the individual cannot be considered Christian, unless it includes the historical Jesus. Bultmann, consequently, was required to relate his own understanding of the relationship between God and the individual to the mission and message of Jesus of Nazareth. And he did this, in *Jesus* in 1926 and subsequently in sermons, articles, and books, by speaking of Jesus' purpose. The historical Jesus' purpose was to raise theological awareness to that level, upon which humanity could recognise the precise importance both of God's eschatological event, and its own eschatological existence. In this way, Bultmann was able to speak of the historical Jesus' role as the precursor of New Testament – and indeed all – theology proper.

It is essential, though, that Bultmann's motives at this point not be regarded too cynically. While it is surely fair to say, with the benefit of hindsight, that Bultmann's Christology was indeed guided by his Lutheranism, it must also be acknowledged that he identified a very important part of the historical Jesus' mission and message with a rigour hitherto lacking in post-Enlightenment Christology. That is, the historical Jesus certainly did call people to a personal encounter with God, and this proclamation certainly was the beginning of what soon came to be Paul's proclamation of the Christ figure itself. As Bultmann states: 'Jesus proclaimed the message; the Church proclaimed him' (Bultmann, 1956, p. 93). Bultmann's answer to the question of the historical Jesus, therefore – that is, to regard as significant solely that element within Jesus' mission and message which referred to the fate of the individual – has its foundation in a significant aspect of the New Testament tradition. But the question that remains is to what extent this interpretation's rejection of so much else of the tradition is justified. As will be seen, in many respects this question must be regarded as at the very heart of any hermeneutic theology.

Bultmann, therefore, was constantly wrestling with the question of the historical Jesus. If he thought he had found its answer, it was because of his conviction that the Pauline and Johannine theologies carried primacy within the New Testament canon, and that Paul and John had understood correctly the nature and extent of God's eschatological act of salvation in Jesus of Nazareth. This conviction was in turn sustained by his belief that Paul and John had understood correctly human existence as being-towards-God, either accepted or rejected. Here, Bultmann could always maintain – quite honestly, given his prior convictions – that Heidegger's phenomenological analysis of human existence did not say anything new to Christian theology, but rather simply elucidated the fundamental – and demythologised – structure of what was to be found in Paul, and especially John, concerning the human predicament.

Chapter 2, consequently, that which was referred to as the human question, was an attempt to demonstrate the way in which Bultmann's theological terminology was established by what the regard as ontological reflection. As Heidegger pointed out, however, theology's ontological reflection is always guided by faith, which for the Christian must at bottom be faith in Jesus of Nazareth. Thus, everything in Bultmann's interpretation of the human question ultimately falls back upon the question of the historical Jesus. If one regards that Jesus as God's Son and Christ, then one is obliged to regard all theology and ontological reflection as ultimately reflection upon the problem of Jesus of Nazareth. In this respect, thinking through Bultmann's theology and its philosophical foundations is rather like an infuriating ascent of a very tall building. No matter how high one climbs, as soon as one stops climbing and enters a seemingly level space, the floor caves in, and down one goes, crashing through floor after floor until finally reaching the basement, the question of the historical Jesus.

If all Bultmann's theology and ontological reflection is at bottom guided and defined by faith, however, what is its meaning? Why is there not simply an expression of a Lutheran Christian spirituality, rather than a phenomenological theology? It seems just to locate an answer to this question in the title that Bultmann gave to the volumes of his collected essays, *Glauben und Verstehen*, which expression can be translated, provocatively but fairly, as faith *seeking* understanding. If such a translation is justified, then one can continue and claim that, fundamentally, what Bultmann was doing throughout his entire career, and what he believed Paul and John also to be doing, was identifying how the individual believes, where 'belief' is recognised as a particular comportment of that individual's entire life, and not simply as a psychological condition. It is here that one sees, once again, the tradition of *Glaubenslehre* to which Bultmann's theology belonged.

The role of theology as Bultmann understood it, therefore, was not so much to elaborate a system in which all knowledge concerning the divine might be located, as to articulate God's will for the individual's eschatological existence, as expressed in the event of divine grace, Jesus Christ. This much – at least from the perspective of Bultmann's supporters – was sufficient to distinguish his work from Barth's massive *Church Dogmatics*, which, rightly or wrongly, was represented as precisely such a system. What one finds in Bultmann's theology, therefore, is a single pathway to the encounter with God. Theology does not teach the individual how to live, in other words. It teaches her how to encounter God's will.

If this is a fair reading of Bultmann's thought, then it places a very heavy onus both upon his own hermeneutics, and upon the hermeneutics of his followers and successors. For it means that the entire question of how the individual believes, if that is to be a genuinely Christian question, must devolve upon the shoulders of the historical Jesus. How does Jesus say the individual must believe, and how is that message subsequently proclaimed by the earliest Christian communities? In other words, theology and its ontological reflection become nothing more nor less than the interpretation of the historical Jesus' eschatological purpose and its complete realisation by the apostles. Faith, if it is to be genuinely evangelical, must be faith in this event or process. Here, neither the traditions of a church, nor indeed ecclesiology at all, are of any significance. What matters is solely the authentic interpretation of the Christological foundations of faith itself; for without that authentic interpretation, that understanding, there can in turn be no such thing as faith.

Chapter 3 elaborated this point at length, in its consideration of Bultmann's understanding of the Christ event as the revelation of the ontological difference, that is, God and humanity, as personal relationship. It was no coincidence, therefore, that Chapter 3 culminated in an exposition of Bultmann's essay 'New Testament and Mythology' (Bultmann, 1948). For the point of demythologising, when all of its different facets are taken together, is precisely to interpret the New Testament's answer to the question 'How does faith work?', regarded as the eschatological question *par excellence*. In the Bultmannian tradition, including the work of his pupils and followers, 'How does faith work?' is the question of hermeneutic theology itself.

Such hermeneutic theology, to reiterate, sets itself an extremely difficult agenda. For it must identify *die Sache selbst*, the meaning of faith as action and event. And it can only do this on the strength of its Christology. That is why this study began with a consideration of Bultmann's answer to the question of the historical Jesus, and why the present chapter, in considering the development of Bultmann's thought into that stream which in the 1950s and 1960s became known in theology as 'the New Hermeneutic', must return to this question. At stake is not simply the fate of Bultmann's own legacy, but also the wider issue of how Christian theology, as critical reflection upon faith, interprets the biblical tradition. This is no longer a matter of simply rediscovering 'what really happened'. No serious theologian today asks that question, nor can theology, still less faith, ever again be reduced to such an arbitrary level, except among fundamentalists. Rather, what is at stake is modern theology's own understanding of hermeneutics itself, and the potential of hermeneutics for any future theological expression of the meaning of faith.

1   Bultmann Replies to His Critics

To a great extent, everything that has been said so far can be summarised by one quotation from Bultmann's brief essay, 'Bultmann Replies to his Critics', published in the first volume of *Kerygma and Myth: A Theological Debate*, in which he argues:

> If the revelation of God becomes effective only on specific occasions in the 'now' of existence [*Dasein*] (as an eschatological event), and if ontological analysis points us to the temporality in which we have to exist, an aspect of existence is thereby exposed which faith, but only faith, understands as the relatedness of man to God. So far, however, from being undermined by a formal analysis of existence, this understanding is in fact illuminated by it, just as it illuminates the question about the meaning of existence and shows that it is really the question about God. (cf. Bartsch, 1964, pp. 195–6)

As the present chapter unfolds, Bultmann's idea of specific 'irruptions' of revelation into human existence, via the kerygma, will take on great importance, not least with respect to his relationship with Heidegger. Within the context of the debate about what came to be known as 'demythologising' (*Entmythologisierung*), however, this quotation is also significant. It is quite clear that Bultmann is willing to compromise neither his own vocabulary, nor his vision of God's revelation in Christ. For we recognise here all of Bultmann's favourite terminology: the 'now' of existence; ontological analysis; the eschatological event; the idea of illumination (see below) – all regarded in the light of faith. Bultmann makes no concessions. He simply reiterates his own position, seemingly oblivious to the compelling arguments given by his critics in favour of clarification. Nor was this atypical. Throughout the 1950s and into the 1960s, when confronted by the findings and advances made by the New Hermeneutic and the New Quest for the historical Jesus, Bultmann remained steadfast.

There are, I think, two possible reasons for this apparent stubbornness. First, Bultmann, as many – including Ricoeur (see below) – would argue, found it impossible to follow through demythologising to its apparently logical conclusion; that is, the 'death' of 'God' as an influence upon human existence. Second, Bultmann's rejection of the New Hemeneutic and the New Quest can be regarded not as a refusal to progress, but as a refusal to abandon the high ground that he had seized with his return to ontological reflection and hermeneutic theory. The first argument rests largely upon the belief – as expressed, for example, by James Robinson – that Bultmann failed to appreciate the significance of the so-called 'later' Heidegger (cf. Robinson, 1963). The second argument, paradoxically (and appropriately), rests upon the conviction that it is only Bultmann who has correctly understood the significance of Heidegger's work on the ontological difference as the foundation of his later writings. Behind the entire question of hermeneutics, therefore, lies the *a priori* question of historical phenomenology. This is the first important point that should be noted. If correct, it means that hermeneutic theology since 1954 has largely been riding a ghost train.

Much of this is not apparent in Bultmann's defence of demythologising, however. It only emerges later on, when his younger pupils – Ebeling and Fuchs in particular – attempt to think beyond their teacher's somewhat entrenched position. Here, Bultmann reiterates again and again his basic argument; that is, that demythologising is necessary to bring to light once more the authentic meaning of eschatology. Thus, Bultmann writes:

> Further, my critics have objected that my demythologising of the New Testament results in the elimination of its eschatology. On the contrary, I am convinced that my interpretation exposes its meaning as never before [!], at least for those who have given up thinking in terms of mythology. (cf. Bartsch, 1964, p. 205)

In so saying, Bultmann believes that he is being true to the Christian faith in Jesus Christ. Hence, when Bultmann writes, that: 'Faith means to exist eschatologically' (Bartsch, 1964, p. 208), he clearly implies that demythologising is a necessary element within faithful existence. It is, in other words, that faith which seeks understanding, not only of the Christian proclamation, but also of contemporary existence. Demythologising, therefore, as a hermeneutic method, is circular. It interprets eschatology both as the purpose of the New Testament narratives, and as the meaning of all human existence. This is the second important point that must be noted.

Bultmann does not simply assert this dogmatically, however. On the contrary, he believes it to be a necessary consequence of the contingency of the manner in which individuals live. In this way, all existence, as in some sense a continuing act of interpretation, is determined by the circumstances in which the interpreter lives. So Bultmann writes that: 'In the first place, it is important to remember that every interpretation is realised by the framing of specific questions, and without this there could be no interpretation at all' (cf. Bartsch, 1964, p. 191). In so far as that act of interpretation is directed towards the kerygma of Jesus Christ in the New Testament and the proclamations of contemporary ministers, moreover, any exegesis of that story cannot be without presuppositions. In his essay, 'Is exegesis without presuppositions possible?', Bultmann writes, therefore, that:

> No exegesis is without presuppositions. The exegete is not a *tabula rasa*, but rather approaches the text with specific questions or with a specific way of raising questions. He or she, in other words, has a particular impression of the subject matter with which the text is concerned. (Bultmann, 1960, p. 142)

A little later in the same article, Bultmann elaborates on this further, stating that: 'A specific understanding of the subject (of a text) is always presupposed by exegesis on the basis of a life-relation to it' (Bultmann, 1960, p. 147). When the subject of the text – be it canonical or exclamatory – is the eschatological purpose of Jesus Christ, then the individual's 'life-relation' to that text is ontologically decisive. Bultmann concludes, therefore, that:

> The purpose of demythologising is not to make religion more acceptable to modern man by trimming the traditonal Biblical

texts, but to make clearer to modern man what the Christian faith is.... The real problem, in other words, is the hermeneutic one; i.e., the problem of interpreting the Bible and the teachings of the Church in such a way that they become understandable as a summons to man.... (For) what matters is that the incarnation should not be conceived of as a miracle that happened about 1950 years ago, but as an eschatological event which, beginning with Jesus, is always present in the words of men proclaiming it to be a human experience. (Bultmann, 1962, pp. 182–3, 184, 193)

'Beginning with Jesus...': once again, hermeneutics is returned to the question of the historical Jesus. In this way, it can be seen that Bultmann's entire consideration of the theme of hermeneutics, guided as it is by his phenomenological, ontological reflection, is at the service of his understanding of faith as faith in Jesus of Nazareth, God's Christ.

Bultmann's thoughts about hermeneutics themselves, though, did not occur in a vacuum. On the contrary, and despite their specific subordination to the expression of his Christology, they take their place in an important history of hermeneutics within Protestant thought, from Schleiermacher to Bultmann himself and beyond. Bultmann's examination of this tradition – and his own theoretical essay into hermeneutics – was his 'The Problem of Hermeneutics' (Bultmann, 1965a).

2   The Problem of Hermeneutics

In itself, however, this essay is something of an anti-climax. Far from presenting any radically new insights, Bultmann concentrates upon elucidating the general history of hermeneutics. Thus, although he begins by referring to the work of Dilthey, Bultmann quickly settles down to the task of naming names within the tradition. He examines briefly Aristotle's formal analysis of the structure and style of literature, before turning to the post-Enlightenment period, in which, he argues, all texts were shown to be historically conditioned. Bultmann comments upon Schleiermacher's linking of psychological considerations with the more grammatical (p. 214), before returning to Dilthey. Here, his brief historical survey serves to cast Dilthey's own developments into sharp relief. In this respect, the key point to which Bultmann seems to be building takes place when he quotes Dilthey, that: 'Interpretation is a work of personal art, its consummate execution being conditioned by the geniality of the interpreter. It is based, therefore, upon affinity (*Verwandtschaft*), intensified via communion with the author and by constant study' (cf. Bultmann, 1965a, p. 215). To Bultmann, this idea still seems too tainted by Schleiermacher's lingering psychologism. He therefore formalises the argument in logical terms, in the process introducing the concept of 'preunderstanding', *Vorverständnis*. If anything, it is the introduction and development of this idea into post-war theology that constituted Bultmann's most significant contribution to modern hermeneutics.

The idea of *Vorverständnis* has already been identified above, in both Chapters 1 and 3. Here Bultmann gives his most succinct definition of the expression: 'The presupposition for understanding (*Vorverständnis*) is the interpreter's existential relationship to the subject which comes to expression – directly or indirectly – via the text' (Bultmann, 1965a, p. 217). By concentrating upon the notion of an 'existential' relationship, rather than Dilthey's idea of affinity or *Verwandtschaft*, Bultmann clearly distinguishes his own understanding of the partiality of hermeneutics from a more aesthetic critique. For Bultmann, interpretation is not so much 'a work of personal art', as an existential engagement that affects the individual's comportment (*Befindlichkeit*) in the world at large, Gadamer's historical aesthetics notwithstanding (cf. Gadamer, 1979). When this existential engagement is with the meaning or purpose of the gospel – and, in truth, this is the only kind of hermeneutics that Bultmann is really interested in – as the moment of encounter with the risen Lord, via the kerygmatic Christ, then the individual's comportment with which Bultmann is concerned is literally regarded as a matter of life and death.

The 'problem' of hermeneutics, therefore, is its partiality. It can never be the value-free practice that many would like to see. But Bultmann does not regard this problem negatively. On the contrary, the problem of hermeneutics, this whole question of preunderstanding, is transformed by him into the effective moment of ontological reflection which is constitutive of faith. Here, faith is not regarded as a psychological acceptance of certain propositions. Faith, rather, is an active decision, an expression of the individual's will towards God, and it is an action that is made – in part at least – on the basis of an intelligent reflection upon the meaning and extent of human existence. This intelligent reflection can be conscious or subconscious, but for Bultmann it must take place.

One can but admire the confidence with which Bultmann asserts this. As with Rahner's understanding of the 'anonymous' Christian, it is emphatically an argument from silence. And yet it addresses a point of fundamental importance for the Christian religion. If Christian faith cannot be such an intelligent reflection, argues Bultmann, then theology has no task whatsoever. Without the requirement of teaching the individual to come to the encounter with God, as Creator, it is reduced to the empty repetition of dogma. It is worth pausing to consider how many of today's theologians can say as much of their work (see below).

Once this point has been clearly made, however, Bultmann's article rather trails off. There are cursory references to the Dilthey/ Yorck correspondence, to Martin Heidegger, and criticism of the so-called Historical School, although here, as elsewhere, many of Bultmann's themes seem to be drawn from Dilthey's own study, *Die Entstehung der Hermeneutik* (Dilthey, 1900). Finally, an odd section at the very end of the piece attacks Karl Barth for his failure to appreciate the significance of hermeneutics in general, and Heidegger's hermeneutic phenomenology in particular. It is an oddly unsatisfactory ending. One misses Bultmann's customary clarity.

There is enough in this article, however, to make it of interest to a philosopher of the calibre of Paul Ricoeur. In his essay, 'Preface to Bultmann' – undoubtedly the finest essay-length introduction to Bultmann's hermeneutics in any language – Ricoeur offers an analysis of Bultmann's position which identifies that one single point which is of the greatest significance for the remainder of the present chapter; that is, the problem of semantics, of the metaphorical description of what came to expression – from the standpoint of faith – in Jesus of Nazareth, prior to the existential encounter (Ricoeur, 1980). That is, Ricoeur recognises the importance of, and holds up for inspection, the question of what one actually says about the historical Jesus in the kerygma, and how that is related to the traditions about that figure which are recorded in the New Testament.

To begin with, Ricoeur reiterates Bultmann's own basic position. He writes: 'If hermeneutics in general is, in Dilthey's phrase, the interpretation of expressions of life fixed in written texts, then Christian hermeneutics deals with the unique relation between the Scriptures and what they refer to as the "kerygma" (the proclamation)' (Ricoeur, 1980, p. 49). This in itself is clearer in many respects than Bultmann's own expressions on this theme. But Ricoeur continues, arguing that:

> The interpretation of the Book and the interpretation of life correspond and are mutually adjusted. St. Paul creates this second modality of Christian hermeneutics when he invites the hearer of the word to decipher the movement of his own existence in the light of the Passion and Resurrection of Christ. (Ricoeur, 1980, p. 52)

This is the biblical basic for Bultmann's entire position, which Ricoeur encapsulates – brilliantly – in the following definition: 'Hermeneutics is the very deciphering of life in the mirror of the text' (Ricoeur, 1980, p. 53). For Bultmann, that is, hermeneutics as existential engagement is the very deciphering of life in the mirror of the kerygma, which itself proclaims God's action on behalf of humanity in Jesus Christ.

Ricoeur's sympathetic and sensitive exposition of Bultmann's main theme, however, gives way in this essay to one fundamental criticism; that is, the very question of semantics and metaphor, as previously cited. For Ricoeur, Bultmann's definition of a Christian understanding of hermeneutics seems entirely justified, and his programme of demythologising seems a sophisticated attempt at its expression (cf. p. 59). There is one problem, though. As Ricoeur rightly points out, it is simply not enough for Bultmann to say that faith, ultimately, can be reduced (in a non-pejorative sense) to the notion of existential encounter. 'Encounter with what?', asks Ricoeur. He recognises Bultmann's answer; that is, encounter with Jesus Christ as story – the kerygmatic Christ – and ultimately as mystery – the risen Lord. But he still maintains that Bultmann's essentially reductive Christology pays too little attention to what Ricoeur refers to as the 'ideality of meaning'; that is, that very content of the kerygma that is proclaimed. In a signal passage, Ricoeur argues, that:

> The entire route of comprehension goes from the ideality of meaning to existential signification. A theory of interpretation which at the outset runs straight to the moment of decision moves too fast. It leaps over the moment of meaning, which is the objective stage, in the non-wordly sense of 'objective'. (Ricoeur, 1980, p. 68).

In other words, what are the stories that we tell about Jesus? And is it really enough to speak solely of Jesus' purpose, as if that purpose were something that could somehow be lifted out of the New Testament, whole, rather as one would fillet a fish? Ricoeur's answer is categorical: no.

Ricoeur adds one more passage of importance before leaving this subject. He writes:

> It is the objectivity of the text, understood as content – bearer of meaning and demand for meaning – that begins the existential movement of appropriation. Without such a conception of meaning, of its objectivity and even of its ideality, no textual criticism is possible. Therefore, the semantic moment, the moment of objective meaning, must precede the existential moment, the moment of personal decision, in a hermeneutics concerned with doing justice to both the objectivity of meaning and the historicity of personal decision. (Ricoeur, 1980, p. 68)

In terms of Bultmann's Christology, we might express this argument in slightly different terms. Bultmann's kerygmatic Christ – his 'story' Jesus – is too pale a character. The individual can obtain no purchase on such an abstracted figure, and so the moment of decision becomes a leap in the dark in a sense very different from, and more negative than, Kierkegaard's. It becomes a leap into ignorance. Or, again to change the argument slightly: one might say that Bultmann pays too little attention to his metaphorical or semantic representation of the story Jesus, because of his conviction that there can be only one way of understanding that metaphorical representation; that is, the eschatological, granted Bultmann's understanding of eschatology. Indeed, Bultmann would even argue that this is not simply one way of understanding that metaphorical representation. It is, on the contrary, the genuine understanding of the human predicament.

That, however, is precisely the problem. Is there only one way of understanding the purpose, content, or meaning of Jesus' mission and message? Or can more be learned of that message by paying greater attention to the metaphorical representation of the historical Jesus? It is at this point that both the New Quest and the New Hermeneutic become significant.

3   The New Quest and the New Hermeneutic

In German (and later, American) theology, both the New Quest (cf. Robinson, 1983) and the New Hermeneutic (cf. Robinson, 1963) originated in Rudolf Bultmann's important essay, 'New Testament and Mythology', (Bultmann, 1948). Although I have already considered this text in depth (cf. Chapter 3), it is worth while adding a few words to consider precisely how these two major developments – 'Quest' and 'Hermeneutic' – evolved out of Bultmann's own work.

Unsurprisingly, reaction to Bultmann's 1941 essay, while initially quite rigorous, died down as the Second World War developed. It is also important to remember that 1941 saw the publication of Bultmann's great *Commentary on John* (Bultmann, 1941), his legacy and manifesto, and a far greater piece than the smaller though pro-grammatic essay. Many people in Germany, regarding Bultmann as primarily a New Testament scholar and realising that the 'New Testament and Mythology' (Bultmann, 1948) piece was in many respects simply the working-out of long-held interpretative prin-ciples, quite rightly hailed the John commentary as Bultmann's greatest work.

After the end of the war, things gradually changed. But the destruction of old Germany, not simply the material damage but also the effective abolition of the old 'mandarin' structure of the German university system (cf. Ringer, 1969) in the creation of the

Federal Republic, hindered the rapid flow of ideas and individuals. One might almost say that the most significant events of these formative years, 1945–50, were the return of Karl Barth to Bonn and his symbolic rediscovery of the bust of Schleiermacher in the town's rubble.[6] Elsewhere in the new Germany, individuals such as Kittel, Althaus, and Hirsch were undergoing varying degrees of duress and de-Nazification at the hands of French and American officials (cf. Ericksen, 1985). In Berlin, people began to remember Dietrich Bonhoeffer. And in the Black Forest, Martin Heidegger sat, prevented from teaching.

In Marburg, by contrast, Bultmann continued his deep and searching analysis of the New Testament texts. In this, his seemingly massive sense of imperturbability in the face of the Second World War – and here one must not forget his statements concerning the First World War (cf. Chapter 1) – one recognises a very disturbing theme in Bultmann's work, which will be considered in depth in Chapter 5; that is, his apparent inability to react in response to social and political events, in public at least, if not in his private life. Here, however, one may be permitted to regard his calm as a positive boon. For it meant that his work on the question of the historical Jesus, from whichever direction he came to it, continued. It was this that provided the impetus to his pupils and younger opponents in the years 1950–65.

A brief survey of the major texts of both the New Quest and the New Hermeneutic, while acknowledging James Robinson's great achievement in making material available to the English reader, must begin with 'a theological debate'; that is, the six volumes of *Kerygma und Mythos*, edited by H. W. Bartsch (1951–6). From the many and varied essays contained within these texts – certain of Bultmann's own contributions were considered above – developed a wave of books and articles, many indicative of the novel developments taking place within German and subsequently American theology. Gunter Bornkamm's *Jesus of Nazareth*, for example (1956), would have been unthinkable in the 1920s or 1930s, such is its 'reconstruction' or 'retrieval' of the historical Jesus. So also Geiselmann's *Jesus der Christus* (1965), at the tale-end of this period. Martin Kähler's famous text, already mentioned, was reprinted twice in 1953 and 1956, indicative of the nature of the contemporary debate. In Austria, K. Schubert edited a collection entitled *Der historische Jesus und der Christus unseres Glaubens* (1962). In the United States, Walker (1969), Perrin (1967), Trotter (1968), Robinson (1963; 1983), all developed ideas and themes first originating in direct debate with the thought and work of Rudolf Bultmann. It is a fitting testimony to his prodigious endeavour.

Pre-eminent among these names must be those of Käsemann, Fuchs, and Ebeling, not, however, because they were the finest of Bultmann's successors, but because they are representative of certain trends that must now be considered in terms of the heritage Bultmann left to hermeneutics.

(a)   Ernst Käsemann

Ernst Käsemann was not, of course, a biblical interpreter in the sense in which one thinks of Bultmann's relationship with hermeneutics. He was, however, arguably Bultmann's finest pupil as a New Testament exegete. It is in this respect that his 1954 lecture, on 'The Problem of the Historical Jesus' (cf. Käsemann, 1964), delivered in the presence of Bultmann himself, becomes significant.

Käsemann – though he begins by stating his belief that all of Bultmann's work is more or less a footnote to Kähler's – certainly has his own specific agenda. One recognises this immediately, when he writes:

We are all without exception concerned at present with the question of a proper understanding of history and historicity which is bound to find concrete, necessary, and, indeed, archetypal expression for the theologian in the problem of the historical Jesus and of his significance for faith. (Käsemann, 1964, p. 16)

So saying, Käsemann reopens a debate that Bultmann himself had surely considered closed. This, of course, does not mean that Käsemann hurtles headlong towards historical excavation and indeed construction of the 'quarry' of the historical Jesus. He too can write that:

To state the paradox as sharply as possible: the community takes so much trouble to maintain historical continuity with him who once trod this earth that it allows the historical events of this earthly life to pass for the most part into oblivion and replaces them by its own message. . . . Mere history only takes on genuine historical significance insofar as it can address both a question and an answer to our contemporary situation; in other words, by finding interpreters who hear and utter this question and answer. (Käsemann, 1964, pp. 20–1)

This, after all, is good Bultmannian (not to mention, Lutheran) theology. And yet, Käsemann is saying and asking more. He is, undoubtedly, asking German theology in the 1950s to *state* more concerning the historical Jesus, and more concerning the authentic nature of that proclamation that lies at the heart of kerygmatic theology. Käsemann can say this, because he believes that the question of the historical Jesus lies at the heart of all kerygmatic theology. In this, he agrees with Bultmann. Thus, he concludes that: 'The question of the historical Jesus is, in its legitimate form, the question of the continuity of the Gospel within the discontinuity of the times and within the variation of the kerygma' (Käsemann, 1964, p. 46).

Käsemann's conclusion raises four very important themes: the identification of the legitimate form of the question of the historical Jesus; the continuity of the gospel; the discontinuity of the times; and the variation of the kerygma. Of these, the latter three are all central to the New Hermeneutic. Käsemann himself simply sketches some preliminary images of the first question. These, however prove to be very significant, and link up with Ricoeur's comments in his 'Preface to Bultmann'. Taken together, Käsemann and Ricoeur point the way forward to both Fuchs and Ebeling, and the contemporary development of hermeneutics in the work of David Tracy.

It will be recalled how Ricoeur called for a reconsideration of that which Bultmann had passed too quickly by. He writes:

The entire route of comprehension goes from the ideality of meaning to existential signification. A theory of interpretation which at the outset runs straight to the moment of decision moves too fast. It leaps over the moment of meaning, which is the objective stage, in the nonwordly sense of 'objective'. . . . It is the objectivity of the text, understood as content – bearer of meaning and demand for meaning – that begins the existential movement of appropriation. Without such a conception of meaning, of its objectivity and even of its ideality, no textual criticism is possible. Therefore, the semantic moment, the moment of objective meaning, must precede the existential moment, the moment of personal decision, in a hermeneutics concerned with doing justice to both the objectivity of meaning and the historicity of personal decision. (Ricoeur, 1980, p. 68)

It is important here to understand what Ricoeur is *not* saying. He is not saying that there is simply one meaning within a text, synonymous – say in the case of the Synoptics – with 'what really happened', and which in some sense can be 'lifted out' of that text, if only one knows the sole, correct and effective hermeneutic method. That would be nonsense, and Ricoeur is too subtle a thinker to fall into that tiger-trap. No, Ricoeur of course acknowledges the necessity of there being more than one 'meaningful' interpretation of a text. But he does so in a very special way. By asserting both the sole semantic meaning of the text – its 'ideality' – and the validity of more than one interpretation, Ricoeur maintains both the integrity of the interpreter – she who must engage with the text in decision – and the integrity of the text's intentionality, understood phenomenologically. This has one important advantage, and one important disadvantage, which, paradoxically, are intimately related.

The advantage is quite straightforward. Adopting Ricoeur's hermeneutic strategy, one can insist upon both a plurality of interpretation, and simultaneously the possibility of identifying a 'wrong' interpretation. For there can be wrong interpretations, interpretations that clearly contradict the 'ideal' sense of a text under discussion. Such a contradiction need not be logical. Indeed, the 'nonsensical' character of an illogical interpretation masks the far more sinister aspects of 'wrong' historical and therefore genuinely hermeneutic interpretation. A simple example will suffice. It is illogical, and therefore nonsensical, to assert that all cats are black. We can ascertain from empirical research that this is not the case. The interpretation that the trial of Jesus, however, as described in the Gospel of Matthew, justifies the punishment and persecution of Jewish peoples, is quite simply wrong. It is wrong in terms of the integrity of the 'ideal' meaning of the text. But it is also wrong, far more importantly, because of its historical (and historic) consequences when individuals and communities identify with it, instigating pogroms and worse. This aspect of hermeneutics is well handled by Ricoeur, and will be returned to below.

Its disadvantage, however, is equally clear. Those without Ricoeur's interpretative subtlety, quite simply, will identify the 'ideal' meaning with the objective truth; that is, 'what really happened'. One sees this development in contemporary biblical exegesis. Under the mistaken assumption that they are conducting empirical research and are therefore being 'scientific', certain scholars attempt to describe the events of Jesus' life on earth, as if they themselves were a part of the story they unfold. This exegesis, it is true, can be conducted with honour. But there are far too many individuals today who cannot see the spectacles perched on the end of their nose, so convinced are they of their perfect eyesight. Biblical exegetes read texts, not the news. And yet it is astonishing how readily this is forgotten.

Turning to Käsemann, it would be wrong to suggest that he has fallen completely into the tiger-trap that Ricoeur has so carefully marked out in the long grass. He does not rush headlong into the business of describing 'what really happened', but, on the contrary, solely makes one or two discreet suggestions. Käsemann asserts, therefore, that the New Testament's texts record the conviction that Jesus understood his mission and message eschatologically (there is no reflection, however, upon this term 'eschatology'). Here, the title 'Messiah' is clearly the correct one with which to anoint the historical Jesus. It is also why theologians today, as well as the first Christians, should be concerned with the question of the historical Jesus, because 'Messiahship' carries soteriological significance.

Käsemann goes further, however. He states, categorically, that: '(But) what is certain is that Jesus regarded himself as inspired' (Käsemann, 1964, p. 41). Here, Käsemann goes beyond the boundaries of the 'ideality' of the text. He makes the mistake of which Ricoeur warns, and has consequently fallen into the tiger-trap. What Käsemann says may well be correct. It is certainly a meaningful interpretation of many biblical passages (e.g. Matt. 12.28), where Jesus appears to receive responsibility from the Holy Spirit. It is, however, hermeneutically 'wrong' to make this assertion as baldly as does Käsemann. Here, surely, Bultmann was correct: how things looked in Jesus' heart we do not know, cannot know, and should not wish to know.

There is, therefore, a very distinct tightrope that the biblical interpreter must walk. Bultmann walks the rope confidently, but he hurries across to the other side far too quickly. Something, consequently, is lost. Käsemann starts out well, but half-way across falls into the abyss. Many contemporary biblical exegetes follow him, lemming-like. And yet Ricoeur has demonstrated the technique with style and panache. Who, then, will follow? With this question, it is time to turn to Fuchs and Ebeling.

(b)   Fuchs and Ebeling

At the very least, the commentator should not be too confused as to whether or not Fuchs and Ebeling *wish* to walk the tightrope; they positively rush to its ladder. Throughout the 1950s and into the 1960s, both men published a stream of articles concerned with the question of the historical Jesus. With Bultmann, without Bultmann, against him and for him, both Fuchs and Ebeling developed their theologies of the Word by means of a detailed consideration of issues raised by the initial demythologising controversy. In every respect, therefore, they are representative – almost pre-eminently so – of both the New Quest and the New Hermeneutic.

It would be wrong, however, for any reader to conclude that the present study constitutes a blanket condemnation of the work of Fuchs, and especially of Ebeling; for this is not the case. On the contrary, here – and in Chapter 5 – I am concerned with the responsibility of contemporary theology to re-evaluate its past, both distant and immediate, and to assess the worthiness of various ways forward. The point of this attempt, with respect to Fuchs and Ebeling, is quite simple: whatever their abilities as philosophical theologians – and Ebeling's work is highly significant in the context of recent Protestant theology – they do represent, in their succession from Bultmann, a reduction of hermeneutic theology to the discussion of Jesus as Word, and the relationship of the individual to that linguistic event in terms of her existential predicament. Here, therefore, is not the place to evaluate the rigour and consistency of their language philosophy; but there can be no real doubt that Fuchs and Ebeling contributed significantly to the drift of hermeneutic theology away from social and political concerns. The point of the present section is to recognise and assess this fact.

Stylistically, Ebeling's work is more restrained than Fuch's. Whereas the latter tends to ride a wave of rhetoric sustained through numerous essays on Christology, the former pinpoints particular concepts and ideas for consideration (cf. Funk, 1966). Ebeling, therefore, proves a more illuminating starting-point than Fuchs. Here, of major significance for Ebeling's theology is his essay, 'The Question of the Historical Jesus and the Problem of Christology' (Ebeling, 1963).

Ebeling begins by claiming that: 'The question of the historical Jesus is manifestly grasped as a theological question only when we perceive that it is aimed at the problem of Christology' (Ebeling, 1963, p. 288). He concludes with the statement that: '. . . the task of Christology is in fact none other than to bring to expression what came to expression in Jesus himself' (Ebeling, 1963, p. 304). In between those programmatic remarks occur other, similar statements, all establishing Ebeling's basic conviction that: 'If it were to be shown that Christology had no basis in the historical Jesus but was a misinterpretation of Jesus, then that would put paid to Christology. . . . The 'historical Jesus' as good as means the true, the real Jesus' (Ebeling, 1963, pp. 289–98).

There is little here that any theologian would wish to argue with, so much so that at times it comes dangerously close to being simply platitudinous. Clearly, Ebeling is attempting to establish a line of continuity between the 'real', the 'true' Jesus, and the individual believer. But he does not do this by means of historical-critical methods of research. On the contrary, instead he uses those methods to discover the heart or essence of the mission and message of the historical Jesus. For Ebeling, this heart or essence is faith. So Ebeling can write, somewhat convolutedly, that:

The point of the Easter story is, that Jesus as the witness to faith became the ground of faith and that those who thus believe are witnesses to faith as witnesses to Jesus. . . . The faith of the days after Easter [including today] knows itself to be nothing else but the right understanding of the Jesus of the days before Easter. (Ebeling, 1963, pp. 301–2)

On the basis of a shared faith, therefore, the individual believer is able to approach the historical, the real, the true Jesus. Indeed, she must do so. For without this understanding of faith, Christology becomes unintelligible, and without Christology the Christian message becomes meaningless. Ebeling places the greatest possible stress, then, on his understanding of faith as the foundation of the relationship between the historical Jesus, the individual believer, and the so-called Christ of faith. He writes: 'The fact that Jesus and faith belong together forms the ground of the continuity between the historical Jesus and the so-called Christ of faith' (Ebeling, 1963, p. 303). In fact, one can say more than that on Ebeling's behalf. One can go as far as to say that Ebeling believes it is possible to do away with the distinction between the historical Jesus and the so-called Christ of faith, that is, the kerygmatic Christ. Instead, on the basis of a historical-critical analysis which uncovers the heart of Jesus' mission and message as faith itself, the individual believer is to be thrown directly into an immediate encounter with the historical Jesus.

Rather than speaking of eschatology, therefore, Ebeling concentrates upon faith. In so doing, he moves away from Bultmann's philosophically established understanding of the eschatological event of revelation, in favour of the attempted rediscovery of Jesus' original confession of faith, which is deemed to be a possibility for the contemporary believer. Again, it is worth noting that for this to be a viable theological alternative, it must be possible to possess absolute knowledge of that confession of faith. In fact, what we do possess are the secondary testaments of other believers to that confession.

Ebeling's, therefore, is very different from Bultmann's Christology. It is worth attempting to establish one or two of the major differences between them. First, Bultmann would never acknowledge this degree of dependence upon the 'heart' of Jesus' own faith or spirituality as the medium through which the individual herself comes to faith. Second, and correspondingly, Bultmann would not allow this degree of creative licence to historical-critical exegesis. The task of such exegesis, on the contrary, is overwhelmingly to identify what the gospel is *not*. These are Ebeling's own developments, and Bultmann cannot follow.

Third, however, is a new, philosophical development. Since it is necessary for Ebeling to insist upon the 'accessibility' of the historical Jesus, and since he regards 'proclamation' as the sole medium by which the gospel is communicated, Ebeling seeks to establish philosophically a level upon which the two – 'Jesus' and 'proclamation' – may meet. This level is language. There are certainly clear signs here of an attempt to develop from the so-called 'later' Heidegger, but essentially Ebeling is simply striving towards consistency. Instead of the perceived 'difficulty' of having to distinguish between the historical Jesus and the kerygmatic Christ, therefore, now one simply speaks of language as the sole basis of encounter between God and the individual in Jesus. This, according to Ebeling, is the only way forward for contemporary theology. He claims that: 'The only thing that can lead us out of the historical difficulty is the view of history which takes its bearings on the word-event (*Wortgeschehen*) and consequently on the linguisticality of reality' (Ebeling, 1963, p. 295).

Certainly, with an expression such as the 'linguisticality' of reality, Ebeling is striving after something perceived in the 'later' Heidegger, and this will have to be considered shortly. But at this stage it is necessary to realise precisely what Ebeling thinks he has achieved. It is, in effect, the (non-pejorative) reduction of the question of the historical Jesus, and thus the question of Christology itself, to the level of language. Henceforth, Ebeling's task will be to elucidate his understanding of *Wortgeschehen* or word-event. In this, we can recognise something that many commentators accuse Bultmann of, but that in fact is not the case; that is, the (pejorative!) reduction of the Christian message to the level of a philosophy. Ebeling is grasping at something important, namely, the nature and role of communication within theology. But in the process, Christian believers are in danger of losing sight of not only the historical Jesus – who is now regarded solely as an (admittedly divine) utterance – but also of the risen Lord, who as Spirit is present in the midst of the world. Bultmann's Christology, by looking away from God in order to recognise, through the medium of the kerygma, the Holy Spirit of the risen Lord in the story of the individual's existence, certainly 'diminishes' the glory of the historical Jesus. This, however, is solely because of Bultmann's concern with the glory of the Lord. Ebeling, by contrast, in seeking to raise up the historical Jesus like the witch of Endor raising up Samuel's wraith, distracts the believer's attention away from her predicament *coram deo*. Certainly, one might agree with Ebeling that 'reality' is 'linguistic'. But what does this mean? And, most importantly, is it a viable, theological analogue? These are questions that are not raised in the 1960s, but that are of central significance for the problems of hermeneutics and of what hermeneutic theology intends to interpret.

In short – and here Ebeling, like others, seems to misunderstand Heidegger – language is primary in neither Bultmann nor Heidegger: on the contrary, it is time that is primary, and therefore the fundamental problem confronting both Bultmann and Heidegger is the relationship between time and eternity, as Chapter 3 demonstrated. This is why eschatology is understood phenomenologically. It is all very well to wish to understand reality linguistically; no one would doubt the sophistication and honour of Ebeling's efforts in this direction. But one is misguided if one regards this as a development of the work of Bultmann and Heidegger: it is not. The fundamental question facing hermeneutics in the twentieth century is how it understands time and eternity, how eternity somehow becomes 'new' in time; Heidegger is not, in other words, an ordinary language philosopher. The question facing any critical theology, therefore, is to what extent the hermeneutic approach to this problem can still be viable today. This is the subject of Chapter 5, and ultimately the aim of this entire study.

The problems one experiences with Ebeling's theology and Christology are dramatically increased when one turns to consider the work of Ernst Fuchs. Here, a cruder philosophical reflection, allied to a less sophisticated Christology, combine to create a most problematic understanding of that 'word-event' which now becomes with Fuchs *Sprachereignis*, or 'language-event'. With Fuchs, one now enters the world of 'speaking' texts and certain knowledge concerning the heart and mind of the historical Jesus.

Fuchs begins in a very similar vein to Ebeling. He states that: 'We must say that just as Jesus was the representative of faith, so faith became the representative of Jesus' (Fuchs, 1964, p. 28). Moreover, 'The so-called Christ of faith is none other than the historical Jesus' (Fuchs, 1964, p. 31). And so, 'It is evident that the quest of the historical Jesus leads to theology rather than diverting from it. The dogmatic continuation of exegetical analysis would have to be a doctrine of the word of God which keeps its sights firmly trained on the historical Jesus' (Fuchs, 1964, p. 31). As with Ebeling, therefore, Fuchs moves towards the formulation of a philosophy of the linguisticality of reality and a doctrine of the Word of God on the basis of faith in the historical Jesus.

One finds at this point in Fuchs's work something always lacking in Bultmann; that is, discussion of what Jesus really believed and thought. This point was made in respect of Ebeling's theology. But with Fuchs it becomes ever more pronounced, and ever more difficult to understand. Essays like 'Jesus and Faith', and 'The Theology of the New Testament and the Historical Jesus', glory in the reconstruction, or retrieval, of Jesus' intentions and convictions concerning faith, his own and that of successive believers (cf. Fuchs, 1964). One's unease with this is not simply due to Bultmannian inbreeding. As stated previously, this so-called historical-critical analysis is built on sandy ground. No one, surely, would now claim that Jesus' mission and message could be reduced to the question of 'faith' alone, as both Fuchs (1964, p. 30) and Ebeling (1963, p. 296) assert. It is simply too Lutheran an understanding to be sustained as critical exegesis. And yet this is the basis of their theological endeavour. The language-event itself in Fuchs, despite his attempts to anchor it in a kind of 'Heideggerian' universality, in which 'language' and 'event' are raised to pristine ontological status, is clearly limited to a very specific understanding of what it is for the minister to articulate the word of the Lord.

With his understanding of the 'language-event', Fuchs moves further than ever away from Bultmann's position. Now, all reality is understood in terms of its 'linguisticality'; that is, language is reality, reality is linguistic. Like Ebeling, Fuchs conflates diversity into one fundamental statement:

> The concept of the situation, which is understood as the essence of the 'language-event', is able to reveal that Jesus' person belongs to the content of his proclamation. This makes it possible to answer the question of how Jesus' person belongs to his

proclamation and to the proclamation of faith in Jesus. Then it
will also be clear why the preaching of faith has a text. (Fuchs,
1964, p. 222)

With this, theology becomes reduced not to the level of interpretation, or hermeneutics, but to that of language-philosophy. In
attempting to develop away from Bultmann, that is, both Fuchs
and Ebeling have essentially betrayed the good intentions of both
the New Quest and the New Hermeneutic. They have moved, that
is, not towards a recognition of the plurality of the life-situation of
the individual, as the locus of time and eternity, but towards its uni-
formity. In so doing, they have dogmatised what in Bultmann –
and Luther before him? – was solely intended to bring the individual to her encounter with the Holy Spirit of the risen Lord. They
have, in other words, made a necessity out of what should be
simply a possibility, and in so doing Fuchs and Ebeling have lost
sight of the genuine prospects for theology of the hermeneutic tradition. In moving away from Bultmann, they have moved away
from the question of interpretation itself, as it must be concerned
with the relationship between time and eternity, and as it is so concerned in Bultmann and Heidegger.

No one would argue that the work of Fuchs and Ebeling was in
any sense illegitimate in its concern with language philosophy.
After all, there are many different ways of speaking about the
relationship between God and humanity. But in so far as it pur-
ported to be a development of Bultmann's own position, the work
of Fuchs and Ebeling disappointed. Rather than a way forward,
it proved to be a dead end. Certainly, it highlights several important aspects of the question of hermeneutic theology. But those
aspects are treated in a perfunctory manner. In the final analysis,
therefore, Fuchs and Ebeling do not constitute an improvement
upon Bultmann's own work.

4   Contemporary Hermeneutics

Fuchs and Ebeling, in other words, failed to see through the task
set (in theory) by Paul Ricoeur; that is, the task of understanding

and interpreting more fully the semantic moment which must of necessity precede the existential moment of encounter. On the contrary, they reduced the existential moment to the semantic moment. The kerygma, therefore, instead of pointing towards something of transcendental significance as it does in Bultmann's theology, became for Fuchs and Ebeling God's revelation itself. Ricoeur's charge, therefore, is still laid at theology's door.

In the years since the 1950s and 1960s, when Fuchs and Ebeling were at the centre of German theology, interest has waned in the question of hermeneutics, at least within theological circles. There has been little coherent, continuous research into questions of historical interpretation, either in West Germany or in the United States of America. In Britain, interest has devolved more or less towards the absorption of literary criticism as the way forward for the reading of texts, a form of interpretation notoriously adrift from genuine historical reflection. That in itself is not necessarily a bad thing. But it does highlight the comparative failure of hermeneutics to assert itself either within the philosophical or theological domain. The only figures who have persisted with questions of historical interpretation are peripheral, in the very best sense of that word: Jacques Derrida, Paul Ricoeur, and, above all, Jürgen Habermas.

Even in itself, this trend is surprising. The forward impetus within theology, West German and American, would have seemed to have been sufficient in the 1960s to maintain the trend towards building systematic theology upon biblical, and in particular New Testament, interpretation. Certainly, the work of figures like Bloch on eschatology, Adorno on aesthetics, Gadamer on hermeneutics itself, and Habermas on history and society, would have seemed to chime in accord with the developments being made by Käsemann, Fuchs, Ebeling, Robinson, and Funk in Bultmann's wake. And yet this was patently not the case. Fuchs and Ebeling disappeared from the scene, the latter returning to questions of Reformation history. Robinson and Funk also faded from sight (though Robinson remains an active theologian). Käsemann, becoming more and more revolutionary, failed to maintain his hitherto exciting understanding of the interrelatedness of exegesis and systematic theology. Across West Germany, Barth's successors, figures like Moltmann and Jüngel, and more anomalous individuals such as Wolfhart

Pannenberg, signalled the end of an era of so-called 'Bultmannian' theology. Hermeneutics itself became more and more the preserve of Roman Catholic figures. In the United States of America, one thinks of David Tracy and John D. Caputo in particular.

In response to this situation, the commentator is required to look at three areas, and this I will attempt to do. First, and most preliminary, one must consider why it was that Bultmann and his pupils were eclipsed in the late 1960s. Then, for the remainder of Chapter 4, I will attempt to demonstrate how Bultmann's own work was somehow abandoned by his pupils, and how, with a little endeavour, its potential can be renewed. After Chapter 5, which develops this theme to arise out of Chapter 4, this will lead towards Chapter 5's conclusion, a preliminary attempt to regard Bultmann's work in the context of contemporary theology. Only then, finally, will it be possible to consider, in this study's Conclusion, how Bultmann's theology might offer an alternative to the dominant theological styles in the contemporary world, those of political and liberation theologies.

(a)   Bultmann's Eclipse

At the very outset, one thing must be remembered: Bultmann was an heir of Liberal Protestantism, of Schleiermacher, Ritschl, and Herrmann. As was stated in Chapter 1, much of his basic theological vocabulary was taken over from this tradition, so much so that one might almost say that the only new 'words' Bultmann learned in his career were 'eschatology', from his New Testament scholarship, and 'phenomenology', from Heidegger. In itself, this may not mean so very much. Certainly, Bultmann belonged to a clearly identifiable theological tradition, but so did Barth, at least until 1919.

It is often said that Barth himself sounded the death-knell of Liberal Protestantism, with his *Commentary on Romans* (Barth, 1963). Yet if this is truly the case, then the death throes of Liberal Protestantism took a further forty years to subside. This, certainly, is an important aspect of the eclipse of Bultmann's work in the late 1960s, and here three quite discernible, though related, trends can be identified. First, the specific theological vocabulary of Bultmann's writings and those of his pupils – vocabulary concentrating upon the individual subject – was overwhelmingly rejected by a movement which, like Barth himself, sought to 'objectivise before I subjectivise' (cf. Jaspert and Bromiley, 1982, p. 106). As will be demonstrated in greater detail in the next section, for better or for worse Bultmann's concentration upon the individual subject, and his apparent rejection of epistemological reflection, became identified – explicitly so by Adorno, in his *Jargon of Authenticity* – with the bourgeois consumerism of post-war European society. (No matter what Adorno's own personal agenda, his critique remains valid for anyone seeking to develop Bultmann's thought – and Heidegger's – in the contemporary context.) In this respect, once again, as in 1919, we find the voice of Barth – and now the new Barthians – raised against the citadels of a complacent culture. Only this time, in the hands of individuals such as Moltmann and Jüngel, that 'Barthianism' is allied with the iron rigour of critical theory. Bultmann, rightly or wrongly – and once again, one must remember Bultmann's loyalty to the past of Herrmann and Harnack – was cast down. This is doubly ironic, if one bears in mind the burgeoning fame in these post-war years of Heidegger, Sartre, and Camus, and the vigorous assimilation during the 1960s of the likes of Hesse and Nietzsche. Bultmann, certainly, 'enjoyed' a period of fame at this time. But even in the hour of his pre-eminence (cf. Rahner's comment in the Introduction), Bultmann's position was being underined. One need think only of Jüngel's step backwards (*der Schritt zuruck*).

Second, and related to the above, in the light of the discoveries at Qumran, and the subsequent 'rediscovery' of apocalyptic and its qualification of our understanding of eschatology, Bultmann's own particular hermeneutic presuppositions seemed more and more outdated. Was the New Testament *really* 'about' the subjective encounter of the individual with the risen Lord as Holy Spirit? Was Sachkritik really the only viable methodology to adopt? Were the Synoptics genuinely as 'untrustworthy' with respect to the fundamental meaning of Christianity as Bultmann intimated, *Jesus* notwithstanding? With all of these questions, biblical exegesis since the late 1960s has arrived at different answers to those provide by Rudolf Bultmann and his followers, figures such as Fuchs and Ebeling. Here, as elsewhere, Bultmann has lost some of his credibility. He may well still be regarded as the greatest New Testament scholar of the twentieth century, but many of his findings and convictions are now regarded as incorrect. (cf. Sanders, 1985, see below).

It is difficult to know quite how to react to this situation, short of simply acknowledging the truth of the matter and moving on. Clearly, Bultmann's position *is* compromised by his overwhelmingly Lutheran reading of Paul and John. Yes, many of his specific analyses of concepts such as New Testament eschatology have been successfully challenged in the light of Qumran. New Testament studies do move on, and figures from the past, be they Strauss, Schweitzer, or Bultmann, cannot expect to be regarded as 'right' in perpetuity.

In Bultmann's case, however, this perfectly reasonable situation has one further, and very considerable, consequence. That is, Bultmann's theology is so closely associated and identified with his New Testament exegesis, self-evidently so, that question marks against his exegesis become, immediately and necessarily, question marks against his theology itself. Certainly, one might indeed say the same thing about Schweitzer or David Strauss. But that does not mitigate the circumstances that have surrounded the reception of Bultmann's thought since the late 1960s. These are now days in which the disciplines, such as New Testament studies and systematic theology, are as separated and arbitrarily distinguished as ever before. Witness the reception of Ebeling and Fuchs, and Boff and Segundo in the 1980s. Any retrieval of the potential of Bultmann's theology must wrestle with this unsettling situation, if hermeneutics is to be both critical of the socio-political context in which human beings find themselves, and of the New Testament, in which we read and hear of the salvation of the world in terms of the relationship of time to eternity.

Third, and perhaps most surprisingly and alarmingly, Bultmann became in the 1960s identified with the so-called 'death of God' theology, because of the manner in which his programme of demythologising had been perceived. There is little that one can say about this turn of events, other than notice that 'death of God' theology has itself died, and that Bultmann himself always repudiated, vehemently, any association of his own work with its position. One might safely say, here, that anyone who regards Bultmann's thought as supportive of the 'death of God', simply has not understood the man or his works.

The 'death of God' movement, however, was indicative of that lack of direction that left hermeneutic theology bereft of guidance in the 1960s, and – with one or two shining exceptions – bereft of leading figures. At this point, one might almost say that theology in the late 1960s was faced with three possible directions in which to move: towards Barth; forward with Bultmann; or forward away from Bultmann. (This is a necessarily crude and arbitrary distinction, but it serves a specific purpose at this stage of our discussion.) Moltmann and Jüngel moved towards Barth, as did Ott in Switzerland and Bromiley in the United States of America. Pannenberg, and 'death of God' theologians like Buri, John Robinson, and Althusser, moved away from Bultmann, though in antithetical directions (Pannenberg could never be regarded as a 'death of God' theologian). Fuchs and Ebeling, as has been observed, attempted to move forward with Bultmann. So did James Robinson and Funk in the United States of America. That attempt, however, failed. This conclusion cannot be avoided. What is now urgent is the task of working out why it failed – already partly achieved – and of working out how it might succeed. There *is* a way forward with Bultmann. It is, moreover, a way forward with Martin Heidegger, and with the best traditions of hermeneutic theology since it was first established by Schleiermacher. It requires, however, a radical reorientation of our presuppositions.

(b) Gadamer and Tracy

A way forward into this attempt is provided by a consideration of two thinkers who have done the most during the last twenty-five years to advance the cause of hermeneutics in general – Gadamer – and hermeneutic theology in particular – David Tracy. The former is, historically at least, by far the closer to Bultmann's own period. Gadamer was at one time a pupil of Bultmann's in Marburg, as he records in his *Philosophical Apprenticeships* (1985). David Tracy, by contrast, belongs very much to the present generation of leading theologians. Gadamer, therefore, can be considered first.

Bultmann's own work on the general theory of hermeneutics has been considered earlier in this chapter. It will be remembered that he spoke out clearly against the view that presuppositionless exegesis or interpretation is possible. On the contrary, Bultmann insisted that any interpretation that one undertook was unavoidably influenced by a preunderstanding (*Vorverständnis*), with which one came to the text in question. In the work of Fuchs and Ebeling, this idea, instead of being developed, was rather coarsened: preunderstanding slipped into (philosophically) the pre-eminence of language, and (theologically) into the overriding analogue of faith. In Gadamer's *Truth and Method*, by contrast, the notion of pre-understanding is developed quite decidely (cf. Gadamer, 1979). This development takes place in Gadamer's theory of the 'fusion of horizons', as the principal event within hermeneutical understanding.

Following on from the preceding chapters, it is not difficult to imagine the basic characteristics of this 'fusion of horizons'. As a hermeneutical thinker, a student of both Bultmann and Heidegger, Gadamer emphasises above all the historical character of knowledge and understanding. He is also at pains to characterise hermeneutic consciousness, this very understanding and knowledge, as openness to both the context within which the thinker or interpreter operates, and the influence of the text to be interpreted. Phenomenologically, this openness is tantamount to both that *intentionality* of objects which Brentano and Husserl spoke of, and that *Gelassenheit* or openness to the event of revelation which Heidegger made characteristic of his own later work. All of these expressions, however, combine into one fundamental insight: that is, that there is no single, absolute reality, that thought can dominate and reflect. On the contrary, our historical understanding of the world in which we exist is in a state of constant flux. Hermeneutics in general is the interpretation of that flux. Hermeneutics as the interpretation of specific texts, however, in so far as those texts have been written, and therefore at some point set down, necessarily involves reflection on the influence upon the present of the past. In this respect, the past, 'energising' or giving meaning to the present through interpretation, exerts a positive influence upon the interpreter, rather than simply vice versa. It is no surprise, therefore, to find that Gadamer can write, that:

In fact, the horizon of the present is being continually formed, in that we have continually to test all our prejudices. An important part of this testing is the encounter with the past and the under-standing of the tradition from which we come. Hence the horizon of the present cannot be formed without the past. There is no more an isolated horizon of the present than there are historical horizons. Understanding, rather is always the fusion of these horizons which we imagine to exist by themselves. (Gadamer, 1979, p. 273)

With this, Gadamer asserts that hermeneutical understanding as the interpretation of the fusion of horizons, past and present, is unavoidable.

It is certainly true that Bultmann's notion of preunderstanding can be incorporated into Gadamer's theory of the fusion of hori-zons. In fact, one might almost go as far as to say that Gada-mer's theory is a development of Bultmann's own notion, if not explicitly then certainly from our perspective as readers of their respective work. The model by which Bultmann understands this occurrence, however, is one of event and decision: the individual comes to the encounter, and her stance or perspective within that encounter is determined by her preunderstanding. Although as hermeneutic theory, therefore, Bultmann's notion employs the ter-minology of reading texts and the words they are made up of, this is simply an expedient way of approaching the issue with which he is really concerned; that is, the existential predicament of the indi-vidual *coram deo*. At no point in Bultmann's work do we find him simply settling at the level of language. Certainly, language is important, because – as kerygma – it is in fact the vehicle by which the individual is made aware of the possibility of encountering the risen Lord as Holy Spirit. But that encounter is never a linguistic event. There cannot be, for either Bultmann or Heidegger, simply a linguistic event, even though it be encountered via language. An event can occur within a linguistic text or context, certainly. Heidegger's interpretations of Trakl, Rilke, and Hölderlin demon-strate as much, in written form and in lecture. There, significance is secured by their exposure of a concealed meaning, and the event of revelation takes place within that exposure. But this is not by any means simply a linguistic occurrence. This is the mistake made by

Fuchs and Ebeling, with their attempt to reduce both Christology and thought to the solitary level of semantic expression.

Significantly, however, Gadamer himself consistently employs a linguistic analogy to bring to light his own understanding of the revelation of meaning. He speaks constantly of knowledge as the product of question and answer (cf. Gadamer, 1979, p. 326), and the Platonic dialogue seems to be his ideal expression of the nature or style of the process of coming to light of hermeneutic understanding. In a signal passage, Gadamer writes, that:

> the hermeneutic phenomenon also contains within itself the original meaning of conversation and the structure of question and answer. For an historical text to be made the object of interpretation means that it asks a question of the interpreter. Thus interpretation always involves a relation to the question that is asked of the interpreter. To understand a text means to understand this question. But this takes place, as we demonstrated, by our achieving the hermeneutical horizon. We now recognise this as the horizon of the question within which the sense of the text is determined. (Gadamer 1979, p. 333)

This is certainly different from both Bultmann and Heidegger. Although it is correct to say that Bultmann often speaks of a question mark, this is always understood eschatologically; that is, the question itself is never presented as an implicit part of the hermeneutic style, but rather as an analogy for the way in which one is challenged by God in the world. It is, in other words, a theological device. Bultmann never elevates it to the level that Gadamer does. On the contrary, Bultmann, like Heidegger, speaks of revelation, exposure, light, seeing: *the analogy is one of visualisation, rather than audition and vocalisation.* Certainly, Bultmann relates his understanding of existence via the medium of the kerygma or proclamation, which, as he explicitly acknowledges, he recognises as a speaking event. But that is not the same as saying that it is a language event in its meaning.

Here, then, is an important development. Gadamer, Fuchs, and Ebeling all pursue the analogy of the vocalisation of the event of revelation, and reduce this to the level of all reality. Bultmann does not. His own understanding, his own analogy, like Heidegger's, is visual. The event of revelation, therefore, is a light: the light of the world. As such, its perception is not simply a case of propositional recognition, but one of imagination. This is not to say that the subsequent reflection upon that perception does not take place in, by, and through language. It does. But that does not by any means imply that the analogy by which we understand the initial process of imagination must be linguistic as well; that is, one of question and answer, of a dialogue between horizons. On the contrary, given the insight that reality is fundamentally 'given' to the individual through language, there is a positive virtue in pursuing that 'given''s understanding by way of an analogy which creates reflective distance between the coming to light of understanding itself, and its subsequent articulation for the benefit of others.

David Tracy's work on the theological or religious classic, in his *The Analogical Imagination* (Tracy, 1981), can itself shed some light on this issue. The 'classic', it will be known, is defined by Tracy as that which can sustain a plurality of interpretations; that is, which can be regarded as nothing less than true, from nothing less than a multiplicity of perspectives. Tracy writes, therefore, that: 'My thesis is that what we mean in naming certain texts, events, images, rituals, symbols and persons 'classics' is that here we recognise nothing less than the disclosure of a reality we cannot but name true' (Tracy, 1981, p. 108). The process by which truth becomes apparent, Tracy names as the journey of intensification and distanciation (Tracy, 1981, p. 248), by which he means something very similar to, if not identical with, Gadamer's theory of the fusion of horizons. In Tracy, however, there is an added dimension; that is, that of imagination, the introduction of which serves Tracy's understanding of the relationship between Christian theology and cultural pluralism. In an important passage, Tracy writes that:

> Imagination is the correlative intensification power which produces in language the meaning which the work expresses. A classic text is produced only when imagination at work, in a work, impels, drives, frees the creator to express the meaning – both the sense and the referent – of the work in the work. (Tracy, 1981, p. 128)

What I want to do in Chapter 5, expressed simply, is to employ Tracy's notion of the role of imagination in hermeneutic understanding and interpretation at the cutting edge of an analogy of visualisation, perception and revelation when approaching the New Testament writings and the classic event that they disclose, the event of Jesus Christ. In this way, I hope to think through the potential that other followers of Bultmann have left unthought. In so doing, it will be possible not only to re-examine Bultmann's work as a New Testament exegete in the light of his more theoretical writings – one of the tasks set by Ricoeur – but also to advance the cause of that hermeneutic heritage that developed in the 1950s, before withering upon the vine in the late 1960s. This is, arguably, the primary, necessary step in returning the problematic of time and eternity to its explicit role in theological reflection. This is the task of critical theology.

5

The Critical Reception

The task of the present chapter is to think through the way in which contemporary theology might return the time–eternity problematic to a central role in reflection. In so doing, I have chosen to engage Bultmann's ideas with those of two of his strongest critics, T. W. Adorno and Dorothee Sölle. Some might feel that this is unjust. The point of the exercise, however, is simple. Rather than bringing down Bultmann's theology, I want to salvage from it what might be useful for contemporary thought. With this aim, there is no sense in avoiding the politicised critiques of Marxists like Adorno, or theologians like Sölle, simply because Bultmann was not a Marxist, or did not write politicised theology. That is the failure of responsibility – and there has been such a failure – which has characterised so much of the secondary reception, not only of Bultmann, but also of Heidegger. I repeat: if one wishes to work with and through Bultmann's thought, and if one feels that it has something to contribute to the contemporary debate, then one is obliged to expose it to the strongest possible criticisms. Hence, the need to engage with Adorno and Sölle.

With this firmly in mind, as the rationale of the present chapter, it is possible to proceed with a constructive argument.

1   Matthew 8.22: The Step Forward

In order to begin this process of constructive argument, Matthew 8.22, the somewhat notorious saying of Jesus to 'let the dead bury their dead', has been selected at this point for several reasons. First, Matthew 8.22 is certainly one of the 'hardest' of all of those sayings of Jesus of Nazareth that are regarded as genuine. If it can be demonstrated that a development of Bultmann's hermeneutic position can facilitate its interpretation – not 'solve' the saying, but highlight a manner in which it can be read meaningfully in a number of different ways – when it is so resistant to interpretation, then one might fairly say – after Tracy – that an advance via Bultmann has been made in the field of critical hermeneutics. Second, Bultmann himself says very little about Matthew 8.22. It is not one of his favourite biblical passages, which predominantly are drawn from the Fourth Gospel and certain of the Pauline Epistles. The selection of Matthew 8.22, consequently, cannot be regarded as in any sense favourable to Bultmann's position. Once again, it represents a highly suitable challenge to the interpreter following on from Bultmann's own work.

One stipulation, and one only, must be made at the outset. That is, any development of the potential of Bultmann's own hermeneutics must be true both to his work as a theologian, and as a New Testament scholar of the highest order.

In his *History of the Synoptic Tradition* (Bultmann, 1972), Bultmann mentions the saying in question, Matthew 8.22, on four occasions. On pages 77, 81, and 119 it receives only cursory consideration. Bultmann asserts that it is indeed an authentic saying of Jesus, one that can justly be regarded as prophetic (cf. p. 119). It also demonstrates the basic characteristics of the 'Old Testament and Jewish' *mashal* (cf. p. 81), and seems to be an exhortation (cf. p. 77) on the part of Jesus to his disciples. In this very simple process of classification, Bultmann does little more than assign the saying to a very broad band of material, which is regarded as genuine and authentic Jesus tradition.

On p. 29, however, Bultmann says more about Matthew 8.22. He writes:

It strikes me as improbable that 'let the dead bury their dead' could ever have been an independent saying: it seems a matter of course that it refers to some specific occasion, though it is impossible to say with any certainty what occasion it was. But that the whole situation is imaginary is even more certain than this, for 'following' is clearly used in its figurative sense, since it was in common use by the Jews as a term for discipleship. That the disciple 'followed his teacher' meant not only that he acquired knowledge from him, but also that he followed his example in practical affairs. Here a concrete situation brings to symbolic expression the truth that 'to follow' Jesus 'sets the disciple free from every duty, permits him no further obligation, but requires of him a surrender securing him wholly to Jesus alone'. (cf. Bultmann, 1972, p. 29)

In a footnote to this passage, Bultmann adds:

It seems completely erroneous to me to trace this saying to an Egyptian fairy-tale, where the dead actually bury the dead.... Neither is it at all clear that...the form of the saying is due to a mistranslation, and to read as the original saying 'leave the dead to their grave digger', or: 'leave the dead to the grave-digger, that he may accompany them'. There is indeed no reason to rob the saying of its paradox, particularly as Judaism also recognised the figurative use of 'the dead'. (Bultmann, 1972, p. 29)

In his treatment of Matthew 8.22, therefore, as recorded here in his *History of the Synoptic Tradition*, one may recognise all of the characteristic features of Bultmann's eschatological interpretation of the New Testament. First, there is close attendance to the *religionsgeschichtliche* background to the saying. Bultmann is concerned with its correct translation, its relations to Egyptian fairy-tales, and Old Testament and Jewish parables. He goes to some length to see it in relation to other sayings of Jesus – as exhortation and prophetic utterance – and he compares Matthew 8.22 with its Lukan parallel, contained within the pericope Luke 9.57–62. Here one may witness Bultmann's careful scholarship, expressed in simple and bold strokes.

There is also, however, what one can now readily recognise as a statement which demythologises this passage; that is, interprets it eschatologically. This is the comment, quoted from Schlatter, that 'to follow' Jesus 'sets the disciple free from every duty, permits him no further obligation, but requires of him a surrender securing him wholly to Jesus alone'. There is nothing here that one need find too surprising. The emphasis upon the personal encounter with Jesus

Christ alone, as the sole mediator of God's grace; the freedom of the individual, which is in fact a frightening and austere gift; the same individual's surrender to one, and only one, authority. This is the stuff of Bultmann's kerygmatic theology, founded upon what he identifies as the purpose of Jesus' mission and message: to call individuals to the kingdom of God, and to exhort them to its service.

The presuppositions that Bultmann brings to the text, therefore, are two. First, there is his customary emphasis upon the existential predicament of the individual; that is, the individual's preunderstanding, *Vorverständnis*. The preunderstanding itself is not a particular way of interpreting this predicament, but rather the claim that the individual is thrust into life without escape, and must therefore address it. It is, in other words, simply the 'given' of human existence, in Heideggerian terms, the 'Da' of *Dasein*, interpreted theologically. Second, there is the prior conviction, as in Gadamer, that this predicament may be addressed via consideration of the past, as recorded in texts, and that such a consideration must be constrained by the best standards of scholarship and exegesis. Hence, Bultmann's efforts in his *History of the Synoptic Tradition*.

There is here, in other words, a combination of two clearly distinct questions. There is the question of the saying's existential significance in the present moment. And there is the question of its internal significance, its context-bound meaning – what Ricoeur refers to as its 'ideal' meaning. The combination of these two aspects can best be described, perhaps, by Gadamer's understanding of the fusion of two horizons. At the very least, at this stage it provides a clear means by which one may appreciate the basic procedure that Bultmann is following.

If one were to follow Fuchs and Ebeling at this stage, a certain reduction or levelling-out of the text would follow. The distinction between horizons, found in Gadamer, would be blurred. As language-event, the exegesis and interpretation of Matthew 8.22 would operate solely upon the level of what both Fuchs and Ebeling refer to as 'reality'. There would be no room, in other words, for Tracy's recognition of cultural plurality and its role in interpretation, and there would be no question of imagination's playing a part in such interpretation. In effect, to follow Fuchs and Ebeling would be tantamount to claiming that: we know, can identify, the meaning of this passage. That would be to return to the very first quest of the historical Jesus, which was so comprehensively condemned by Schweitzer.

This is not true to Bultmann's own hermeneutics, nor to its potential. What I want to do now is to see how Tracy's understanding of imagination and cultural pluralism can realise aspects of Bultmann's hermeneutics hitherto overlooked. It is a question of teasing out the subtleties that are contained within, yet that have remained unrecognised, even by Bultmann himself. In this, hermeneutics may become genuinely critical within theological reflection.

At this stage, I do not wish to say anything positive or negative concerning Bultmann's own work on Matthew 8.22. In the light of Martin Hengel's brilliant study of this text, *The Charismatic Leader and his Followers* (Hengel, 1981), one might wish to question aspects of Bultmann's *religionsgeschichtliche* analysis. Moreover, in view of the criticisms advanced by David Tracy and others regarding Bultmann's theology of a rather monolithic faith, one might want to examine this second issue. But not here. That might reasonably be held over until the following Conclusion. Here I wish to consider solely the structure of that moment in Bultmann's thought in which hermeneutic understanding comes to light.

It was noted above that there was, using Gadamer's expression, a fusion of horizons at this moment of hermeneutic understanding; that is, two theoretically identifiably separate elements were brought into intimate relationship in the instant of interpretation: the exegesis of the past, and the perception of the meaning of the present. The relationship between the two is symbiotic: each, in effect, changes the other, at least in terms of hermeneutic understanding.

This, however, is insufficient. For what results in fact is what one finds in Bultmann's own hermeneutics: historical-critical exegesis combined with one dominant analogy for its theological interpretation, in his case the analogy of existentialist interpretation or demythologising. That is, there is in Bultmann's hermeneutics the implication of plurality, in so far as he recognises at a theoretical level the partiality of interpretation itself. In practice, however, this is forgotten. The New Testament becomes, in effect, a manual for individual, subjective existence. It is from precisely this caricature that Bultmann's thought must be rescued.

To do this, we need to acknowledge two things. First, that both historical-critical exegesis *and* an analogous interpretation are both relevant, but that Bultmann's own method – demythologising – must not be accepted as the only legitimate one. Second, that these two styles of interpretation must be applied to each of the two contexts in question. In other words, there are four 'horizons', not two, involved in hermeneutical understanding; that is, four, not two, elements within that 'fusion' we may call hermeneutic understanding. They are:

1   Historical-critical exegesis of the text.
2   Religious-philosophical interpretation of the dominant analogy at work within that text.
3   Historical-critical exegesis of the context in which the interpreter is operating.
4   The application of a recognised and designated analogy for the expression of the interpretation itself.

Not surprisingly, these four elements require a little unpacking.

Historical-critical exegesis of the text (1) involves, straightforwardly, the *religionsgeschichtliche* analysis, in so far as it is possible, of the motifs, symbols, events, and utterances described within it. Of course, no historical-critical findings can ever be described as absolute. At best, they are simply very probable. This stage, therefore, is not the same thing as the misguided attempt to discover 'what really happened' in first-century Palestine. Rather, this stage is a question of what one may refer to as allowing the text to speak in its own language; that is, the recognition of the validity of that which Bultmann referred to as 'myth'.

The religious-philosophical analysis of the dominant analogy at work within a given text (2) – that is, Ricoeur's 'ideal' meaning – is something that exegetes too often forget, leading them to regard their 'findings' as absolute 'facts', when in fact they can be no such thing, at least, not within the compass of our identifiable knowledge. On the contrary, such a religious-philosophical analysis, as a historical consideration of the analogy at work within any given text, must be concerned with the style with which that text has been worked together. It is, in other words, an analysis of the apparent narrative structure, which recognises the text as the production of a particular community. Unlike redaction criticism, however – which would seem to serve the same purpose – such a religious-philosophical analysis would not be concerned to identify the nature of the community, but would rather recognise the sovereignty and purposiveness of the text. Again, like the first stage, it would allow the text to speak with its own voice. But it would move towards recognising that voice as itself an interpretation, one representation among several, which the author(s) has here been responsible for articulating.

Theologically, therefore, 'analogy' is being used in the sense of the reflective means by which an individual – or more likely, group or community – arrives at a particular understanding of its relationship with God. Conventionally, therefore, it applies to questions of theological method. All meaning, fundamentally, is the product of analogy and, therefore, of theological method (cf. Tracy 1981). Philosophically, of course, it is precisely this method of analogy, as the making-present of meaning, that addresses the time–eternity problem so central to Bultmann's own, and indeed all, Christian theology. Without analogy, therefore, it becomes impossible to speak of God's eternal will in Christ in the kind of non-objectifying language that Bultmann – and all hermeneutic theology, including critical theology – seeks.

The historical-critical analysis of the context in which the interpreter is operating (3) must take into consideration the social, political, historical, and economic constraints that impinge upon the interpreter's context and the process of interpretation itself. This is an important, indeed, crucial, aspect of the interpreter's task which is so clearly lacking in Bultmann's own hermeneutic understanding, to its detriment. In effect, it takes into consideration Tracy's concern with the role of cultural pluralism within hermeneutic theology. In so doing, it also refers hermeneutic theology away from its task of enunciating its own 'grammar', and towards the task of speaking historically and meaningfully about God's action in the world.

Finally, the expression of a recognised and designated analogy (4) brings to understanding – and this is the theologian's hermeneutic task – the particular perspective from which the other three stages of hermeneutic understanding itself are perceived, and the particular perspective from which theology wishes to speak – in non-objective terms – of God's eternal will to act in time. In Bultmann's own hermeneutic theology, this stage of interpretation is muddled. Instead of recognising the partiality of the particular analogy of subjective existence with which he operates, he asserts it simply as the single, dominant understanding of life confronting humanity. This is a mistake. As there can be no one, single understanding of God's action in the world, but there is rather a series of analogies (which of course must be evaluated), a series of recognised perspectives from which to undertake hermeneutic theology (some of which will be ecclesiastical), so there can not be one, single understanding of humanity with absolute authority. Bultmann refuses to accept that. Consequently, his hermeneutics ultimately fails.

This presentation might seem unduly to confuse matters. But that need not be the case. On the contrary, set out in this fashion, hermeneutical understanding can be regarded as a simple yet subtle tool with which to express one's own particular theological position. It serves, in other words, an ontological purpose, but it does so in such a way as to recognise the necessary relativity of ontologies. This is not, of course, an epistemological relativity, although epistemologies play an important role in both the religious-philosophical analysis and the expression of any chosen analogy. Rather, ontological relativity is a consequence of hermeneutic understanding. And *that* is the promise or potential of Bultmann's thought upon which I wish to elaborate.

With respect to Matthew 8.22, we can see how these four stages in the fusion of the horizons – we may preserve Gadamer's terminology for the time being – might operate. The historical-critical exegesis (1) remains more or less as Bultmann and Hengel leave it, with the proviso that such exegesis is the reading of a text, rather than an attempt to identify 'what really happened'. The religious-philosophical analysis (2) considers the implications of the narrative itself: the key words and expressions used, their relation to other areas of religious and theological importance in the texts of the period, and the apparent intentions of the writers of the text. Again, the relativity of the information gleaned must be preserved. Taken together, these two stages should serve to open up the text both so that it can communicate aspects of its own ideal meaning, and itself be regarded in a new light.

Likewise, the third and fourth stages: they prepare the interpreter to perceive the point of engagement between his own critical context and those aspects of the meaning of the text that have been revealed in stages one and two. With respect to Matthew 8.22, the interpreter must naturally consider the question of the social, economic, politicial and historical (3) relevance of death and burial in his or her context. This may seem pedantic. It is, however, an inevitable consequence of the cultural pluralism of the contemporary world. Only after this has been achieved in stage three, can stage four bring to expression the theological analogy that any one interpreter might wish to employ (4). One can see here the problem with an interpretation such as that of Fuchs and Ebeling: their existential concern with faith *per se* simply glosses over the very real, material impact of motifs and events such as death and burial. This is something that hermeneutic theology must strive against.

One or two examples might be instructive at this point.

Naturally, the interpreter operating in a Western, first-world context will conduct stage one with the tools adopted from historical-critical studies, as it is classically perceived. Overwhelmingly, these will be regarded as 'empirical', or 'scientific', and therefore 'trustworthy'. The interpreter must recognise these limitations for what they are; that is, already the first signs of the partiality of interpretation. This will also be the case in stage two, where specific understandings of 'religion' and 'philosophy' will be brought to bear. The interpreter must acknowledge this. In such fashion, it is possible to assert that stages three and four are already impinging upon stages one and two even in the formulation of their most basic terminology. Such is the nature of hermeneutic understanding. And so we may recognise what Gadamer referred to as the fusion of horizons: that symbiotic relationship between the different stages of interpretation in which each asserts its intentionality upon the other, so that in practice neither stage remains as clearly delineated as is possible in theory.

Quite obviously, therefore, 'death' and 'burial' will mean different things, too, in our Western culture. The interpreter must recognise this trend for what it is, and evaluate her interpretation accordingly. We would have to acknowledge very different trends in the work of, say, a Central American interpreter. There, different understandings of all four stages might be in operation. The predominantly Western model and appreciation of empiricism, for example, which plays such an important role in European interpretations of historical-critical exegesis, might well be replaced in a Central American context by a set of materialist categories for textual understanding. Even the structure of hermeneutic understanding itself, as described here, cannot be asserted absolutely. All that one can say is that, given our Western tradition of hermeneutics, it seems to be an advancement on positions hitherto held.

All of this is complex. A simile for this structure itself, therefore, might be enlightening. In the following, I am attempting to maintain my distinction between the kind of word-obsessed dialectical or dialogical models one finds in Gadamer, Fuchs, and Ebeling, and the revelation/visualisation models one finds in the Bultmannian/Heideggerian tradition.

Instead of the fusion of two horizons, therefore, I propose that we imagine the process of hermeneutic understanding as the movement or passage of light between two 'windows'. One 'window' looks on to the text; the other looks on to the context in which the interpreter operates. Stages one and three 'construct' the 'frames' of their respective 'windows'; their analyses structure the perceptions of stages two and four. Those latter stages themselves (2 and 4) are in fact the effort of perceiving or 'looking through' the said 'windows'. And, as with the positions we adopt before windows in mundane existence, so the 'positions' we adopt in relation to the 'windows' of hermeneutic understanding affect that which we 'see' or 'perceive'. In other words, the analogies we adopt determine what it is that we can see through the 'windows' that we have attempted to 'frame'.

We can see how this works with reference to the question of the historical Jesus. Historical-critical exegesis establishes a window on to the texts which tell stories about him; but that is all. Likewise, socio-political and historical-economic analyses establish a window on to the context in which we wish to see Jesus of Nazareth in his soteriological significance (given that we are Christians). What we actually see, however, depends upon how we look. If we gaze from the perspective of the subjective individual, we will see that Bultmann sees. If we gaze from the perspective of the liberation of the oppressed poor of third-world nations, we may see what Leonardo Boff sees. If we gaze from the perspective of the sacramental community, we may see what Yves Congar sees. And so on.

The process of hermeneutical understanding, therefore, is on this model the process or movement of reflection, refraction, and illumination. Some things are lost when we look. We do not perceive everything in any one given interpretation, nor can we expect to. Some of our interests, in other words, are reflected, in so far as these to begin with were recognisably prejudiced. One thinks here, for example, of certain attempts in Liberal Protestant life-of-Jesus theology to portray the Messiah as something akin to a romantic poet-philosopher. Others are refracted; that is, they become something we did not expect. One may consider, here, the fashion in which the political convictions of theologians concerned with the oppression of their communities, must adapt their attitudes when confronted by certain of the sayings of Jesus. In other words, one discovers something. This, too, is part of the process of hermeneutic understanding. And, finally, some things are illuminated. We may see, strangely and wonderfully, a figure whom we can recognise as meaningful for the context in which we live. Such a figure would be Jesus of Nazareth, in one of his many guises. Hence, as reflection, refraction, and illumination, hermeneutic understanding involves the symbiotic relationship of several strands of interpretation and exegesis, analysis and consideration, which can be identified and conceptualised. In theory, the theologian must reflect upon the distinct stages which, in practice, often become one single series of statements.

That such reflection did not take place in the late 1960s, however, indicates the failure of hermeneutic theology to elaborate upon its own promise. In the work of such figures as Ebeling and Fuchs, as has been seen, this failure went unnoticed. Certain writers, though, were not so discreet. In the following section, a consideration of the work of T. W. Adorno and Dorothee Sölle will draw out this more critical aspect of the reception of Bultmann's theology.

What has been achieved hitherto, therefore, is the identification of a space in which hermeneutic theology can grow and develop, so as to fulfil not only its own pedagogic intent – as in Bultmann's theology – but also its responsibility towards the cultural relativity of contemporary theology, as Tracy's *The Analogical Imagination* makes clear. The aim of the simile here elaborated, therefore, is not to justify any one particular analogy or theological method, any one way of interpreting the story of Jesus and the Christian faith of the individual believer. It is not, in other words, an attempt to justify liberation or political theologies, or a-political theologies. On the contrary, it seeks simply to highlight the need for theology to teach those to whom it would speak. Today, this means that a genuinely critical theology must seek, pedagogically, to speak of cultural pluralism and socio-political concerns, not simply in order to advance a particular position – though that may be the case – but to bring people to the encounter with the risen Lord, as that event in which God's eternal will to act in time comes to expression.

The remainder of Chapter 5 will attempt to develop this possibility – fundamentally, stage three in the simile outlined above – via a consideration of the work of T. W. Adorno and Dorothee Sölle, and their criticisms of Bultmann's theology with respect to such socio-political concerns and questions. Some of the preparatory work for this effort, however, was accomplished above. The matter of defining four horizons or variables in the process of hermeneutic understanding, for example, though necessarily inexact – and hermeneutics must be an inexact science – was part of the process of teasing out the critical potential of hermeneutic theology in general and Bultmann's hermeneutic theology in particular. It is worth while recalling those four variables here:

1   Historical-critical exegesis of the text.
2   Religious-philosophical interpretation of the dominant analogy at work within the text.
3   Historical-critical exegesis of the context in which the interpreter is operating.
4   The application of a recognised and designated analogy for the expression of the interpretation itself.

With respect to Bultmann's own theology, it was possible to arrive at the following conclusions. First, Bultmann recognised the importance both of the historical-critical exegesis of the text, and of the religious-philosophical interpretation of the dominant analogy at work within the text; that is, stages (1) and (2) above. One can see this at work in his studies, *The History of the Synoptic Tradition* and *Primitive Christianity in its Contemporary Setting* respectively. Thus, one might say that to a certain degree, Bultmann succeeded in defining or constructing one of the 'frames' of the hermeneutic 'windows', and of adopting a clear stance with respect to it.

What happened next in Bultmann's thought was, essentially, a mistake. Instead of recognising the necessity of a detailed analysis of the socio-historical context in which the interpreter finds herself, and of the partiality of all analogies by which one interprets anything, Bultmann conflates stages (2) and (4) above. That is, he designates his own particular religious-philosophical interpretation of the gospel as *the* meaning of the New Testament, and, therefore, as the only analogy by which any interpretation may become meaningful. The effect of this development is dramatic. Meaning becomes divorced from the social and political arena in which individuals live, being elevated rather to a plane upon which all theology is reduced to the expression of a fundamental challenge to decide for or against God's event, Jesus Christ. Subsequently, hermeneutic theology, even in the work of such an intelligent thinker as David Tracy, becomes essentially illiterate, and therefore redundant, though Tracy's more recent work has corrected this tendency (cf. Tracy, 1987). It fails to listen to the extraneous noises of existence, and so cannot teach. And its failure to teach, ultimately, is its failure to be genuinely critical.

Simply stated, the work of Adorno and Sölle considered below attacks the manner in which Bultmann implicitly conflates stages (2) and (4), thereby failing to consider stage (3); that is, the question of the critical analysis of the interpreter's social and historical context. In so far as the present chapter represents a move towards a genuinely critical theology, it is, in effect, an attempt to undo Bultmann's omission.

2   T. W. Adorno

It is curious to note that Rudolf Bultmann, so clearly the last scion of Liberal Protestantism and yet – so clearly – concerned with twentieth-century philosophy in the shape of Heidegger's hermeneutic philosophy, was contemporaneous with such figures as Walter Benjamin, Max Horkheimer, and T. W. Adorno, and that he lived to see the great days of the Institute for Social Research and its partial eclipse – with Adorno's demise – in the 1960s. Curious, because Bultmann fails to make any mention of their work. It is this failure on his part that introduces the critical reception of Bultmann's theology by Adorno and Dorothee Sölle.

In 1927, the year in which Bultmann wrote his important essay on Christology (at the age of 43) and the year in which Martin Heidegger published *Being and Time*, Theodor Wiesengrund Adorno submitted his first *Habilitationsschrift*: he was 24 (cf. Adorno, 1973, pp. 79–322). This work was not accepted by the philosophy faculty of Frankfurt aM University. Subsequently, however, after coming under the influence of the leading literary critic and intellectual figure Walter Benjamin (1891–1940), who was to have such a profound effect upon the development of literary criticism in the twentieth century, Adorno became one of the leading writers of the Institute for Social Research, the so-called Frankfurt School. In this guise, Adorno contributed greatly to the critical reception of the German idealist tradition in the twentieth century, as well as developing his own aesthetic theory.

It may seem strange at first sight to highlight Adorno's work in a study of Bultmann's theology. The two men seem never to have met, and there is certainly no effort on Bultmann's part to understand or accept the work of any modern philosopher after his encounter with Heidegger in Marburg (despite his skilful debate with Jaspers). On the contrary, once he had established the ontological reflection and the event theory that were to serve as the foundation of his Christology and therefore of his entire theology, Bultmann turned away from philosophy.

Adorno, however, *did* concern himself with Bultmann's work, in so far as he regarded Bultmann as one of the (albeit minor) propagators of what he (Adorno) referred to as the 'jargon of authenticity' (cf. Adorno, 1973, p. 77). Adorno's critique, therefore, is directly and explicitly concerned with Bultmann's theology, and so is highly significant at this stage of our examination of its reception. To ignore Adorno's critique – on the grounds, for example, that he is a Marxist and therefore inevitably antipathetic towards Bultmann's position – is simply to ignore the challenge to Bultmann's theology of contemporary reflection.

Jargon der Eigentlichkeit: Zur deutschen Ideologie (*The Jargon of Authenticity*) was first published in Frankfurt aM in 1964 (cf. Adorno, 1973). Written as an explicit attack upon the work of Heidegger and Jaspers and the mediation of their ideas via various cultural phenomena, *The Jargon of Authenticity* was originally conceived as part of Adorno's important philosophical study, *Negative Dialectics*, but grew too large to be included in that work and so was published separately.

The Jargon of Authenticity is apparently a book without any definite structure, being devoid of chapters or section headings. It seems to exist, rather, as a 140-page pamphlet or *Flügschrift*. This initial impression, however, is misleading, for there is in fact a very clear order within the text, which is fashioned in accordance with some of the most significant themes of Adorno's philosophical work. After a lengthy passage examining the extent of the 'jargon' itself in post-war West German society, therefore, and a consideration of the ideological impact of this particular brand of philosophising upon West Germany, Adorno quickly settles to a systematic exposition of the basic terminology of the 'jargon of authenticity': existence, Being, care, decision, authenticity, encounter. In this way, Adorno exposes its basic *constellation*, this being made up of the particular points within 'existentialist' philosophy (as Adorno characterises the work of Heidegger and Jaspers) which are of primary importance. Then, in his subsequent commentary, Adorno identifies what he terms the *forcefield* which operates between those points ('constellation' and 'forcefield' are key terms in Adorno's immanent critique of the particularity of cultural phenomena). It is this forcefield that Adorno specifies as the ideology of existentialism.

Adorno's, then, is a destructive commentary. He attempts to identify all of the central themes or motifs of the jargon, to isolate them from each other, and thereby to disconnect them from the forcefield that gives them their power. By 'switching off' the forcefield, moreover, and identifying the jargon as propaganda, Adorno hopes to destroy its power and to remove it from the exalted plane upon which it has been placed by the philosophers of existentialism, Heidegger and Jaspers, and their acolytes, including Rudolf Bultmann.

It should be noted at this point that Adorno sweeps aside Heidegger's lingering claim to be the thinker who returns to the primal revelation of Being. In so doing, Adorno also brings into question Bultmann's claim to be the theologian who has articulated anew the essential message of the New Testament kerygma, in so far as the specific terminology that Bultmann uses in his theology echoes the terminology condemned in *The Jargon of Authenticity*. In the light of Adorno's study, in other words, it is no longer possible to regard Bultmann's theology solely upon its own terms. Rather, it is time to consider the ideology inherent in Bultmann's position. In this respect, it is now necessary to overturn the distinction between Bultmann's phenomenology proper, and so-called existentialism, which was made in the earlier exposition of his theology.

Quite simply, Bultmann's ontological reflection attempts to be purely phenomenological, in so far as that implies a fundamental analysis of the meaning of existence and the event or *Ereignis* which brings to light that meaning. In practice, however, that attempt fails. For the terminology in which that fundamental analysis is expressed – existence, Being, care, decision, authenticity, encounter – carries with it an ideology that smothers the good intentions of phenomenology. Or rather, phenomenology itself, when interpreted as fundamental ontological reflection, smothers itself as it falls victim to its own impossible goal. Paradoxically, therefore, Bultmann's theology is existentialist – in Adorno's pejorative sense – as it seeks to be phenomenology.

Bultmann's phenomenological analysis of historical existence, in other words, is not existentialism. Its ideology, however, is. This, ironically, is the result of Bultmann's refusal to say anything about the practical aspects of theology. In effect, by leaving a vacuum at this point, and by refusing to speak meaningfully and pedagogically about the practical task of the individual believer, Bultmann abdicates responsibility for the fate of his hermeneutic theology. For when a vacuum is deliberately left, one cannot be surprised if it is filled by something unforeseen. One might say, therefore, that although Bultmann is not an existentialist, in so far as he does not seek to articulate a psychology of the individual subject (as one finds, say, in Kierkegaard or Sartre), his is, paradoxically, an existentialist theology, where that expression is referred to his theology's ideological implications, and understood pejoratively. The force of Adorno's critique, of course, is that existentialism can only be understood, as ideology, in such a pejorative sense.

In general terms, therefore, Adorno's *The Jargon of Authenticity* represents an important challenge to Bultmann's theology. More specifically, however, it calls attention to two significant aspects of Bultmann's methodology, which Adorno considers by means of a detailed examination of the particular terminology of the jargon of authenticity.

In so doing, Adorno refers to *The Jargon of Authenticity* as a 'metacritique', by which he means that it goes beyond an analysis of philosophy *per se*; that is, philosophy as it would like to regard itself, into its historical and socio-political context. In other words, Adorno identifies the existentialist philosophy that is the subject of his analysis as itself a cultural phenomenon, and refuses to allow it to maintain its own aloofness to the material world.

There seems to be a very definite attempt here by Adorno to distance the notion of metacritique from that of 'critique', which has such a very distinguished place in the history of German idealism (cf. Connerton, 1980, pp. 17–18). This idea seems to have been a popular one among members of the Institute for Social Research: in his *Knowledge and Human Interests*, for example, Habermas states that Marx conducted a 'metacritique' of Hegel (cf. Habermas, 1975, pp. 25–42). For Adorno, this claim to be conducting a metacritique means that he insists upon a position outside of the tradition of German idealism. Observing 'from without', as it were, it is in this sense that he is able to write objectively of the jargon of authenticity.

Adorno's intention, therefore, is clear. He is conducting a remedial or corrective analysis of the jargon of authenticity, a destructive retrieval or interpretation of its structure and content. The notion of metacritique, in other words, whatever else it might be intended to convey, cannot escape from its own pedagogic meaning. As Adorno seeks to dismantle the scaffolding of existentialism, he seeks also to instruct contemporary society in the ways of (meta) critical thinking. Implicitly, therefore, he is assuming the mantle that Bultmann (and Heidegger) placed upon their own shoulders; that is, the mantle of the teacher.

The Jargon of Authenticity, then, is a metacritique of the reification of language in (Adorno's) contemporary German philosophy, which for the purposes of this text Adorno identifies as the existentialist philosophies of Heidegger and Jaspers, the former being his primary target. By 'reification', Adorno means the suppression of the heterogeneity of language in the name of identity – the identity being Heidegger's, whereby language *per se* has exalted status as the House of Being – in other words, the shelter or shade in which Being comes to light, that is, appears. In other words, the authentic meaning of language for Heidegger (and therefore for Bultmann; cf. Chapter 3) as the event of revelation is ontologically prior to the objective description that might appear to be the primary function or use of language.

It is this process of reification, of artificially raising language to non-existent 'levels', which is the basic method by which the jargon as ideology achieves its objective; that is, that which Adorno identifies as the thoughtless acquiescence of people in the existentialist philosophy, and its socio-political, cultural, and economic expressions. (Adorno leaves aside at this point the question of the deliberate manipulation of people by Heidegger, despite the latter's involvement with National Socialism under Hitler.) This reification, Adorno claims, destroys the social basis of language, distorting its cultural content, and thereby making it subordinate to propaganda. With respect to this point, Trent Schroyer writes, in his foreword to the American edition of *The Jargon of Authenticity*, that:

> Adorno's reconstruction of Heidegger's philosophy attempts to show that it becomes an ontology that retreats behind, rather than overcomes, the tradition of transcendental philosophy. In the universalisation of transcendental subjectivity into *Dasein*, the empirical is totally lost and, so Adorno claims, an essence-mythology of Being emerges. (Adorno, 1973, p. xvi)

Hence, the manipulation of language in the name of a particular form of philosophical propaganda leads to its distortion. In this fashion, far from language being the House of Being, argues

Adorno, it becomes the refuge of ideology. This is the basic argument and conclusion of Adorno's analysis of the jargon of authenticity.

The implications of this argument for any appreciation of Bultmann's theology are immediately apparent if one reconsiders his Christology, as examined above in Chapter 1. Although Bultmann asserts that it is in the ordinary language of the pastor that the individual encounters the story of Jesus Christ, the eschatological encounter with the risen Lord, which is ontologically prior to but semantically later than the actual proclamation of that story, can only be experienced as an event of revelation *in terms of that individual's* Dasein. For Bultmann, this means that even though the actual proclamation of the Christian gospel takes place semantically in the story of Jesus Christ, that story is told solely with respect to the purposiveness of Jesus' life in terms of the individual's eschatological existence. There is no attempt by Bultmann, in other words, to say anything about the *content* of Jesus' message in terms of its references to specific situations and circumstances. On the contrary, everything is effectively reduced to the level of the individual's encounter with a question mark, a demand for a decision that itself cannot be judged by the standards of those material decisions made in the ontic world. On the basis of Adorno's metacritique, therefore, one can now say that Bultmann's insistence upon the ontological significance of 'correct' or 'authentic' language amounts to the construction of an ideology which sets its own agenda and, in the process, answers its own questions without any meaningful reference to the specific and peculiar within social existence. As will be seen below, this is precisely the issue that Dorothee Sölle finds most compelling.

This is an important point. The West German society that Adorno is implicity criticising for being duped by the jargon of authenticity is the West Germany of the 1950s and 1960s, when Bultmann's theology and its impact reached its high-water mark. In effect, Adorno's metacritique of this jargon amounts, in terms of Bultmann's theology, to the claim that it simply accommodates the *Angst* of the immediate post-war consumer society being created there, without making any contribution to its social and political rebuilding. If this claim is justified, then Bultmann's theology is reduced to something like the expression of bourgeois anxiety when confronted by economic instability. His preaching itself becomes nothing more than rhetoric, the empty and endless repetition of questions and suggestive answers which, like lost souls, can find no home in contemporary society. One might almost say that Bultmann, in his attempts to understand contemporary philosophy (Heidegger) in terms of Christian faith and thereby proclaim the gospel in the modern world, succeeds solely in repeating the errors of those theologians who signed the Manifesto of the 93 Intellectuals in 1914, in support of Kaiser Wilhelm II's war policy.

With these more general considerations in mind, it is now possible to turn and consider Adorno's more specific charges against the jargon of authenticity.

Adorno first attacks the jargon and its sponsoring philosophies by considering the question of transcendence. For it is a consequence of the apparent overcoming of the fundamental subject–object dichotomy of epistemological idealism by phenomenology, which itself is held responsible for Heidegger's so-called existentialism, that transcendence is no longer included methodologically within that dichotomy, but is a question for the subject alone. In other words, transcendence becomes a theme of human self-consciousness (in a non-psychological sense), so that Adorno can write that: 'In the jargon transcendence is finally brought closer to men: it is the Wurlitzer organ of the spirit' (Adorno, 1973, p. 17), where 'spirit' is not any form of Hegelian *Geist*, but rather such human self-consciousness. Transcendence therefore becomes not a logically distinct category or condition, but an abstracted, ontological possibility for the individual who cannot realise that possibility in the ontic world alone, but solely through meaningful encounter and decision. Thus, Adorno claims that: 'Complete demythologisation totally reduces transcendence to an abstraction' (Adorno, 1973, p. 31). In the process, any discussion of a distinction between ontic and ontological on the basis of transcendence is evacuated of all meaning.

This is the first part of Adorno's metacritique which can be directed at Bultmann's theology; that is, that through his insistence upon the claim that salvation is not to be found in the ontic world but through an eschatological encounter with a Christ figure who can only be encountered on a level which transcends the ontic world, Bultmann has reified salvation itself into one abstracted ontological possibility, the other being inauthenticity and, presumably, damnation. In so doing, Bultmann reduces eschatology to a meaningless expression, with lasting implications for his Christology. By reducing eternity to a matter of immanence in the individual's encounter, argues Adorno, Heidegger, and by implication Bultmann, abandons the material reality of existence as existence *in time*, whatever Heidegger's, and Bultmann's, attempts to give time primacy in his thought.

As a consequence of this treatment of transcendence, Adorno writes, there is a corresponding rejection of the ontic world. The reduction of the one to a meaningless level results in the same treatment for the other, when they are both engaged in a symbiotic relationship. All that remains is the subjective, divorced from the social and political realities that render it intelligible in dialectic. He writes: 'By means of the magic formula of existence, one disregards society' (Adorno, 1973, pp. 68–9). That is, by raising up transcendence, Heidegger and Bultmann cast down the ontic world, with – on Adorno's terms – consequently no regard for ethical, social, and political matters. On the contrary, the only concern that the jargon now has with society is its own self-preservation and propagation within that society. This is perhaps paralleled in Bultmann's theology, where it is only by constant and unremitting affirmation of the decision when confronted by the kerygma, that the individual believer is saved. The believer, then, has only to decide, continuously. There is no other point to the ontic world than to provide a meaningless forum or locus for this encounter to take place. Schroyer writes, therefore, that: 'One needs only to be a believer: the objective content of belief has been eclipsed in the subjectivisation of objective content' (Adorno, 1973, p. xiv). In the process, the pedagogic intent of Christianity – which must, surely, be insisted upon – is abandoned to the individual's imagination; that is, her self-understanding. There remains no material or concrete referents for ethical conduct. On the contrary, they are demythologised out of significance, if not existence.

The importance of Adorno's analysis of the jargon of authenticity, therefore, is in its criticism of the impact of Bultmann's theology, and its ideology, upon Western society. For example, it casts a very different light upon the following passage from Bultmann's essay 'The Sermon on the Mount and the Justice of the State' than

was perhaps hitherto possible: 'What God demands is not the renunciation of justice in the sense of the ordinances that regulate the
community, but rather the renunciation by the individual of his
rights in the concrete moment; i.e., of his use of the ordinances of
justice to further his own interests against his neighbour' (Bultmann, 1960, p. 204). What God wants, Bultmann seems to be saying in the light of Adorno's metacritique, is the abdication by the
individual of her social and political rights as a citizen, in the name
of authenticity. This in itself is sufficient to denounce a theology
which proved itself incapable of any meaningful resistance to
National Socialism, as James D. Smart has recognised. He writes:
'Nevertheless, Bultmann's remarks in *The Task of Theology in the
Present Situation* (1933) show disturbing parallels to the thinking of
Gogarten (a National Socialist) and would not be likely to build
any significant barriers against the rising tide of totalitarian nationa-
lism' (Smart, 1967, p. 217). On a first consideration, this might
seem unjust to Bultmann's avowed intent; that is, to proclaim the
gospel in terms of its eschatological purposiveness. But when considered in context – and one must keep in mind that Bultmann was
the leading New Testament theologian and exegete throughout the
years, 1933–45 – the readiness with which that theology loses its
anchor in society is worrying. One recalls here his apparent uncon-
cern at the First World War. In the final analysis, Bultmann's theology cannot but be judged by his response to National Socialism,
its causes and its after-effects, as Adorno rightly asserts. Again, I
must insist, this is not a matter of judging Bultmann personally,
with the benefit of hindsight. But at the same time, the stakes are
high: anyone who seeks to understand the human situation in terms
of time and eternity, and thereby follows Bultmann at any point,
must acknowledge this lack on the part of his theology, and
attempt to correct it. Bultmann's own situation, and his courageous
attempts to help his own students and friends – witness the testimony of Hans Jonas and Hannah Arendt – mitigates one's criticisms of his theology to an important degree. But there can be no
such latitude allowed to theologians today, unless they too are
confronted by the direct possibility of persecution and death. This
is not the case in Western Europe or North America.

If this is correct – and surely it must be so – what seems to be
required for Bultmann's theology to have any lasting significance in

the contemporary world is a means by which his formal event theory can be 'politicised' in a Christian sense, to avoid the unwanted ideology of existentialism. For, justified or not, it is the charge of existentialism – of the abandonment of theology to subjectivism – that Bultmann's theology must be defended against.

The only viable defence of Bultmann's theology, however, is in its assertion that it is the historicality of existence which is the plane upon which theology must operate. And in the light of Adorno's metacritique, and the preceding consideration of the hermeneutic heritage of Bultmann's theology in Chapter 4, it must now be asserted that historicality must be considered in terms of its social and political qualities. To retrieve the critical potential of Bultmann's own hermeneutic theology, therefore, one must dismantle the a-political scaffolding in which it is clad, and return once again to the question of the historical Jesus.

3   Dorothee Sölle

Karl Barth, in other words, had a point: for although he misunderstood the nature and intention of Bultmann's theological method, Barth correctly foresaw its consequences; that is, the reduction of the Christian faith to an a-social, a-political, a-practical comprehension, acceptance, and decision for a formal event theory, abstracted from the material world. In this, Bultmann was unable to discern an effective role for the eschatological event in the material and social life of the individual. Or better, he was incapable of bringing such a role to theological expression, given his own philosophical rubric. Like Kierkegaard in Adorno's estimation, Bultmann reduced the individual, and her vitual concerns, to the bourgeois *Angst* of one living in a technocratic age. In this respect, Bultmann's understanding of the role and purpose of the Holy Spirit (which is often overlooked) is also defined by his dominant philosophical-ideological concerns, and so becomes axiomatic for this stage of the present critique of Bultmann's theology. He writes:

And so the power of the 'flesh' is manifested in the fact that it binds man to the transitory, to that which in fact is always past, to death, so the power of the Spirit is manifested in the fact that it gives the believer freedom, opens the way to the future, to the eternal, to life. For freedom is nothing else than being open for the genuine future, letting oneself be determined by the future. So Spirit may be called the power of futurity. (cf. Moltmann, 1967, pp. 211–12)

It is this conclusion of Bultmann's that must be challenged. Is the Holy Spirit to be reduced to the role of wet-nursing the individual's quest for identity? Or is the Spirit the divine power for change, in the name of the crucified God? The answer to this – in terms of hermeneutic theology – lies in a renewed consideration of Bultmann's understanding of eschatology, in the light of the discoveries of the present chapter.

Certainly, much has already been said concerning Bultmann's understanding of eschatology. Chapter 1, for example, established in some detail the distinction that Bultmann made between eschatology and apocalyptic, by which he – erroneously, in the light of more recent research (although this might be a matter of discussion and debate) – understood straightforwardly the objective description of the Divine. In this way, his work as a biblical exegete could be seen to be the attempt to distance the historical reality of Jesus of Nazareth's life in first-century Palestine, from the eschatological significance of his purpose as God's event of saving grace. Similarly, Chapter 3 established this particular understanding of eschatology in Heidegger's phenomenological interpretation of the event of revelation. Here, then, the future of which eschatology presumably spoke was not an objective moment of materialisation, but rather the revelation of a transcendence that gives ontological meaning to the present. Thus did the eternal 'invade' the present moment.

In so far as this effort was intended to preserve the gospel from the dangers of cultural relativism, such as it had suffered – or so it seemed to Bultmann – at the hands of Liberal Protestantism, it is possible to appreciate its sincerity. Moreover, it had an earnest pedagogic intent or purpose; that is, to educate the individual into believing, and understanding, that the reality of God's saving action on her behalf was not to be reduced to any material gains which might accrue in the interim. On the contrary, the individual's existence was always in doubt. The purpose of Bultmann's understanding of eschatology, therefore, was to demonstrate precisely how this element of doubt, in the present moment, was in fact the realisation of God's will for the individual's future. Hence, the role of this understanding as eschatology, rather than any other Christian doctrine.

The consequences of this position, however, negated the sincerity and pedagogic intent with which it was advanced. As Adorno demonstrated, evacuating the transcendent of any material significance likewise evacuated the material of any ontological relevance. That is, the ontological relationship that Bultmann – following Heidegger – sought to establish between the transcendent and the material, in the eschatological event of revelation, simply reduced both elements to the level of ciphers. In Christological terms, with the risen Lord reduced to the status of an intuition, the historical Jesus too is diminished. Jesus of Nazareth then becomes simply the necessary precursor of a future that turns out to be the best possibility of the present. Eschatology, divorced from the realm of hope and effective change, no longer speaks of a future that may be realised once and for all, in the form of the kingdom of God. Finally, the Holy Spirit serves simply to usher in not the hoped-for future, but an already-realised past, somehow returned to the present in every fresh moment. This is not a theology that aims to teach the individual to come to the encounter with God's eschatological event. It is a theology that evades its own pedagogic responsibility, by evading the material reality of human existence. Such – according to his critics – was the tragedy of Bultmann's theology, in so far as it rested upon an attenuated understanding of eschatology.

As Jurgen Moltmann has ably demonstrated. (cf. Moltmann, 1967), this basic understanding of eschatology as a doctrine not concerned with some objectively future realm but with the significance of the transcendent for the present moment, owes much to the ideas generated by Kant's important essay, 'Das Ende aller Dinge', first published in 1794 (Kant, 1947, pp. 31ff). In Bultmann's theology, however, the historical implications of this understanding of eschatology and the transcendent are developed more completely than in Kant's work, because of his understanding of Heidegger's phenomenology. Nevertheless, this debt to Kant's earlier work goes some way towards explaining Bultmann's lack of concern with social, economic, and political matters. His philosophical rubric, in which the eschatological is reduced phenomenologically to the plane of a transcendent event or moment, simply will not allow him to show any concern for the socio-political. He is restricted, effectively and solely, to the subject.

The return to Kant, however, demonstrates the step that must be taken to rescue Bultmann's theology from this philosophical 'slough of despond'. One must, in some way, alter the understanding of his event theory; that is, one must 'politicise' or 'revolutionise' it, by replacing the phenomenological reduction of a transcendental analysis of *Dasein* with an immanent critique of the social reality of human life. In other words, one must restore to eschatology its original relationship with *hope*, as the fundamental meaning of its futurity. In Christological terms, this restoration goes hand in hand with a renewed consideration of the title 'Messiah', and its application to the historical Jesus. As will be seen below, in the conclusion to the present chapter, to a great extent this has been the implicit nature of the reception of Bultmann's Christology by contemporary theology.

This will not, it must be emphasised, in any sense alter Bultmann's understanding of Christology or his event theory of the essential relationship between God and humanity, in so far as that event theory presents a formal understanding of the *manner* in which one may meaningfully relate the human to the divine, time to eternity; on this, there can be no misunderstanding. On the contrary, it is a way of developing beyond Bultmann's established position. By changing Bultmann's emphasis upon the individual subject to an emphasis upon the social group, one might be able to liberate Bultmann's event theory, thereby allowing contemporary theology to establish a doctrine of the power and ability of the Holy Spirit to teach and to effect change. What is being called for, therefore, is not a rejection of Bultmann's theological method, his event theory proper, but rather a rejection of that element within his philosophical rubric which ordains as its practical significance the ideology of existentialism which Adorno has identified and condemned in *The Jargon of Authenticity*. In this way, it might be possible to define a pedagogic role for the doctrine of eschatology in a contemporary theology of the Holy Spirit.

If we look at contemporary theology, and its work on the doctrine of Christ, we can see how eschatology, which under Bultmann was divorced from material reality – despite his claims that in reality his understanding of eschatology was the only one that gave meaning to material existence – is returned to the realm of hope for, and expectation of, a kingdom of God in the power of the Holy Spirit, which will effect real and lasting change in the material world. To illustrate this point, one need only look at the work of liberation theologians such as Gutierrez or Leonardo Boff (see below). Similarly, in Schillebeeckx's Christology, the image of Jesus as the eschatological prophet is concerned to highlight the socio-political and economic dimensions of the Christian doctrine of eschatology. In this respect, contemporary theology, wittingly or unwittingly, has reacted against Bultmann's at times anaemic theology to realise its potential as a direct challenge to the Christian individual or group to act in a political dimension, and for effective change. Thus is the pedagogic intent of Bultmann's theology transformed – and thereby kept alive – in contemporary thought.

The theologian who has examined this possibility most radically with respect to Bulmann's Christology is Dorothee Sölle. Sölle states that: 'More and more it appears to me that the move from existentialist theology to political theology is itself a consequence of the Bultmannian position' (Sölle, 1974, p. 2). To support this claim, Sölle refers to a sociological report into the effects of Bultmann's theology among the pastorate of the German Lutheran Church. She writes:

> The sociological study by Goldschmidt and Spiegel, *Der Pfarrer der Grosstadt* (1969), concludes that pastors who embrace the theology of Rudolf Bultmann place greater emphasis upon the formation of political opinion within their congregations and on the public responsibility of faith than do church officials with more conservative theological ties. (Sölle, 1974, p. 3)

Pedagogically, of course, this is certainly a favourable development, namely, that Bultmannian theology should teach Christian believers to appreciate their social responsibilities. But it is a definite paradox. For if so-called Bultmannian pastors are concentrating upon the formation of political opinion, then it is by no means certain that they are doing something that Bultmann himself would have approved of, from a theological perspective. What they would appear to be doing, on the contrary, is politicising (perhaps unwittingly) the eschatological event that Bultmann himself would claim to have uncovered by means of phenomenological interpretation.

Sölle's argument is that this is a consequence of Bultmann's existentialist position. We may go further, however, and argue that this is an *essential* consequence of Bultmann's theology if it is to be, at all, theology in any Christian sense. An event theory in itself is insufficient. A genuine theology must give the event theory work to do.

Such work, as has been indicated throughout this chapter, must be regarded in terms of the social, political, and economic challenges both of the contemporary situation, and the mission and message of Jesus of Nazareth. In effect, this means that the moral and ethical charges inherent in Bultmann's theology, which there are limited solely to the individual's self-realisation, must be liberated for the sake of the community at large. Ethics, in other words, can no longer remain the preserve of the individual. It becomes, at last, the domain of the Church in the power of the Spirit (cf. Sauter, 1988).

Bultmann himself would no doubt argue that this is an invalid step, bringing theology back into tension with the very elements of material existence that make it partial and relative. But in this respect, Bultmann himself is an unreliable witness at the trial of his own theology, and his testimony should be questioned

The task of theology in the present situation, therefore, is to radicalise Bultmann's statement that: 'It suffices to recognise that faith in God and nationality stand in a positive relation, insofar as God has placed us in our nation and state' (Bultmann, 1960, p. 159), so that Christians engage in a constant critique of society's structure, rather than passively acquiescing in its destabilisation, as arguably theologians such as Bultmann did in 1933. That Bultmann would not have approved of such a programme, given the nature of his Lutheranism and its doctrine of the two kingdoms, is incidental. The present task is to move beyond Bultmann's established position.

This means, of course, that theology today can no longer lay claim to any form of absolute status as it did in the 1950s and the 1960s, both in the work of Bultmann and of Karl Barth. On the contrary, theology, in so far as it seeks both to teach a specific community and to articulate that community's hopes and fears in terms of its Christian faith, must be contextual and therefore relative. This does not mean that it may create new doctrines, simply to serve the propaganda of a given situation. But it does mean that it must, in all sincerity, interpret the doctrines of the Church in the light not of one attenuated understanding of the gospel, but in the light of the gospel's work in its own specific context. This is an aspect of contemporary theology, and its development away from Bultmann's absolutism, which will be considered briefly in the conclusion to the present chapter.

The necessity of this approach to Bultmann's work has been recognised before. In an article concerned with Bultmann's theology, and quoted by Sölle, M. Herrmanns argues that: 'Thus even the existentialist interpretation with its exclusive interest in the individual and the possibility of authentic existence plays directly into the hands of Fascism' (cf. Sölle, 1974, p. 8). Sölle argues that Bultmann's obsession with the kerygma has in fact blinded him to the significance of *Jesus* the individual, which is ironic and tragic given the nature of his Christology. If Bultmann had been able to give as much attention to the actual words of Jesus as he did to their supposed purposiveness, argues Sölle, then he would have recognised the political nature of the foundation event of Christianity as a historical religion. She writes:

In distinction to theological language, which has supposedly been depoliticised but thereby in fact has become subservient to the prevailing interests [also Adorno's point – see above], the language of Jesus is always both religious and political, encountering the whole individual in her environment. (Sölle, 1974, p. 36)

That is, Jesus' *own* – admittedly religious – claim is conditioned by social and political factors. This is of the essence of calling oneself *Messiah*. By proclaiming a Christ figure that the individual can only encounter subjectively, Bultmann has lost the understanding of Jesus as Messiah which makes sense of eschatology and hope and, finally, theology's pedagogic intent. This is the final insult of the transcendentalisation of eschatology. It results, moreover, in the peculiar spectacle of a theology incapable of hearing the voice of its own, modern age, so concerned is it to hear the authentic Word. Solle writes:

> It seems to me that political theology, not kerygmatic neo-orthodoxy, draws the logical conclusion from Bultmann's situational thinking, because it strives to hear precisely the questions posed by the current situation and to analyse them exactly, so that theologically 'correct' answers are not handed out again and again as kerygma to questions that are not even being asked. (Solle, 1974, p. 22)

One is left, therefore, with the fundamental requirement of modernity, if theology is still to be theology of the event of God's grace and love in Jesus Christ; that is, to think and proclaim the historical Jesus as Messiah. Sölle concludes:

> That God loves all of us and each and every individual is a universal theological truth, which without translation becomes the universal lie. The translation of this proposition is world-transforming praxis. . . . The letter of Christ that we ourselves are is further written (II Cor. 3:3) and further received and read. There is no other letter capable of replacing the letter of Christ that we are. (Sölle, 1974, p. 107)

That is, contemporary theology must return in the power of the Holy Spirit (cf. Sauter, 1988) to the question of the historical Jesus, there to rediscover a Christian understanding of the Messiah.

Conclusion: Bultmann and Contemporary Theology

The Introduction to this study began with the audacious claim – supported by an authoritative statement by the late Karl Rahner – that Rudolf Bultmann's thought is of signal importance for the future of contemporary theology. Chapters 1–3 attempted, in the light of this, to elucidate the basic structure of Bultmann's theology, and its philosophical foundations, so as to reveal the nature of his lasting contribution; that is, his understanding of the eschatological event as the heart of any theology that seeks to bring the individual to the encounter with God. Continuing this theme, Chapters 4 and 5 highlighted the shortcomings of Bultmann's own work in this area, whilst striving to rescue his event theory for contemporary theology.

When Rahner wrote in 1968, it might fairly have been said that Bultmann's popularity was still near or at its peak. The decade of the 1960s had seen the continued hermeneutic activity not only of Fuchs and Ebeling in West Germany, but also of James Robinson and Robert Funk in the United States of America. Similarly, research in the areas of New Testament and intertestamental literature wrestled with many of the questions posed by Bultmann's own work. Finally, though somewhat dubiously, 'death of God' theology, in part taking its lead from one particular interpretation of Bultmann's work, was at its zenith. In all of these areas, the decade of the 1960s remains an impressive monument to Bultmann's endeavours, fully justifying Rahner's optimism.

If one surveys the contemporary theological scene, however, all has changed. Today, the work of hermeneutic theology has largely declined, commensurate with the growth in popularity of 'deconstruction' and post-modernist literary theories. Fuchs and Ebeling, in West Germany, and Robinson and Funk in the United States of America, have largely disappeared from view. Significantly, following Rahner's statement, it is left to such Roman Catholic writers as Tracy, O'Meara, and Caputo to continue work in this area. In Britain, whilst several leading figures profess interest in hermeneutics, no one theologian can claim that she or he is formulating an hermeneutic theology. The theological scene, so to speak, has moved on.

The situation is similar in biblical studies. Whilst no one today would seriously argue that Bultmann's case against presupposition-less exegesis is invalid, his concern for such questions as that of the historical Jesus, and the role of mythology in the New Testament writings, is for the most part ignored, eviscerated by the tidal wave of historical-critical research in the wake of the discoveries at Qumran and the subsequent, renewed interest in the significance of the intertestamental writings for our understanding of the New Testament. The question of the historical Jesus, if it is considered at all in any theological sense, is to be found in the writings of such figures as Leonardo Boff, Edward Schillebeeckx, and Albert Nolan. Once again, it comes as no surprise that these individuals are Roman Catholics. One of the remarkable features of the reception of Bultmann's theology is the continuing interest felt by Roman Catholic writers.

Finally, 'death of God' theology is itself no longer a viable, theological option, its advocates themselves either dead or forgotten. God, to be sure, lives on – but has to face renewed questioning from those impatient with suffering and injustice throughout the world. Again, liberation and political theologies enjoy a high profile in this respect.

To all intents and purposes, therefore, it might appear that Rudolf Bultmann has indeed been forgotten by contemporary theology. This may be so, in a superficial sense. Certainly, in Britain at least, the centenary of his birth in 1984 was given little attention. Barth, by contrast, enjoyed far greater retrospective consideration, indicative perhaps of the different attitudes in Britain towards these two figures.

Beyond this superficial level, however, much of Bultmann's work and influence remains. Here, briefly, I want to consider two areas – biblical studies and systematic theology – in which it is possible to trace elements of Bultmann's theology. Whilst contemporary theology may not be the living embodiment of Bultmann, therefore, there are areas in which his influence can still be felt. In identifying them, we move one step nearer to a genuinely critical theology.

The point of this brief section, therefore, is not so much to link Bultmann's theology with particular contemporary figures, as to sketch some very general areas in which aspects of Bultmann's legacy are too often overlooked. It is, therefore, something of a coda to Chapter 5 proper. Nevertheless, in so far as it returns to aspects of the critique so far, it may prove enlightening.

(a) Biblical Studies

In his brilliant study, *Jesus and Judaism* (1985), E. P. Sanders writes that: 'It is the purpose of the present work to take up two related questions with regard to Jesus: his intention and his relationship to his contemporaries in Judaism' (Sanders, 1985, p. 1). These are literally Sanders's first words on the subject of Jesus and Judaism (in this text). They indicate, therefore, the goal and sense of purpose that characterise that study; that is, to argue for a degree of historical knowledge and certainty concerning the historical Jesus and his religious context hitherto unachieved.

In this, one might sense a rejection of Bultmann's own approach to questions of historical-critical research. Certainly, it is true that Sanders calls into question many of Bultmann's own findings. Indeed, it might be fair to say that Sanders overwhelmingly rejects Bultmann's entire position, in the search for a clearer understanding of Jesus' intention.

This does not mean, however, that Sanders is guilty of what Bultmann would have referred to as 'life-of-Jesus' theology. He, like Bultmann, is not concerned with how things looked in Jesus' heart, and the entire question of religious feeling or sentiment simply does not arise in his work. On the contrary, Sanders is concerned to arrive at historical facts about Jesus of Nazareth. Certainly there is little or no philosophical reflection upon the expression 'historical fact', but this does not call into question the honourable nature of the quest. It is not, in other words, a theological interpretation of the New Testament.

Sanders, therefore, like Bultmann in one of his roles, operates according to the rubric of historical-critical research. In this, he is typical of much of the biblical studies being undertaken today, especially in the English-speaking world. Certainly, scholars like Sanders arrive at very different conclusions to those of Bultmann. But in so far as they are all conducting historical-critical research, it is possible to recognise a definite degree of continuity.

There, however, the similarities end. For as was observed in Chapter 1, Bultmann's historical-critical research, centred as it is upon the question of the historical Jesus, is never simply an end in itself. On the contrary, it is always at the service of his theological and therefore pedagogic intent. Sanders, by contrast, and other scholars who share his general methodology, have no such theological intent. They simply aim to discover more about Jesus of Nazareth.

Undoubtedly, from the perspective of a scholar such as Sanders, it is precisely Bultmann's theological intent, and its presuppositions, that intrude upon his historical-critical research, to such an extent that the image of Jesus of Nazareth that one finds in that research is attenuated and distorted (cf. Sanders, 1985, pp. 26–34). This, as was demonstrated in the consideration of the work of Ebeling and Fuchs in Chapter 4, is a serious, and valid, charge. Protestant – and in particular, Lutheran – theology was guilty, especially in the work of Bultmann and his followers, of failing to recognise the invidious nature of this influence.

Apparently, therefore, Sanders and Bultmann stand as antitheses, one to the other. This, however, is not the case. Granted that on questions of 'historical facts' there may be no room for reconciliation between the two, still Bultmann and contemporary hermeneutic theology can learn from the most recent historical-critical research.

It will be remembered that, in reducing his treatment of the question of the historical Jesus to a consideration of his eschatological purpose, Bultmann had nothing to say about Jesus' social and political message, rather being directed towards the individual's ontological comportment *coram deo*. As Chapter 4 developed, specifically in its consideration of the work of Käsemann and Ricoeur, it was shown how it is this failure on Bultmann's part that evacuates his Christology of socio-political significance, thereby condemning it to the criticisms to be found in Adorno and Sölle. That is, it was Bultmann's failure to attend to the semantic representation of the image of Jesus that allowed his theology to fall into the trap, the ideology, of an exclusive devotion to existentialism.

In effect, this accords with the criticism of a study such as Sanders's *Jesus and Judaism*; namely, that Bultmann's theology interferes with his historical-critical work. Contemporary research, therefore – with its quest for objectivity – can act as a possible corrective to Bultmann's inadequate image of Jesus, if only in response to the question of the historical Jesus.

Certainly, this does not mean that one may simply replace Bultmann's with, for example, Sanders's image of Jesus. Rather, it should be possible to develop Bultmann's image in the light of more recent research. At bottom, therefore, the purpose of contemporary historical-critical research can be regarded positively rather than negatively; that is, not as identifying what theology may not say, but as helping it to say what it wants to say. Historical-critical research, in other words, helps theology to draw better pictures. Specifically, and in the light of contemporary research, this means drawing out those socio-political aspects of Jesus' mission and message that Bultmann's theology ignored, to its lasting detriment.

In the light of the critique contained in Chapter 5, in particular its four-stage simile by which one may understand the process of hermeneutic understanding, we might say that contemporary historical-critical research may act to inform Bultmann's work in stages one and two – which concentrate attention upon the 'window' of first-century Palestine – so as to clarify stage three; that is, the construction of the second 'window', the socio-political analysis of the interpreter's own historical context. Certainly, this is not to say that Sanders, or any other contemporary scholar, takes this step. But in so far as theology can learn from the scientific study of the world of the New Testament, it may well be in the area of the construction of images of the historical Jesus.

(b) Systematic Theology

This, of course, is relatively simplistic. After all, such historical-critical research has always served theology proper in this fashion. One might almost argue that the Evangelists acted in precisely this fashion, drawing on traditions of Jesus' life and work to structure their theological statements.

That it is introduced at this stage in the present study, however, is significant, for it helps to identify one way in which Bultmann's work runs on into contemporary theology. In other words, in highlighting this possibility of the application of corrective pressure to Bultmann's Christology, we are raising up for consideration further possibilities for theological endeavour.

In fact, if one looks at the contemporary theological scene, one can see precisely this trend in progress. This can be demonstrated simply by turning and considering several recently published books. The short guide, *Introducing Liberation Theology* (Boff and Boff, 1987), by Leonardo Boff and Clodovis Boff, uses some basic findings of recent research to illustrate its conviction that 'the poor and persecuted Nazarene' (Boff and Boff, 1987, p. 31) challenges contemporary society to address the plight of the oppressed. Similarly, Albert Nolan's *God in South Africa* (1988) employs such techniques and findings to support his challenge to the evil that is apartheid.

The clearest example of this trend in systematic theology, however – though also its most problematic example – is the work of Edward Schillebeeckx. Most recently, his *Jesus in our Western Culture: Mysticism, Ethics, and Politics* (1987), demonstrates powerfully and straightforwardly the manner in which Schillebeeckx combines recent historical-critical research with his own understanding of the theological significance of the Christ event. He writes:

> Originally the term 'Jesus Christ' was not a proper name but a double name which at the same time expresses a confession, namely the confession of the earliest Christian community: the crucified Jesus is the promised Messiah, the eschatological anointed of the Lord: 'God has made him Lord and Christ' (Acts 2.36; see Rom. 1.3–4). That 'Jesus Christ' is a confessional name provides the basic structure of all Christology; this confession is the foundation and the origin of the New Testament. Without this confession we should never have heard of Jesus of Nazareth. That Jesus thus became known in our history is essentially also dependent on the Christian confession. But in turn this confession points to a being from our human history, Jesus of Nazareth. This confession is as it is because Jesus of Nazareth was the sort of person who could evoke it. (Schillebeeckx, 1987, p. 15)

Certainly, it would be relatively easy to question some of Schillebeeckx's statements concerning matters of research, as has been the case throughout his theological career. But that would be to miss the point. Schillebeeckx uses recent historical-critical research to bring to expression his own theological position. At the very least, therefore, and in pedagogic terms, he cannot be accused – as can Bultmann – of neglecting the adequate delineation of his image of Jesus. On the contrary, the individual is left in little doubt as to the evidence Schillebeeckx adduces for his Christology.

Overwhelmingly, therefore, what one sees in the contemporary world are theologians employing such research to support their work, specifically in terms of the socio-political element within Jesus' mission and message. In other words, and as a corrective to previous practices, writers like Boff, Nolan, and Schillebeeckx have turned their attention to Jesus' activity as liberator and prophet. Notions of eschatological restoration, consequently (cf. Sanders,

1985), are given theological legitimation in their application to specific socio-political contexts. This development may at times take a libertine view of the constraints of historical-criticism. But that, fundamentally, is a risk that all theology must take.

Again, this may not say very much about the reception of Bultmann's theology in contemporary circles. Nevertheless, it is sufficient to demonstrate the manner in which aspects of Bultmann's theology that appear inherently problematic, are in fact already being overcome by modern theology. The work of rehabilitating Bultmann's theology – or, rather, the concerns of that theology – has therefore already commenced.

This, however, is all that can be said at the present time. Chapter 5, constrained by the requirement of considering the work of Bultmann and his followers, has at time been highly critical. This was a necessary, but essentially limited, task. What now remains, in the light of the findings of the present chapter as well as the comments of this conclusion concerning contemporary theology, is to relocate Bultmann's pedagogic intent, the role of his theology as *Glaubenslehre*, in the 'spaces' left for it by such writers as Schillebeeckx, Nolan, and Boff. Granted that there is still a role for a theology that calls the individual to the encounter with the risen Lord, therefore – in other words, that within liberation and political theologies attention must still be given to the Christian believer and how she comes to faith, and that understands that encounter in terms of the problematic of time and eternity – the task that remains is to consider the possible application of Bultmann's theology to this role. What remains, in other words, is a final consideration of Bultmann's theology as a critical theology of *education*. This is the task of the following Conclusion.

Conclusion: Towards
a Critical Theology

In moving towards an explicitly critical interpretation of Bultmann's theology, Chapter 5 was concerned, at the same time, to
look for its best possibilities. Ultimately, this concern took the form
of an attempt to identify points of contact between Bultmann and
contemporary theology, specifically in the areas of biblical studies
and systematic theology. There was a definite limit, however, to
what that consideration could actually achieve. The facts of the
matter are that Bultmann's theology is not, today, widely received.
Nor is there any indication that this situation will change in the
foreseeable future. On the contrary, Bultmann, like Herrmann
before him, seems to be lost to the present moment.

The present Conclusion, therefore, must step back from the
ambitious claims that seemed about to be advanced at the end of the
last chapter. At the very least, those claims must be tempered by
the knowledge that, at best, what is being offered here cannot be
as radical as Bultmann's own programme of eschatological interpretation. There is no scope in contemporary theology for such an
absolute endeavour.

What will this Conclusion attempt to achieve, then? First, it will
attempt to draw together the central themes of Bultmann's theology, as they have been discovered in this study, as they form
themselves around the central question of theology's role as education. Second, it will attempt to guide that question itself towards
its logical and necessary terminus. In other words, Bultmann's theology, finally, will point its own way out of its present predicament.
It can only be, in other words, a preliminary Conclusion.

The notion of theology as in some sense education, or *Glau-benslehre*, as Chapter 1 stated, was an important element within German Protestant theology from Schleiermacher onwards. To a great extent, therefore, this aspect of Bultmann's thought agrees with the theology of his Liberal Protestant predecessors. The Christologies of such individuals as Herrmann and Harnack, for example, can be regarded as attempts to discover in the question of the historical Jesus an example and a teaching that would be effective in the daily lives of Christian believers. Despite their methodological differences, therefore – and Herrmann's or Har-nack's psychological concerns with the inner disposition of Jesus of Nazareth are very different from Bultmann's own interpretation of the Christ event – it is possible to see how Bultmann stands in that tradition of *Glaubenslehre* identified above. The link is one of peda-gogic intent.

As Chapter 5 demonstrated, however, this intent was fatally flawed, in so far as it failed to consider the seriousness of the socio-political context in which any such theology must operate. That this failure, though, was in itself axiomatic for his theology, Bultmann himself attests, in an introductory remark to his opening lecture of the 1933 summer semester in Marburg. He states:

> Ladies and gentlemen. I have made a point never to speak about current politics in my lectures, and I think I shall also not do so in the future. However, it would seem to me unnatural were I to ignore today the political situation in which we begin this new semester. The significance of political happenings for our entire existence has been brought home to us in such a way that we cannot evade the duty of reflecting upon the meaning of our theological work in this situation. (Bultmann, 1960, p. 158)

'The significance of political happenings for our entire exist-ence...': and yet a consideration of these found no place in Bultmann's own theology. It is as if, in his concern to understand the manner in which the individual encounters eternity in the moment, that moment has been evacuated of all temporal signifi-cance. That is, despite Bultmann's obvious, explicit concern with the problem of time and eternity, his understanding of time is curiously slight. Such a flaw in Bultmann's theology cannot be overlooked here.

In this, the task of the present Conclusion – to draw out the ethical imperatives of Bultmann's theology – is opposed by Bultmann himself. We are turning, therefore, to waters in which Bultmann never sailed: that is, questions of ethical conduct and the active role of the individual in society. Granted that Bultmann's ontological reflection, as examined in Chapter 2, did not consider the individual in such terms: still this remains the task of any responsible theology. In this respect, one may only wonder why Bultmann did not follow Herrmann's lead on this point (cf. Chapter 1).

Theology, in other words, can and should tell people what to do. We see this today in Central America, in Europe, and in South Africa. This understanding, moreover, is implicit in that tradition of *Glaubenslehre* to which Bultmann belonged. Again, therefore, one wonders why Bultmann was so reticent about something which, logically, was implicit in his entire theological position.

Chapter 3, at least, indicated that this was the case. The eschatological moment of decision, despite its logical or formal appearance, remains for Bultmann always simultaneously a moment in a temporal sense – problems with Bultmann's handling of temporality notwithstanding. It is established in a concrete event in the continuum of time; that is, the proclamation of the Christian gospel, even if its ontological status cannot be reduced to that concrete event. In this way, again as Chapter 3 indicated, Bultmann was able to identify a definite relationship between Christian belief in a Creator God, who establishes the temporal world, and the eternal moment of eschatological encounter, in which the decision for or against God's Will is to take place. On this, Bultmann writes: 'That God is the Creator means that man's action is not determined by timeless principles, but rather by the concrete situation of the moment' (Bultmann, 1960, p. 159). The decision for God, therefore, is established in so far as God encounters the individual in her temporal reality, as a whole person. This was demonstrated in Chapter 3. Time and eternity, in other words, are always present now in the moment of encounter. Hence – crucially – the question of revelation is reduced to the question of what is new each moment.

In this way, Bultmann's understanding of faith, like his Christology, could not be reduced to the psychological categories of an irrational belief in some form of theistic idealism. He writes:

'Belief in God does not speak of soul-sparks and soul-essences, but of the whole individual' (Bultmann, 1965a, p. 8). Bultmann's, therefore, is not a theology – and not a Christology – that emphasises certain aspects of the subject at the expense of others. At the very least, he makes a genuine attempt to consider the individual in her entirety, her complete historicity. Bultmann is not, in other words, an anti-materialist, despite the very partial understanding of the world in his theology. The question that remains, however, is whether or not that partial understanding can still be tolerated.

What this study attempted to do, therefore, throughout Chapters 1–5, was to highlight the integrity and cohesion that characterise Bultmann's theology. It is important to emphasise this aspect of his thought, for it is easily overlooked, especially if his Christology has been reduced in commentary to a simple form of docetism. As Chapter 5 demonstrated, however, Bultmann's event theory, ultimately, makes such an attempt meaningless, in so far as his immanent critique of the individual's historicity does not consider the social, economic, and political context in which that individual finds herself.

On this reading, what one finds finally in Bultmann's theology is that he is solely concerned with the individual's *Geschichte*, despite the lip service that he pays to *Historie*. When faced by such disasters as National Socialism – or even the First World War, as Chapter 1 indicated – such an attenuated interest in *Geschichte* is simply insufficient. It is in this sense that Bultmann's theology implies an existentialist concern – understood in Adorno's pejorative sense – despite the fact that Bultmann stands at some remove from such figures as, for example, Sartre and Camus. Bultmann writes that:

> This surrender to the claim of the moment is not to be thought of simply as the abstract, negative recognition of human finitude; on the contrary, it involves the positive recognition of the claims of the Thou as the criterion of my finitude, and their fulfilment; i.e., love. Neither is it to be thought of simply as the negative acknowledgement that I am not master of my own fate; rather it involves at the same time the positive recognition that I exist for the other person. (Bultmann, 1965a, p. 12)

However, the concrete predicament of the individual is not for Bultmann a matter of social, economic, or political action, but rather is concerned with the comportment of the individual towards her God and her neighbour. This is the concrete specificity, as Bultmann understands it, in which the moment of decision is established, expressed now in terms of love. Quite simply, therefore, Bultmann is asserting that to love God is to love one's neighbour, and that this love is a question of ontology and of comportment, rather than any psychological understanding or empathy, or indeed any programme of radical social action involving that neighbour's material existence. Though doubtless Bultmann would not wish to deny the importance of good works, therefore, they nevertheless have no significance for his understanding of grace. On the contrary, his own sense of the fundamental Lutheranism of the gospel means that Bultmann is unable to escape from the iron grip of the *sola fide*.

Certainly, as the final few pages of Chapter 5 attempted to indicate, it is important to acknowledge that what Bultmann is trying to say here is not wrong or inherently bad. On the contrary, it is clearly important for the newly converted Christian individual to be reminded that she has definite responsibilities with respect to her neighbour, and that these, as Jesus of Nazareth stated, are in many respects definitive of the Christian faith. And yet, at this moment of pedagogic intent – that is, at this moment of decision in which the individual is called to specific behaviour – nothing is said regarding what such love actually means in practice. That is, Bultmann fails to articulate any specific course of action for the newly converted Christian. It is as Trent Schroyer indicated, as recorded in Chapter 5: in the moment of decision, it seems that one has only to decide to decide.

The impact of Bultmann's phenomenological reduction, in other words, in which encounter and decision appear to be attitudes rather than actions, is in effect to deny the individual any moment of epistemological reflection; that is, a moment of knowing or learning how to behave. There is no room, consequently, for the individual to learn through practice precisely how dangerous faith can be. Even in historical terms, therefore, the individual does not know anything. She cannot ascertain any concrete form of behaviour from her predecessors in the historical churches of the Christian religion. The moment of decision, Bultmann seems to be claiming, is simply not concerned with such matters, even in a preliminary sense; that is, as guides on the pathway to God. Bultmann's moment of pedagogic intent, on this reading, is curiously anti-educational. It leaves the individual, once the decision has been made for or against God, to fend for herself. The minister brings the individual to the encounter with the kerygmatic Christ. But after that. . .there is nothing.

Despite his comments concerning the doctrine of the Holy Spirit, therefore, as examined in Chapter 5, Bultmann is silent as to the real significance of the life of God in the life of the individual. In this, as stated above, he is fatally silent concerning the dangers of belief. This is his greatest mistake. For the danger of faith is the cost of discipleship. If nothing else, it is this that theology must teach the individual.

The danger of faith, in this sense, can be understood as risk or venture. Faith as venture, in other words, implies the premise that faith is not automatically ensured once-and-for-all in the moment of decision; that it can, in fact, be lost, or forfeited, and that the individual can come to destruction through the encounter with faith.

Bultmann seems to share this understanding of the double-edged nature of faith as venture. Hence, when the individual decides for God, and for salvation, this implies for Bultmann something more than simply a quantifiable alteration in ontological status. It implies an entirely new way of life, in which life itself may be lost. The decision of faith must recognise this. In this recognition, for Bultmann, dwells understanding. Faith, therefore, is never simply a 'leap in the dark'. For such ignorance would hold no fears. On the contrary, Bultmann writes: 'And even if faith can in some sense be spoken of as a "leap in the dark", still it is impossible to understand it as, when, say, I stand at a crossroads and, lacking a signpost, venture to strike out in a certain direction and thus risk arriving at my goal or missing it' (Bultmann, 1960, p. 55). On the contrary, faith is a matter of life and death.

All of this brings us back to the ontological reflection undertaken in Chapter 2. It comes as no surprise, therefore, to find that Bultmann can write: 'Therefore, talk of faith as venture is legitimate only when what is meant by it is that faith "ventures something". Not to venture faith itself, but to venture in faith' (Bultmann, 1960, p. 55). For this reflects his understanding of the eternal nature of the moment of decision, in which, in faith, the individual must always return to the encounter with God in Christ. To venture in faith, therefore, is to risk such a return.

With this return to the world of Chapter 2, however, comes a degree of resignation, if not despair. For it seems certain that Bultmann is, effectively, unwilling or incapable of going any further. Hence, he can write: 'For faith does not mean to accept the proclamation of God's forgiving and to be convinced of its truth in general, but rather to regulate one's life by it' (Bultmann, 1960, p. 56). Again, therefore, one discovers that faith, for all of its mystery, is nothing more nor less than the matter of right living. In the light of Bultmann's comments concerning the relationship between the Creator God and the individual, as considered in Chapter 3, this may be an adequate way of understanding that relationship. But it possesses no sense of danger, of loss and destruction. Demythologised, certainly, the Christian gospel is revealed as challenge. But the cost of failing in that challenge seems neglected in Bultmann's theology.

What one finds there, consequently, is the revelation of the previously-concealed individual by means of a movement or passage, in the eternal moment of decision, in which the individual must decide ever again for the risen Lord, and to manifest this decision in her daily existence within a community of neighbours. The goal of this passage – to be free, 'in Christ' – Bultmann characterises as: 'release from all worldly conditions and radical openness for encounters with God in all that comes' (Bultmann, 1960, p. 241). But it is precisely this 'release from all worldly conditions' which, ultimately, is the root inadequacy of Bultmann's theology. Thus, although he can write that: 'No, I "have" faith only when I have it ever anew in my duties and exigencies' (Bultmann, 1960, p. 57), he can never say what those duties and exigencies actually are. They seem to be deciding to decide, in perpetuity. Certainly, Bultmann is correct to emphasise the contingent nature of faith, in so far as faith is venture and therefore never an absolute certainty. But even when faith is not certain, the Christian still has a task and a duty. For even if faith is irretrievably lost – is it ever? – the Christian's duty, to take up her cross, remains the same. Bultmann himself, however, seems to be lost in a conceptual miasma of his own construction which represses any natural expression of a conviction with respect to such a Christian duty or 'workload', by which one might understand a task that the Christian is set. The cost of discipleship, then, is for Bultmann theoretically terrible. But in reality it fades away as one considers it, rather like the Cheshire Cat (cf. Chapter 1).

In the final analysis, in other words, Bultmann's theology loses its way. It seeks to speak of a pathway to God, by means of the process of encounter and decision in the eternal moment. Certainly, this question of the relationship between time and eternity is absolutely crucial to the entire story of modern philosophy and theology, and indeed the fate of literature in the twentieth century: one thinks, immediately, of Proust's *Remembrance of Things Past*, Joyce's *Ulysses*, and Eliot's *Four Quartets*. (Here in literature the centrality of the problem becomes almost embarrassingly obvious. There remains to be written, however, an important study of this problem as the philosophical basis of critical theology). Arguably, no theologian has perceived this quite like Rudolf Bultmann. And yet this emphasis upon the passage of the individual, from inauthenticity to authenticity, is fatally flawed, in so far as it fails, utterly, to consider the *rites* of that passage. This may appear strange, at first sight. For if Bultmann's event theory is about nothing else, surely it is about the rites of passage, understood as the process of encounter and decision?

But this is not the case. Throughout the present study, throughout its attempt to elucidate the theology and philosophy of Bultmann's thought, the constant struggle between the material and the historical, in Bultmann's sense of the term, has been kept to the fore. Chapter 1, consequently, raised the question of the historical Jesus. Chapters 2 and 3 considered the negative role of *Historie* in Bultmann's phenomenological event theory. Chapter 5, ultimately, returned this event theory and confronted it with the social, economic, and material reality of its own world.

Yet, finally, it must be acknowledged, this attempt has failed. Bultmann's theology, despite its apparent pedagogic intent, simply floats away from the everyday world of the individual believer. In this is its greatest danger. If it is to make any further contribution to contemporary theology, Bultmann's thought must be anchored in the real world. Time is primary, certainly; this much modern theology has learned from the mistakes of its idealist parents; that is, those who turned to the construction of the world in terms of the subject's mental faculties. But time must be grounded in the material circumstances of human existence. If nothing else, the aim of this book has been to demonstrate not simply how Bultmann's theology used to work, but how it might work once again by returning it to the encounter, not only with God in Christ, but also with God in the everyday events of human life. This is the task of a genuinely critical theology.

Notes

1 The pun is Robert Morgan's.
2 Bultmann's 'confession' was made in a private interview with Professor Gerhard Sauter, from whom I learned of it.
3 I am grateful to Professor John Heywood Thomas for introducing me to this interpretation of Kierkegaard's philosophy.
4 The idea of reduction/realisation comes from Gerd Buchdahl's brilliant essay on Kant: 'Reduction-Realization: a Key to the Structure of Kant's Thought', in *Philosophical Topics*, 12–2 (1981).
5 I am greatly indebted to Mrs Doreen Duncan, widow of the late Canon C. H. Duncan, for permission to quote from her husband's private correspondence.
6 The bust remains in Bonn, in the safe keeping of Gerhard Sauter.

Bibliography

1 Primary Sources

(a) Rudolf Bultmann (1884–1976)

1917: 'Die Bedeutung der Eschatologie für die Religion des Neuen Testaments', *Zeitschrift für Theologie und Kirche*, 27, pp. 76–87.

1921: *Die Geschichte der Synoptischen Tradition*, Göttingen.

1926: *Jesus*, Berlin.

1934: *Form Criticism*, Chicago.

1941: *Das Evangelium des Johannes*, Göttingen.

1942: review of W. Nestle, 'Vom Mythos zum Logos', *Theologische Literaturzeitung*, 67, pp. 146–7.

1948: 'Neues Testament und Mythologie', in *Kerygma und Mythos*, I, ed. H-W. Bartsch, Hamburg, pp. 15–53.

1953: *Theologie des Neuen Testaments*, Tübingen.

1954: 'History and Eschatology in the New Testament', *New Testament Studies*, 1, pp. 5–16.

1955: *Essay Philosophical and Theological*, London.

1956: *Primitive Christianity in its Contemporary Setting*, London.

1957: *History and Eschatology*, Edinburgh.

1958: *Jesus Christ and Mythology*, New York.

1960: *Existence and Faith*, London.

1962: review of S. Ogden, 'Christ without Myth', *Journal of Religion*, 42 pp. 96–102.

1964: *Glauben und Verstehen*, I (5th edn), Tübingen.

1965a: *Glauben und Verstehen*, II (4th edn), Tübingen.

1965b: *Glauben und Verstehen*, III (3rd edn), Tübingen.

1967: *Exegetica*, Tübingen.

1968: *Glauben und Verstehen*, II (5th edn), Tübingen.

1969: *Faith and Understanding*, London.

1971: *The Gospel of John: A Commentary*, Oxford.

1972: *The History of the Synoptic Tradition*, London.

1975: *Glauben und Verstehen*, IV (3rd edn), Tübingen.

1980: *Glauben und Verstehen*, I (8th edn), Tübingen.

1984: *Theologische Enzyklopädie*, eds E. Jüngel and K. W. Muller, Tubingen.

(b) Martin Heidegger (1889–1976)

1954a: *Vom Wesen der Wahrheit*, Frankfurt aM.

1954b: *Vorträge und Aufsätze*, Pfüllingen.

1962: *Being and Time*, London.

1972: *On Time and Being*, New York.

1973: 'The Problem of Reality in Modern Philosophy', *Journal of the British Society for Phenomenology*, 4–1, pp. 64–71.

1975: *Early Greek Thinking*, New York.

1976a: *Wegmarken* (Gesamtausgabe 9), Frankfurt aM.

1976b: *Die Grundprobleme der Phänomenologie* (Gesamtausgabe 24), Frankfurt aM.

2   Secondary Sources

Adorno, T. W., 1973, *The Jargon of Authenticity*, London.
Asendorf, U., 1971, *Gekreuzigt und Auferstanden*, Hamburg.

Barash, J. A., 1988, *Martin Heidegger and the Problem of Historical Meaning*, The Hague.

Barr, A., 1954, 'Bultmann's Estimate of Jesus', *Scottish Journal of Theology*, 7–4, pp. 337–52.

Barth, K., 1962a, 'Rudolf Bultmann: An Attempt to Understand Him', in *Kerygma and Myth*, II, ed. H-W. Bartsch, London, pp. 83–132.

Barth, K., 1962b, *Theology and Church: Shorter Writings 1920–1928*, London.

Barth, K., 1963, *Der Römerbrief*, 1st edn, Zürich.

Bartsch, H.-W. (ed.), 1964, *Kerygma and Myth: A Theological Debate*, I, London.

Boff L., and Boff, C., 1987, *Introducing Liberation Theology*, Tunbridge Wells.

Bornkamm, G., 1960, *Jesus of Nazareth*, London.

Boutin, M., 1974, *Relationität als Verstehenprinzip bei Rudolf Bultmann*, Munich.

Cairns, D., 1960, *A Gospel without Myth? Bultmann's Challenge to the Preacher*, London.

Caputo, J. D., 1985, *Heidegger and Aquinas*, New Haven.

Colette, J., 1965, 'Kierkegaard, Bultmann, et Heidegger', *Revue des Sciences Philosophiques et Théologiques*, 49–4, pp. 597–608.

Collingwood, R. G., 1926, *Some Perplexities about Time – With an Attempted Solution*, London.

Collins, J. D., 1983, *The Mind of Kierkegaard*, Princeton.

Connerton, P., 1980, *The Tragedy of Enlightenment: An Essay on the Frankfurt School*, Cambridge.

Diels, H. (ed.), 1951, *Fragmente der Vorsokratiker*, I, 6th edn, Berlin.

Dilthey, W., 1900, *Die Entstehung der Hermeneutik*, Berlin.

Dilthey, W., and Yorck, P., 1923, *Briefwechsel zwischen Wilhelm Dilthey und dem Grafen Paul Yorck von Wartenburg 1877–1897*, Halle.

Dyson, A. O., 1974, *The Immortality of the Past*, London.

Ebeling, G., 1963, *Word and Faith*, London.

Elrod, J. W., 1975, *Being and Existence in Kierkegaard's Pseudonymous Works*, Princeton.

Enslin, M. S., 1962, 'The Meaning of the Historical Jesus for Faith', *Journal of Bible and Religion*, 30–3, pp. 219–23.

Ericksen, R. P., 1985, *Theologians under Hitler*, New Haven.

Evang, M., 1988, *Rudolf Bultmann in seiner Frühzeit*, Tübingen.

Fisher, S., 1988, *Revelatory Positivism? Barth's Earliest Theology and the Marburg School*, Oxford.

Franz, H., 1961, 'Das Denken Heideggers und die Theologie', *Zeitschrift für Theologie und Kirche*, 58–2, pp. 81–118.

Fuchs, E., 1951, 'Bultmann, Barth, und Kant', *Theologische Literatur-zeitung*, 76–8, pp. 461–8.

Fuchs, E., 1964, *Studies of the Historical Jesus*, London.

Funk, R. W., 1966, *Language, Hermeneutic, and the Word of God: The Problem of Language in the New Testament and Contemporary Theology*, New York.

Gadamer, H.-G., 1976, *Philosophical Hermeneutics*, Los Angeles.

Gadamer, H.-G., 1979, *Truth and Method*, 2nd edn, London.

Gadamer, H.-G., 1985, *Philosophical Apprenticeships*, Cambridge, Mass.

Geiselmann, J. R., 1965, *Jesus der Christus I: Die Frage nach dem historischen Jesus*, Munich.

Habermas, J., 1975, *Knowledge and Human Interests*, London.

Harnack, A. von, 1957, *What is Christianity?*, New York.

Haug, H., 1958, 'Offenbarungstheologie und philosophische Daseinsanalyse bei Rudolf Bultmann', *Zeitschrift für Theologie und Kirche*, 55–1, pp. 201–53.

Hengel, M., 1981, *The Charismatic Leader and his Followers*, London.

Herrmann, W., 1927, *Systematic Theology*, London.

Herrmann, W., 1966, *Schriften zur Grundlegung der Theologie*, I, Munich.

Herrmann, W., 1967, *Schriften zur Grundlegung der Theologie*, II, Munich.

Hobbs, E. C. (ed.), 1985, *Bultmann Retrospect and Prospect*, Philadelphia.

Hough, W. E., 1956, 'The Significance of Bultmann', *Baptist Quarterly*, 16–8, pp. 343–55.

Ittel, G.W., 1956, 'Der Einfluss der Philosophie Martin Heideggers auf die Theologie Rudolf Bultmanns', *Kerygma und Dogma*, 2–2, pp. 90–108.

Jaspers, K., 1954, *Rudolf Bultmann. Die Frage der Entmythologisierung*, Munich.

Jaspers, K., 1978, *Notizen zu Heidegger*, ed. H. Sauer, Munich.

Jaspert, B. (ed.), 1977, *Karl Barth/Rudolf Bultmann: Briefwechsel 1922–1966*, Zurich.

Jaspert, B. (ed.)., 1984, *Rudolf Bultmanns Werk und Wirkung*, Darmstadt.

Jaspert, B., and Bromiley, G. (eds), 1982, *Karl Barth/Rudolf Bultmann: Letters 1922–1966*, Edinburgh.

Johnson R. A., 1974, *The Origins of Demythologising: Philosophy and Historiography in the Theology of Rudolf Bultmann*, Leiden.

Jonas, H., 1977, 'A Retrospective View', *Proceedings of the International Colloquium on Gnosticism*, Leiden, pp. 1–15.

Jonas, H., 1982, 'Is Faith Still Possible? Memories of Rudolf Bultmann and Reflections on Philosophical Aspects of his Work', *Harvard Theological Review*, 75, pp. 1–23.

Jones, G., 1988, 'The Play of a Delicate Shadow: Bultmann and Hesse in the Magic Theatre', *Journal of Literature and Theology*, 2–1, pp. 96–111.

Jüngel, E., 1976, *Doctrine of the Trinity*, Edinburgh.

Jüngel, E., 1985, *Glauben und Verstehen: Zum Theologiebegriff Rudolf Bultmanns*, Heidelberg.

Kähler, M., 1964, *The so-called historical Jesus and the historic, Biblical Christ*, Philadelphia.

Kant, I., 1947, *Zur Geschichtsphilosophie*, ed. A. Buchenau, Berlin.

Käsemann, E., 1964, 'The Problem of the Historical Jesus', *Essays on New Testament Themes*, London, pp. 15–47.

Kegley, C. W. (ed.), 1966, *The Theology of Rudolf Bultmann*, London.

Kierkegaard, S., 1940, *Stages on Life's Way*, Princeton.

Kierkegaard, S., 1941, *Concluding Unscientific Postscript*, Princeton.

Kierkegaard, S., 1980, *The Concept of Anxiety*, Princeton.

Kierkegaard, S., 1985, *Philosophical Fragments*, Princeton.

Kirchhoff, W., 1959, *Neukantianismus und Existentialanalytik in der Theologie Rudolf Bultmanns*, Heidelberg.

Korner, J., 1957, *Eschatologie und Geschichte; eine Untersuchung des Begriffes des Eschatologischen in der Theologie Rudolf Bultmanns*, Hamburg-Bergstedt.

Macquarrie, J., 1955, *An Existentialist Theology*, London.

Macquarrie, J., 1960, *The Scope of Demythologising*, London.

Malet, A., 1969, *The Thought of Rudolf Bultmann*, Shannon.

Malevez, L., 1954, *Le message Chrétien et la mythe: la théologie de Rudolf Bultmann*, Brussels.

Marle, R., 1956, *Bultmann et l'interpretation de Nouveau Testament*, Paris.

Miegge, G., 1960, *Gospel and Myth in the Thought of Rudolf Bultmann*, London.

Moltmann, J., 1967, *Theology of Hope*, London.

Mussner, F., 1957, 'Der historische Jesus und der Christus des Glaubens', *Biblische Zeitschrift*, 1, pp. 224–52.

Nolan, A., 1988, *God in South Africa: The Challenge of the Gospel*, London.

Oden, T. C., 1965, *Radical Obedience: The Ethics of Rudolf Bultmann*, London.

Ogden, S., 1962, *Christ without Myth; a study based on the theology of Rudolf Bultmann*, London.

O'Neill, J., 1970, 'Bultmann and Hegel', *Journal of Theological Studies*, 21, pp. 388–400.

Ott, H., 1955, *Geschichte und Heilsgeschichte in der Theologie Rudolf Bultmanns*, Tübingen.

Ott, H., 1959, *Denken und Sein. Der Weg Martin Heideggers und der Weg der Theologie*, Zurich.

Owen, H. P., 1957, *Revelation and Existence: A Study in the Theology of Rudolf Bultmann*, Cardiff.

Painter, J., 1987, *Theology as Hermeneutics: Rudolf Bultmann's Interpretation of the History of Jesus*, Sheffield.

Pannenberg, W., 1967, 'The Revelation of God in Jesus of Nazareth', in *New Frontiers in Theology II: Theology as History*, eds J. Robinson and J. Cobb, New York, pp. 101–33.

Perrin, N., 1967, *Rediscovering the Teaching of Jesus*, London.

Perrin, N., 1979, *The Promise of Bultmann*, Philadelphia.

Pöggeler, O., 1978, 'Being as Appropriation', in *Heidegger and Modern Philosophy: Critical Essays*, ed. M. Murray, New Haven, pp. 84–115.

Rahner, K., 1968, 'Theology and Anthropology', in *The Word in History: The St. Xavier Symposium*, ed. T. P. Burke, London, pp. 1–23.

Rahner, K., 1972, *Theological Investigations*, 9, London.

Reichenbach, H., 1958, *The Philosophy of Space and Time*, London.

Richardson, W. J., 1963, *Through Phenomenology to Thought*, The Hague.

Richardson, W. J., 1965, 'Heidegger and Theology', *Theological Studies*, 26, pp. 86–100.

Ricoeur, P., 1980, *Essays on Biblical Interpretation*, ed. Lewis S. Mudge, London.

Ringer, F. K., 1969, *The Decline of the German Mandarins: The German Academic Community 1890–1933*, Cambridge, Mass.

Roberts, R. C., 1977, *Rudolf Bultmann's Theology: A Critical Appraisal*, London.

Robinson, J., (ed.), 1963, *New Frontiers in Theology I: The Later Heidegger and Theology* (with J. Cobb), London.

Robinson, J. (ed.), 1983, *A New Quest of the Historical Jesus*, Philadelphia.

Rupp, G., 1977, *Culture-Protestantism: German Liberal Theology at the Turn of the Twentieth Century*, Montana.

Sanders, E. P., 1985, *Jesus and Judaism*, London.

Sauter, G., 1988, *In der Freiheit des Geistes*, Gottingen.

Schillebeeckx, E., 1987, *Jesus in our Western Culture: Mysticism, Ethics, and Politics*, London.

Schmithals, W., 1968, *The Theology of Rudolf Bultmann: An Introduction*, London.

Schnübbe, O., 1959, *Der Existenzbegriff in der Theologie Rudolf Bultmanns; ein Beitrag zur Interpretation der theologischen Systematik Bultmanns*, Göttingen.

Schubert, K., 1962, *Der historische Jesus und der Christus unseres Glaubens*, Vienna.

Schwan, A., 1976, *Geschichtstheologische Konstitution und Destruktion der Politik: Friedrich Gogarten und Rudolf Bultmann*, Berlin.

Schweitzer, A., 1954, *The Quest of the Historical Jesus*, London.

Sheehan, T., 1979, 'Heidegger's Introduction to the Phenomenology of Religion, 1920–1921', *The Personalist*, 60–3, pp. 312–24.

Smart, J. D., 1967, *The Dividend Mind of Modern Theology: Karl Barth and Rudolf Bultmann 1908–1933*, Philadelphia.

Sölle, D., 1974, *Political Theology*, Philadelphia.

Spiegelberg, H., 1960, *The Phenomenological Movement: A Historical Introduction Vol. I*, The Hague.

Stegemann, W., 1978, *Der Denkweg Rudolf Bultmanns: Darstellung der Entwicklung und der Grundlagen seiner Theologie*, Stuttgart.

Thiselton, A. C., 1980, *The Two Horizons*, Exeter.

Thomas, J. H. 1973, 'Kierkegaard's View of Time', *Journal of the British Society for Phenomenology*, 4–1, pp. 33–40.

Todt, H. E., 1978, *Rudolf Bultmanns Ethik der Existenztheologie*, Gutersloh.

Tracy D., 1981, *The Analogical Imagination*, London.

Tracy D., 1987, *Plurality and Ambiguity: Hermeneutics, Religion, Hope*, London.

Trotter, F. T. (ed.), 1968, *Jesus and the Historian*, Philadelphia.

Walker, W. O., 1969, 'The Quest for the Historical Jesus: A Discussion of Methodology', *Anglican Theological Review*, 51, pp. 38–56.

Weiss, J., 1971, *Jesus' Proclamation of the Kingdom of God*, London.

Wrede, W., 1971, *The Messianic Secret*, London.

Wyschogrod, M., 1954, *Kierkegaard and Heidegger: The Ontology of Existence*, London.

Young, N. J., 1969, *History and Existential Theology*, London.

Index